Small School
Big Dreams

David Michael Ribich

Copyright page:

ISBN: 978-0-692-04281-6

Small School Big Dreams By: D.M. Ribich

Reader Discretion is Advised

It is often said, "It takes a special kind of crazy to be a distance runner." I add to that by saying it takes a special kind of crazier crazy to read about a distance runner (especially if you are reading about me). What you will read may sound informal, incomplete, grammatically incorrect; but what you read is also what I thought, did, and spoke during the day. It is all accurate and if you have ever heard me speak, you know all of this adds up. I am sure you hear my one of a kind voice narrating this very part to you. Enjoy the read and if at any time something I said sticks out to you then make a mental note. Shoot, make a physical note, underline it, highlight it, rip out the page for all I care. I just hope what you read inspires you and transcends track and field. Feel free to message me too and share some of your thoughts! Text, direct message, letter, messenger pigeon, any way works! This is a journal, I want it to be personal, I want you the reader to be involved.

Special Thanks to:

Teammates: Dustin Nading, Alexander Holmberg, Samuel Naffziger, Zachary Holloway, Brady Beagley, Riley Anheluk, Tyler Jones, Aaron Whitaker, Josh Dempsey, Parker Marson, Justin Crosswhite, Hunter Mosman, Sawyer Heckard and Stephen Fey,

Family: Geneva Reinheardt, Michael Ribich, Madison Ribich, Falk Thieme, Olivia Woods

Coaches/university staff/agents: Dan Moody, Kevin McCadden, Michael Johnson, Randi Lydum, Lonny Sargent, Michael Feuling, Paula Baldwin, Emily Plec, Danny Mackey, Chris Layne

AND EVERYONE APART OF MY COLLEGIATE CAREER NOT MENTIONED

Cover Photographers: Paul Merca & J.r. Masters

Table of Contents

Introduction Part I

I am not sure what to put in this portion of the journal because if you're a reading this journal like I read books I rarely ever read the introduction. To start, if you don't know who I am, my name is David Ribich. If you don't know when I was born, I was born December 27th, 1995 in La Grande, Oregon. With that being said, now you know my birthday and gifts are appreciated. I have an incredible family: Geneva Reinheardt (mother), Madison Ribich (sister), and Michael Ribich (father). My family started in Summerville Oregon, then transitioned to Glide Oregon for a few years. In the year of 2000 we moved to Wallowa County and settled in the small city of Enterprise, Oregon.

Enterprise is NOT a spaceship and it is not a rental car service. Enterprise is a town of two thousand people where the cattle and livestock outnumber the people 7 to 1. Enterprise is a place where the nearest Walmart is 70 miles away -- one direction. A place where no stop lights hang from the wires, no stores are open past 9pm. It is a place where I went to kindergarten with 24 of my 36 graduating classmates as a senior in High School. Enterprise is a place where I attended church to see the county after a week of farming, work, and school. A place where the community carried me to reach my potential. A place where if I or anyone did one thing wrong, the town would hear about it. Enterprise is a place where my lifelong friends reside because it is a place, we will call home.

For those "meeting" me for the first time in this journal, I will catch you up to date on who I was as a child, to who I am today. As a child I was the energetic spunky kid that the teachers warned each other about during their summer breaks. I wrote my name on the board just as much as I did on papers as a kid. Not because I was bad but because I was so energetic. My 2nd grade teacher Mrs. B told me once that the book "No David" was written about me. In 4th grade, I put a grasshopper in my friend Callyn's desk and got detention.

Jump to my 6th grade year, it was my last year to play the sport I loved the most, soccer. Due to the small size of Enterprise soccer wasn't offered after 6th grade. Growing up our school counselor advised my mom to take me into the doctors for ADD or ADHD medication, my mom refused and so my wild days continued (thankfully). 7th grade I started cross country in the fall and gave up my love for soccer. I dedicated my first ever cross-country race to my 1 year old puppy Akia (Japanese for "strong warrior"). Him and I were playing catch in my front yard after my first day of Jr high, when I accidentally threw the ball too far precisely at the time a truck came barreling around the bend running over my puppy right before my eyes. The man driving the truck offered to give us a new puppy because his family just had a new batch and I looked at him and said "No! I have a dog and you just hit him." Due to that dedication to Akia that chocolate lab of mine helped me win my first ever cross country race. Was that puppy story completely relevant? Maybe not in detail, but in spirit he helped me win my first ever race.

Moving on, after that race in Elgin I was strongly advised by my coach to continue running. The decision to continue was decided after some contemplation of joining a club soccer team in the fall, thankfully I continued to run. As an 8th grader I set the goal of winning state cross country as a high schooler! On my last day of Jr high I got detention. Callyn and I wanted to see if I could fit into a locker, so we tucked myself in one and she kicked the door shut locking it. She says it was accident but that's okay because I deserved it in response to the 2004 Grasshopper/desk incident.

Going into my freshman year at Enterprise High School I was a small kid. Small kid with big ambitions. However, high school is such a blur in the timeline of life, but it is an incredibly important few years. Going into high school I was 4"10 and weighed 86lbs. I always told people I was 5ft, but I wasn't. I ran cross country in the fall, rode the pine in basketball in the winter, and ran track in the spring.

When I got my drivers permit in February, I had to use phone books to see over the steering wheel and was advised by the DMV to not drive bigger vehicles like trucks, SUVs, etc. My freshman year of athletics I was injured in the fall for cross country. I played JV basketball in the winter and then qualified for state in the 3000m and 1500m in the spring. There I finished 7th in the 3000m and 9th in the 1500m. As a Sophomore, I was finally 5ft tall and I weighed 98 lbs. This year I lied and told people I was 100lbs. I took my neighbor to prom as a sophomore and didn't need a phone book to drive anymore. In the fall, I finished 7th in small school state cross country 1A/2A/3A. Started JV basketball in the winter and finished 4th in 3000m at state and 6th in the 1500m.

After my sophomore year I was still a pretty small kid but knew after that year I wanted to run in college, so I packed up a portfolio and traveled to universities in Oregon and introduced myself to schools, so they can put a face to the name, if I was even on their radar. I visited Oregon State,

Eastern Oregon University, and Western Oregon University. This summer I also attended Steens Mountain Running Camp for the first time where I developed even further as a high school runner. My junior year I was slowly developing 5'6 weighed 110lbs and began to really improve athletically. In the fall I was runner up in Oregon State 1A/2A/3A cross country. In the winter I didn't ride the pine as much in basketball, started JV, sat varsity. Spring, I finished 2nd in the 3000m and 3rd in the 1500m at the state meet. My senior year I won state cross country in the fall, started varsity basketball in the winter and went on to win the 1500m, 3000m, 4x400 relay for Oregon classification 1A/2A/3A that spring. February of that year I signed with NCAA Division 2 Western Oregon University. I was one of the 36 graduates from Enterprise High School in the class of 2014. When I graduated, I was the 64th best 1500m runner in the state of Oregon, and the 162nd best 800m runner in the state of Oregon.

Introduction Part II

During my freshman year at Western Oregon University, I was still on that small-town mindset; where my eyes really weren't open to the real-world lifestyles. A lot of new things were seen during my first year in college and a lot of decisions had to be made to succeed and continue following my dreams. As a freshman at WOU, the fall was an adjustment period. I came from a small school where I thought I was a big deal. I quickly realized I was a small fish in a big sea. It took some adjustments but having juniors and seniors on the team like Brady, Sam, Zach and Riley made the transition easy. At the West Regional Championships that fall in cross country I finished 52nd, far off a qualifying spot for the national meet. In my first indoor track season I ran 4:13 in the mile. I was shocked, I was just 3 seconds off my high school PR in the 1500m but ran an extra 109m! That race gave me the confidence that I could potentially be a factor as a collegiate athlete. In high school, I never ran indoor track so this whole experience was new and running that fast, that early, was an incredible motivator for the upcoming year. I surprisingly won our 1500m conference title as a freshman that spring and ran a PR of 3:50.58.

As a Sophomore at WOU I qualified for the national championship for cross country in the fall by finishing 13th In the West Regional Championships, 29 places ahead of last year's finish. Finishing 13th was a shock for a lot of people including myself, all I tried to do was latch on to the front pack and race the final 2k. I did so and earned an individual qualifying spot for the national championships in Joplin Missouri. In my first National appearance I finished 67th. My roommates at the time: Zach, Brady and Rachel made the drive from Oregon to Missouri to watch me race. Having those familiar faces made the world of a difference. That championship was the first of many my parents and family traveled to throughout my collegiate career. Florida, Kansas, South Carolina, Missouri, Indiana it doesn't matter the location they make it work. That race made me hungrier than ever to return to a national championship.

Winter of my sophomore year I qualified individually for the mile and was a part of the Distance Medley Relay team (destiny because my initials are DMR I suppose) where we finished 5th at the national championship coming in ranked 10th, Earning my first Division II All-American honor. Prior to the DMR, on the same day I qualified for the mile final, this race was my first ever preliminary round experience where I finished 3rd, auto qualifying for the final. The next day I finished 4th in the indoor mile earning my first individual All-American accolade. My time in the prelims of 4:06.36 stood as my sophomore PR and a new school record.

Fast forward to outdoor track, I ran a big PR at Azusa Pacific running a time of 3:43.42 in the 1500m and barely winning my heat. That time became a new school and conference record. Again, a surprise to many including myself that I would run a 5 second PR (Two weeks prior I ran 3:48 at Stanford). My coach, Michael Johnson (A.K.A Johnson, Coach, or Papa J) told me that day at Azusa one of the most important words of my career. He said, "David now and for the remainder of your career however long that is just Be David". Now it didn't make much sense at that time, but you'll read when I figured it out. Later that year I was 5th in the outdoor 1500m final at the national championships. My senior teammate Sam Naffziger finished 8th, both of us earning individual Division II All-American honors. That summer I trained intensely to be ready once fall rolled around. Mission one of junior year: qualify for cross country nationals.

Junior year was a successful year on and off the track. After qualifying for nationals as a sophomore in cross country, I was hungry for more this year. In my mind I was hungry for a top 10 finish and All-American honor. Quite ambitious for a guy that just finished 67th right? To summarize that goal didn't happen but the result changed my perspective of the sport entirely. I ended up getting hurt mid-October because I wanted to get a workout record. Arrogant right? I cruised the last 5k of our 9 mile "Shady" loop in roughly 14:30. I finished that day feeling like the fittest man in the world. My double that night resulted in me limping back home unable to put any weight on my Achilles tendon. That day on, I was working out in the pool and working out on treadmills for 5 weeks. The diagnosis was inflaming or straining my Achilles, honestly don't remember because I was so zoned out sitting on the medical table. Under great coaching, trainers and medical staff, I was able to race the championship portion of the season

The day before our conference championships I ran outside for the first time in 4 weeks. I thought it's go time, I feel fresh, I feel good, I feel ready. Next day for our conference championship I finished 5th, a year prior I finished 4th. This was the first time in my entire career that I had gone "backwards" in performance. Once I got to the regional championships in Billings Montana, I finished 15th where I missed being an individual national qualifier by just six seconds in the 10k. At the time I was devastated, now I am so thankful for that setback. I was ticked off at myself for not digging deep and qualifying. I thought "You're **** runner David, how could you expect to get top 15 at nationals if you can't even make it out of your region."

Weeks went by until the start of December when I realized how selfish, and egotistical I had been about focusing only on my goals. I got so caught up with the achievements and the trophies that I failed to realize how far I had come and how I was taking so many of my pervious achievements for granted. From freshman year of high school to that fall I had been relatively injury free and nothing could stand in my way of my dreams. Every year had been an improvement until this year and I truly believe my improvement for the future was emphasized because of this season. Watching the cross country national meet that year is when I came to terms that I would much rather be 199th at nationals than sitting from home watching others succeed. It put my previous year of 67th into perspective, making me appreciate that small accomplishment much more.

After the upsetting finish to the fall, I told my coach some of us guys will be staying in Monmouth over December to train for indoor track. My purpose was to find that love again, feel the stress-free elements of being able to wake up and run without any other commitments. The ability to enjoy the process. The month of December was one of my favorite months of training and it set myself and the other guys up for an incredible year. Josh, Dustin, and AJ the three others that stayed were a huge reason to why I was able to find the love again in the process and not the result. We worked hard every day to achieve the goals we had in mind, but each individual day was the focus. Being able to wake up and see each other struggle and thrive in a workout made every day worth it. We laughed, learned and grew together so much during that winter break and after December, I learned that there's a lot more to the sport than the hardware or victories. Thanks to a supportive group of friends, family and incredible girlfriend, I was able to grow a lot more than I could have imagined after a "defeat".

That indoor track season was nothing but incredible, the four guys that stayed and trained (myself included) broke the Division II national record in the DMR and won the DMR national title. Dustin and I went 4th and 3rd in the indoor mile, Josh finished 6th in the 800m final, and my girlfriend finished 6th, her teammate 5th in the 800m final. We were 5/5 on individuals making the final at the national meet and bringing home an All-American accolade. The men's team consisting of us four finished sixth as team at the indoor national meet. The highest GNAC men's team finish ever.

Fast forward to the spring the ball kept rolling. I forgot about the expectations, the accolades, and just started to race. Now I'm not a guru, nor do I know it all, but I can tell you that racing each race like it was my last and enjoying the process; gave me the strength to run all the way to July. I won my first individual title in the 1500m at the NCAA Division II National Championships in Bradenton, Florida. After the race I got drug tested for the first time and felt pretty cool. Once in the testing room the man asks, "Whenever you are ready, we can go into the bathroom and pee."

As energetic as I was, I said, "Let's go now! I could totally pee."

We walk into the bathroom, I face the man and try to pee into the cup, maybe 5 milliliters fill the bottom of the cup and I say, "dang, I was really expecting more."

The man replies, "Is that all you got?"

I quickly respond as immature as I am, "You're talking about the pee, right?"

We both laugh and walk back to the testing room. After that pointless story lets get back to the intro, we are almost caught up to the journal entries so keep grinding through this intro! Summer of 2017 we go into Portland Track Festival and I was in the office when J. Marcus was talking with my coach Johnson. The conversation pans out and Marcus asks if he should put me in the fast heat, Johnson replies no. put him in the second fastest heat. Given this conversation was on speaker I sat and listened to Johnson pulling me out of the fast heat. Why did he do that? Don't worry folks, I'll get to that. Now it's the day of Portland track, everything is healthy, body feels great, I'm feeling a sub 3:40. We go into the race, I end up barely winning it and running 3:39.56. After the race, I asked my coach why he didn't put me in the fast heat and he said, for that reason (pointing to the time board). You had the opportunity to control your heat, control your fate, and you capitalized, our next talk will be USAs, go cool down and keep being David.

Running History and Progress

Pre-College

2009 (7th)

1500m 5:24.70

800m 2:50.0

2010 (8th)

Injured because spring powered doggie door hit me in the Achilles. Ouch.

2011 (9th)

5000m 17:52.8

3000m 9:38.59

1500m 4:27.83

2012 (10th)

5000m 16:31.0

3000m 9:10.68

1500m 4:20.38

2013 (11th)

5000m 16:08.2

3000m 9:05.20

1500m 4:18.68

800m 2:06.1

2014 (12th)

5000m 15:58.0

3000m 8:57.32

1500m 4:10.45

800m 2:03.99

College Career

WOU Freshman

10000m 32:08

8000m 25:38

5000m 15:02

3000m 8:36.35

Mile 4:13.84

1500m 3:50.58

800m 1:54.78

WOU Sophomore

10000m 30:12

8000m 24:38

5000m n/a

3000m n/a

Mile 4:05.21

1500m 3:43.41

1000m 2:28.83

800m 1:52.63

WOU Junior

10000m 30:36

8000m 24:04

5000m n/a

3000m 8:13.94

Mile 4:02.30

1500m 3:39.56

800m 1:49.41

WOU Senior

10000m 29:49

8000m 24:47

5000m n/a

3000m 7:50.81

Mile 3:58.88

1500m 3:37.35

1000m 2:21.38

800m 1:48

Part I: Summer

June: USA's

July: Steen's Mountain Running Camp

August: Pre-season

6.20.2017

Sunday/Monday of declarations into USAs was rough. I was refreshing the page every 5 minutes. I left the page open and went to practice, my last quick workout before USAs -- if I got the opportunity to go. It was my worst workout ever. Johnson stopped the workout after the 3rd rep and told me to go cool down because I was having a terrible time, physically and mentally. I hadn't slept or ate much the last 48hrs and apparently it showed. Knowing that they usually only take top 30, I locked in my final resting place of 33rd on the declaration list. Once I was there, I had given up. I went into the shower, turned on my 1500m playlist music and sat on the floor, letting the hot water roll off my skin. After about 20 minutes I had come to terms with not going. I told myself -- David you are getting too caught up in the result and not the process again. You are forgetting the last 8 months of incredible experiences you've had with your team and friends. Achieving goals you worked for all year, USAs was a bonus, that meet is for professionals, it's all good, you'll get it next year.

Two hours later I was unpacking my bag in Monmouth and got a text that forced me to repack my bags. My roommate Tyler texted me saying, "Congrats you are in!" Confused I messaged Drew Windle and he said, "You're in the meet dawg. Congrats! I watched your race in Portland, close like that and you'll be in the final! Good luck this week!" My world flipped, I was so pumped. Turns out I made it in from politics and scratches, they ended up taking 37. I told myself to enjoy every moment of USAs and keep it in perspective how lucky I am. I am traveling down with Brady Beagley our Assistant Coach, my old roommate, and great friend. He deserves opportunities like this to coach me at these meets and I am so thankful I get to share this opportunity with him. Johnson is driving down from Monmouth and will meet us there tomorrow night. We are staying in one of the designated meet hotels so that'll be cool to see big time athletes around the hotel.

6.21.2017

This is my first ever USA experience and you could say I am getting the full experience. My prelim heat is with Centro, Murphy, Wheating, Fleet, some big names. All in all, I have zero expectations for tomorrow I just want to race. This log came to me before I left for Sacramento and thought it would be a good idea to jot down some thoughts and words about USAs while I am here, maybe I will continue this all year who knows. Blah Blah Blah, back to prelims, first and foremost RACE ignore the name, their achievements *cough* Olympic Gold medal *cough* and race. Take advantage of being the third heat and burn the hell out of your feet.

Premeet with Brady Beagley:
25 min run, 3x120s @ 16.2,16.4,15.9, 1x500 broken @ 26(200)/jog 180/16.2(120), 1x200 at 24.3

6.22.2017
Mileage 6

Prelim: 5th in the heat, 3:40.95 small q for the finals on Saturday

What the heck? Are you kidding me? There I was feeling good with a lap to go and I was just thinking holy cow, I could do this. Incredible experience and excited to race the best come Saturday. After watching the first two heats, I knew I just needed top 6 to advance onto Saturday so I focused on that and was just ready to kick if I was in a sticky situation. Wheating took it out and kept the pace honest, I feel bad he didn't advance for multiple reasons, he is a 1500m fan favorite, he is a good racer, and he paced out the third section helping me make the final.

Out of my heat was: Centro, Murphy, Prakel, Hunter, Myself, Saarel (off petition) and Gregorek. Gregorek had a wild kick. Going in with 200m to go Murphy clipped me a bit and he flies past I thought mid race "Wow I just got clipped by Clayton Murphy" and I kept on swinging wide into the final stretch, for a moment I thought I might win the heat. Going into the final I just want to forget the names again and race. I finished the prelim and just stood in lane five waiting for my name to pop up on the board like really? Is this a joke?

Morning: 12 min run and drills
7:45pm: Warm up for race, ice bags in hand
8:25pm: Stood in waiting room forever in spikes corralled like chickens.

One of roommates from last year Zach also surprised me, he flew down and traveled 16 hours and walked into my hotel room. Life is good.

6.23.2017

Mileage 6

Today I am thankful for one more day of competition before I call my junior year. 12 min AM run, saw Emma Coburn running around the park, Brady and I joked like we were going to turn around with her, but we would have gotten dropped. She was cruising.

The best part about today was watching the women's 5k and watching Jerry Schumacher coach of Shelby Houlihan and Bowerman Track Club. Shelby's twitter is @Shelbo800 but I think she needs to update her twitter name to Shelbo5000. So, to explain, I was on the same bleacher side by the Bowerman coaches and as Shelby races to the line for victory in the women's 5000, Jerry jumps with joy hugging colleagues. I find that so incredible because he has had so much success as a coach, but still it looked like this was his first win. Making me believe he cherishes every win with full heart. It is an unusual sight because so often coaches play it cool, shake hands, nod heads, say great work etc. but Jerry showed so much raw emotion that it was truly inspiring.

Tomorrow's final I have goals in mind but one goal I have after the race is to find Jerry Schumacher and Danny Mackey to introduce myself. Going to bed with a full heart and a clear mind. Excited to toe the line and race against the nation's best.

25 min afternoon run, a little toasty in temperature
3x120s @ 17.3, 16.2, 16.2 good pickups for tomorrow

6.24.2017
Mileage 6

Well you already know I made the final, it's 9:21 PM roughly 5-6 hours before the final. Too early for exact math. The craziest part about making the final is I am not top 13 in the country on paper. 20 other guys have every right to be in that final as I do. I am going to soak in this opportunity and hopefully showcase WOU, Enterprise, and myself. I have no idea how this final will go down if it goes out piss slow I might just take it cause why not? I think my fitness level is strong enough that I could go sub 3:40 today if needed. The prelim a few days ago felt like a prelim and not like it was 1 second off my PR. I really wonder what kind of fitness I am in. I will then look for the coaches (Mackey and Schumacher) it will be a hot game of where's Waldo but hopefully I can find them.

Putting tonight aside it has been an incredible year. A national record, two national titles, Indoor & Outdoor Track Athlete of the year for Great Northwest Athletic Conference, Male Athlete of the Year for GNAC, almost a year with my girlfriend, life is too good. Today is a go out and race kind of day. Next log I will be on the plane talking about the final.

6.24 Continued

Well this log is on the plane, post final. Finished 9th and I have a lot of mixed feelings for being the 33rd guy in to the meet finishing 9th in the USA final. Is it wrong for me to say I wish I placed higher? The race started out slow and I was hip one and boxed from the gun. No matter my positioning the whole race I had nowhere to go, someone was always boxing me. With 600m to go Blankenship made a massive surge to the front, first three could respond, but everyone else had to play catch up. I was caught behind too many bodies to make up the ground.

After the race, I walked into the tent and talked with Josh Thompson and Quigley, two Bowerman athletes. I walk through the interview portion hoping I would get stopped for a few words...nope just kept walking. Looking back at that, I am so glad I didn't get interviewed because in the chaos of people around the track I slip and slide in between the crowd and walk right past Schumacher. I passed him and froze. "Screw it, just talk to him" I said that out loud and turned around, I yelled "coach" he kept walking, "hey coach" kept walking, then I was like, "Jerry" finally he turned around, we talked briefly nothing to serious. I just wanted to put my name and face together and officially meet him. We talked for a few minutes and he said he was ecstatic to talk with me which was great to hear.

After that I returned to my "fan section" -- hugs and high fives all around. My girlfriend Olivia who I am sure you will read about quite often surprised me and traveled with my mother and Zach's mom to Sacramento. An 11-hour drive for her and a 16-hour drive for my mom. Olivia bless her soul made this experience 10x better just seeing her before my final.

My last lap was 54.04.

6.25.2017

After Sacramento, my heels are sort of raw which is interesting because I only did the 1500m. After a full day to relax and reflect on the race I can say I am content with 9th. I am not sure if it is just me or it is like this for everyone, but after big championship races the two days after I am in a slump. Tired, drained, almost depressed. I think it is just coming off of a super structured high stress environment into a relaxed no worry in the world gives a weird signal to the body.

When running a race, I encourage you to reflect on every aspect of the race, the time, the place, the tactics, so many unsaid accomplishments come from races. In my case, my last 800m in the USA final was 1:52.95. My PR last year as a sophomore in college was 152.62. That stat changed a lot of my thoughts about the race and leaves me happy and hungry for more. Take away as much as you need from a race to make it a positive experience...

W: 20min AM run solo / 30 min PM run with Josh (my roommate) and Dustin (fellow DMR guy).

6.26.2017

For the summer months, I am not doing any workouts just runs so a lot of my logs will be insight/thoughts more so than core workout material. If you want to get to the workouts go to late August or September.

Today I concluded my junior year of track. Next time I wear the big red W I will be announced as a senior. These first 3 years have gone by so fast that I am sure this next year will be a blink of the eye. I guess some words of advice are cherish every moment, live in the moment, and reap the benefits you are given day by day. As a Division II athlete take in all the positives and ignore the rest. If you get gear and get scholarships, why waste it? Four years goes by a lot quicker than you would think so take advantage of it. There will be times when temptations sway you to live the college life and that's fine, just know college athletics is not going to wait for you to figure it out.

On any major decision ask yourself "What's the benefit?" If you can't think of any sound reasons and you aren't trying to convince yourself, chances are it's not beneficial. For example, I scratched a meet in Canada this morning, the Harry Jerome Track Classic. The race was getting paced for 3:36 but I passed on it. I couldn't think of too many benefits, a PR maybe? But sometimes it's best to stop when things are getting good. It is like ice cream, like cookie dough. You take a big bite and inside that bite is a thick gooey piece of dough. The next bite also has dough. Do you double back two delicious doughy bites or wait for a later bite to indulge that dough? I just came off USAs healthy and ready for more, which leaves me in a good spot going into my senior year. Also, I am a broke college student and my cars tags are expired and I don't have $80 to get them renewed. Maybe that is a reason I am not going to Canada.

6.29.2017

Ta-da three days have passed and I haven't logged so let me catch you up:

Tuesday- Ran 20 mins
Wednesday- Off day
Thursday- Ran 20 mins

For the past three and the next seven I will be in my ten day break period where I let my body kind of find itself again. I am thankful to be in a program where we work hard and recover harder. This last year was a none stop grind and being able to just relax and put in super easy miles is incredible. Tonight was an easy 3 mile run on our cross country course. Super soft surface with AJ (400m leg in DMR) and Dustin. Friends like them don't come around often. Finding people with like passions makes the work to achieve life goals easy.

Tomorrow will be another regular run and Saturday I'll try for 30 mins one of these days I need to go to DMV and get my tags renewed.

25 mile week

7.3.2017

Mileage 7

Sorry for the inconsistency -- I didn't want to bore you with my down period life where I am just eating Oreos, watching Netflix, and getting blizzards at 9:30pm. The last few days haven't been anything incredible, 30 min run on Saturday, Sunday I ran 20 mins. It is already July and I am ready to rock and roll workouts. Yesterday I watched the men's 1500m TrackTown Summer Series race and Blankenship won. One of the guys was gunning for a world standard, but with 350 to go he yelled an explicit word starting with F, rhyming with Truck and stepped off the track.

There was a lot more to that race than the time and I hope kids took the positives away from that meet. I also talked with Drew Windle. He approached me, well, we sort of met eyes and I walked down to him. He won the 800m at the race in Portland and just recently qualified for worlds to represent USA in the 800m. He is a Division II guy from Ashland, he told me if I have any questions or concerns about post collegiate running let him know and he will help me out. That's what I love about running, and the Division II success stories like Windle, they are in it to help everyone succeed.

Today's work at the Nike World Headquarters in Beaverton:
40 min run
2x200 @ 25.3, 24.7|2x120s @ 16.2, 16.3

To start, I lied to a security guard, so Olivia and I could get into the campus. I was a little turned around once we got on campus, but thankfully Woody Kincaid came to the rescue and showed us to the track. Another Bowerman guy and host of the podcast, Price of the Mile, check it out. We talked back and forth until we got to the track to see Clayton Murphy working out with Alberto Salazar, a big secret in the running world that Murphy is working out with Salazar. It was super awkward like I just walked in on an affair. I put my bag down by the track and ran out with Olivia, I explained the whole thing to Olivia, her response was, "Don't forget to introduce me to people, like you always do." Looks like I forgot too... Olivia and I have been dating for one year tomorrow, fourth of July so that'll be fun, the whole country is celebrating us. Right?

7.7.2017

Mileage 7

Last four days consisted of good runs and lots of fun. Didn't log anything due to being so busy, I promise I will log more frequently once I am not in this down period. Tuesday 4th of July Olivia and I worked at a party and made some good money. I ran 20 minutes nice and easy then celebrated America (Olivia and Is 1 year). Wednesday the 5th, even though I was running around working on my feet I felt great, so I went 50 mins nice and easy at 7:15 pace. Thursday the 6th I took off, just hung out with Olivia's family and Friday (today) I ran 35 mins. As I said, pretty fun last few days of runs and activities.

My packing for Steens Mountain Running Camp has begun, for those of you who don't know what Steens is, it is a high altitude running camp for high school athletes. The camp is located 70 miles southeast from Burns Oregon resting at 7500 ft elevation on the Steens Mountains. I will be up there for three weeks where I will be setting up camp the first week, week two session 1 I will be a counselor to 20 high schoolers, week three session 2 I will be a coach for a counselor with a new group of athletes.

Today Andrew Wise, a writer for Citius Mag, released an article titled, *The Strange Magic of Division II*. I really enjoyed the article and I encourage you to read it or find it online. The message in the article shouldn't be the negatives of Division 2 It should be what you can do with your given situation. I sent Wise a response article to his post, let's see what happens with it. He is also interviewing me tomorrow, so we will see how that goes.

24 mile week

7.8.2017

You know, I was super satisfied with my race at USAs. Then I talked with my high school coach on the phone and he started talking about tactics, how boxed I was in the final and overall the entire race. I got amped talking with him like dang, I want to run again, give me another shot! Just got to be patient and learn from the final and move on, I was a nobody in that race and it would have been cool to just take the lead like I said I would. High school coach said, "If you had been in the back by Ben and followed his move up, no worse than 6th." Maybe he was right, maybe he was wrong, all in all I always appreciate his words and am excited someday to get another crack at USAs.

Currently in Portland leaving for Steens bright and early with David Laney. Laney is a pro trial runner for Nike and a good friend of mine. I am sure I will talk about him a lot throughout the next few weeks. On the drive up here to Portland, I talked on the phone with Andrew Wise for Citius Mag. It was a solid 40 minute phone interview and I think a lot of good things were talked about. To start, I talked about how when you line up along the starting line, forget the jerseys, forget the divisions and race. This goes from professional down to high school because ultimately if you are toeing the line next to someone, they want to race.

As a Division II athlete I enjoy lining up next to Division I and pros just for the chance to really race some of the best in the country or world. The first time I raced a field of professional runners was at the University of Washington in an indoor meet. I was racing people like Andrew Wheating of Nike, Brannon Kidder of Brooks, Eric Avila of Hoka One One, Harun Abda of Oregon Track Club, Justyn Knight of Syracuse. A good overall field. I fully expected myself that day to go sub 4 minutes in the mile. This heat had twelve sub 4 minute milers and I really thought this was a good chance. We go through 800 in 2:05 and I run 4:02.4. After the race, I was pretty pissed off at the heat because I relied on them, and their jerseys to get my job done but, it was won in 3:59. They have all done the whole sub 4 gig so to them this was just another race to win. For me it was a big opportunity that I wasted because I got caught up in the expectations of a race. I got caught up in the fact that they were professionals. That race was what prepared me for the USA prelim. Because my prelim, I didn't care about the jersey, I was ready to race. Line up and give yourself credit that you deserve to be there and race. No matter the division or separation.

I also talked about how moments before I was sent to the starting line of the 1500m final at USAs an official stopped me and said, "Go Badgers." I replied, "Go Wolves." Given the Western W does look a lot like Wisconsin I just let it go. I won't spoil the article, give it a read on Citius. Anyway, this was a long post, not sure if I will have time to run or log tomorrow so next post will be Monday.

7.10.2017
Mileage 5

First day of camp setup complete. My hands are cut, sore and tired. It was a long day and a lot of hard work was put into the camp. I feel like we accomplished a lot already on the first day. This morning, I woke up at 6am to the chirping of the birds and the rising of the sun. So poetic I know. I ran an easy 5 miles to just get used to the elevation and air. It's great to work up here with Cole Watson (pro trail runner for Hoka) and Laney. We set up our tents next to each other, we have a little village going.

Today Harland gave me my tent assignment and I will be with the small school guys. I am extremely excited for next week already because well, I was/am a small school guy and it will be nice to be with a familiar group. Hoping tomorrow is another 5 miles in the AM.

7.11.2017
Mileage 5

I am writing in the journal with a lot of daylight left in the day. I am sitting on the ridge top in the truck with Laney and I cannot believe how much I missed him. He is a humble, quiet, hardworking guy that never talks about his success and accolades. He hands out Nike gear to campers and people like it is an endless supply. He is a co-owner of a company called Trails and Tarmac that specializes in private coaching and running. He is up here replying to his athletes while I write in my journal and count the rodent holes on the dirt road that I will be filling sometime this week.

In terms of fitness ran another easy 5 miles today up to Fish Lake and back. 10 miles in two days both runs at 7:20s, yes! I am getting fit! My watch said I took 50,481 steps today. Not sure how accurate but I was on the move for 11 hours and 35 minutes. 6 AM run, 7;30 breakfast, 8-12 work, 12-1 lunch, 1-5 work so I wouldn't be surprised if that was true. Today's workload consisted of digging trenches out from around the tents so if it rains, the rain will go into the trenches. Tomorrow will be another good day of work, nothing else to report other than I love this place.

7.12.2017
Mileage 8

Even though the last two days have been hard manual labor I decided to get up a little earlier and do a workout, 8-mile morning here is how I broke it up. 4 mile run down to the uphill 5k start line at 6:35s, 1 mile up beat at 6:05s, 3 mile cooldown back up to camp at 7:00s. It was a doozy; longest run I have had in a couple weeks.

After the workout, we worked till 1 then headed down to wild horse lake it is about a mile hike down off the summit and the water is freezing cold! Can only stay in it for maybe 20 seconds before you feel like you're dying. I hiked up one of the mountain sides, more like rock climbed because I wanted to explore what looked like a cave. Once I got within 20 feet of this "Cave" it turned out to be a shaded rock.... I used all that energy for that. My mistake. Tomorrow will be another 5 mile run to fish lake to work out the workout from today.

7.15.2017

A recap of the last three days:

Thursday: 5 miles worked on final preparation for campers

Friday: Ran in the AM, then double again that night, we woke up 4:15 to watch the sunrise, I mean sure it was beautiful but 4:15? Ugh. 6 miles on the day.

Saturday: Today ran 45 mins at 6:22s in Burns nothing too crazy. Tonight, we have the annual barbeque for staff of the camp and I am excited to see everyone again after the year. Steens is so special because the people are absolutely incredible. When I was at USAs I sat with Ty, the 5th 6th 7th man for Steens, and a massage therapist for Nike. He is traveling to London after Steens for the World Championship. I also heard Dave Frank, the coach at Central Catholic High School in Portland, a national powerhouse for high school running. I remember running down the backstretch to the start of the prelim to hear Frank yell, "Let's go DAVID RIBICH FROM ENTERPRISE!!!" it was just what I needed going into the prelim. I just wanted to further explain how awesome these people are. Here is the weekly schedule:

Sun-Campers Arrive
Mon- Acclimation for Campers
Tues-Big Day (27-mile run/hike/climb)
Wed- much needed recovery day
Thurs-Cross Canyon
Fri-Olympics
Sat- Campers depart
Sun-Repeat above week for session 2

7.16.2017

Mileage 5

Today is the first night of camp and I feel bad writing because my light is on and the whole tent of 20 guys is trying to sleep. Explain to me why the first night of summer camp, you go straight to bed, these guys didn't even talk amongst themselves. They seem excited but disciplined for the week, they must be returning campers knowing they need all the strength they can get come Tuesday. I am a co-tent assistant with Jared Hixon a NAIA 1500m National Champion for Southern Oregon University. Current member of Team Run Eugene. I have not talked with him much, but he seems like a great guy. Also ran 5 miles this morning, can't forget about that!

7.17.2017
Mileage 8

Today was a good day, camp went through acclimation drills this morning, food was great and the tent is phenomenal. I think it will be a pretty good week with these guys. Usually on the first day you have a straggler, but everyone seemed to be moving right along. Lying in my cot right now everyone is so quiet. All the returners know what is coming tomorrow for the big day and really set the tone for lights out. I myself have been assigned group 4. I won't be with group 4 until after the campsite and after the 14-mile hike.

After the 14-mile hike, groups will split into group 1, group 2, group 3, and group 4. Group 1 will 60/60 out to the waterfall for seven miles. These means they will run for 60 seconds then walk for 60 seconds, all the way there. Group 2 will be doing 60/120-minute run, two minute walk, all the way to the waterfall. Group 3 will be doing 60/180. In the first three groups if they are going too fast a camper may hop off the trail till the group goes by so they can wait on the trail for the next group. Group 4 will be walking the whole way out.

In previous years I have either led group 1 or swept group 2, this is my first year being back with group 4 and I am excited because I am trying not to do workouts till august. I want to postpone the start of my season as long as a I can. I have heard a lot of "horror stories" and it involves poop, pee, puke, tears. So hopefully we will have some good action to report.

7.18.2017
Mileage 14?

Well after 21 miles of hiking and 7 mile run back to camp, I can tell you my legs feel great and my feet feel broken. Took over 61,000 steps today with 15 hours and 18 mins of movement. According to my polar watch. Today I swept group four and to be honest I don't have much to report. No puke, poop or pee. What I saw was strong relentless high schoolers battling their demons through the canyon and up the mountain side. The only campers in previous years I had been with had been the ones who are attempting group one. Never at this camp have I been with the kids struggling to take a single step after the hike.

Today I had one of my campers from my tent with me on the seven-mile hike. His name is Alex and he is one of the strongest guys in my tent. We were hiking and at mile 4 his quad started cramping. When I mean cramping, I mean visibly I could see his quad tensing up and pulling up his leg. All he did was grimace and wait for it to pass before he took another step closer to the waterfall. It was a humbling experience being with group four because I saw a different side of the camp. I am so thankful for the opportunity to help Alex and the other campers in group four make it out.

Group four companions, if you are reading this one year after our big day, I can still say today that you, group four, are the strongest ones at camp. Ron and Harland, camp director and founder, came up to me and asked if I wanted to be the guest speaker tomorrow night and I accepted. It's a 50-minute block. Let us see if I can fill the time. Unsure on my mileage on today, I will just call it 7 miles.

7.19.2017

Mileage 8

The day was overall success, 8 miles at 7:10s with our last 3 miles at 6:35s this elevation makes it seem a lot faster but felt good. Best part apart today was my opportunity to speak. Seriously, like what a night, I was honored with the task of speaking to the camp. I was supposed to speak for 40 minutes, I did my first speech run through earlier today and it was 13 minutes. I then said o well I'm sure I can talk more once I'm up there. Guess I was right, I talked from 8-9:05 and took questions till 9:30. 90 minutes of speaking. The whole thing was incredible. I started with explaining my development and transitioned into my college years. I wish someone recorded it so I could at least look back at it years to come and hear what I had to say word for word. My main points focused around "BE YOU" and enjoy the process not the result.

Being yourself is something I really value now; I never understood at the time when Johnson told me. At Azusa Pacific my sophomore year I jumped from being a 3:48 guy to a 3:43 guy. After the race Johnson said, "you know what I'm going to tell you now?" I quickly responded, "go cool down, get ready for the next one?" he replied, "no, Be David. Just keep being you." At the time I kind of chuckled and was like, okay? That's kind of weird. Until I went to USAs I knew exactly what he was talking about. When you are toeing the line, whether it is at a dork meet, dual meet, home meet, District meet, State meet, National meet whatever. Toe the line as YOU. If you toe the line as somebody else, you won't make it very far. Simple as that, when you warm up, how you present yourself, be you. Don't change your persona on race day. Everyone is different in the world so use that to your advantage.

When I walked into the holding area before the USA prelim I saw a bunch of robots wearing different branded gear. Everyone was doing the same thing, talking the same way, puffing their chests the same way, it just looked silly. I sat down in a chair talked with Engles a bit, Thompson a bit, Hunter a bit. Those guys seemed pretty cool. As heat 2 was on the track, I was standing next to Matthew Centrowitz. Ring a bell? Olympic Gold medalist? Yeah him. We were standing next to each other and a bunch of kids had their phones taking pictures of I assume him. So, I looked at him and said, "they taking pictures of you or me?" he looked at my feet, my bib, my jersey, my face and replied, "definitely you."

I just sort of blurted that out standing next to him because that's me! No matter who that person would have been I would have said that, being in that holding area I felt like I needed to be myself in order to succeed. Everyone seemed to be acting like everyone else. How you act leading up to a race greatly impacts the performance. If you are lacking a bit of confidence, puff your chest up, lift your chin and walk around like you own the place. A saying I always liked was "Fake it till you Make it." Leading up to races I have my insecurities like everyone else, but I try my hardest to hide them, or fake it till I make it.

My next focus was enjoying the process and not necessarily the result. I said that because my junior year was a roller coaster. From being the most fit I had ever been in the fall, to getting hurt, to relocating that fire. I learned a lot. In the fall, I got so caught up in nationals, the accolades, the awards that I forgot the value of each day. From December to June it was all about the process and everything seemed to click. I also talked about the declaration period for USAs and how I was in the biggest slump I had ever been in. For some reason "being just out" at the time was enough to jeopardize my performance.

This was another example of when I was thinking about only the result and forgetting that I just had an incredible last 6 months of running.

The campers were all ears and even asked questions at the end that were fun to answer, “where do I see myself in two years?” “what’s my favorite workout?” “how do I manage school and athletics?” “which pros were nice and which pros were mean?” I would totally answer those, but you know, those answers are Steens Mountain Exclusives. Had to be there. I also developed a title for this journal, “Small school, Big Dreams” or something of that fashion.

Tomorrow we are running cross canyon and starting the Olympic competition. Hoping for a fast and healthy cross canyon. Goodnight.

7.20.2017

Mileage 9

Thursday at Steens, warm up with 60/60s for 3 miles to the start of cross canyon, hike as a tent for 3 miles in, race across the canyon for 3 miles then a 3-mile run back to camp. For those of you reading this that don't know what Cross Canyon is; it's a 5k race from one edge of a canyon to the other, no course, no map, all you see are the buses far off on the other side. You must compete as a tent and everyone finishes together, no one left behind. During the race the counselor (me) gives a quote to the campers, the quote is usually 20+ words. I run down the line of campers giving each of them one word to remember, then, at the end of Cross Canyon we get back in order from the start and everyone says their one word forming the quote. If you have one mistake, whether it is missing a word, messing up a word, you get thirty seconds added to your overall time. It's a game changer. So today, I had a pretty good feeling going into it because of how cohesive the guys have been all week.

You could say my feeling was accurate because we ended up winning the whole thing! The tent stayed together and were so supportive the whole time. I am so happy we pulled together as a tent and won. These guys deserve it. We are going into the Olympic competition tomorrow in first place, let's see if we can get the job done.

7.21.2017

Mileage 9

Well we didn't end up winning the backpacks, but we got third! All In all, incredible experience. I love these guys up here and it's a place I can call home. The staff and atmosphere make me love every second of it up here. I miss my girlfriend and I hope she can someday come up here with me. Next year will be interesting because I am not sure what I will be doing post collegiate. This might be my last night as a counselor because next week I have been offered a coaching position for a tent meaning I will be staying across the creek in my own tent.

Tonight, the camp did skits and I got roasted pretty good. It's all fun and the skits were great. One guy, named Ty would always say "Hi I am David Ribich, buy my book it's on sale." It was all fun and I told him he will get the first copy. Julian Heninger ended up winning the backpacks again this year and Julian if you are reading this in 2018 or whenever, I'm still bitter that you won this go around again. Next week I'm rooting for Gabe.

The last exciting thing that happened today was the uphill coffee cake 5k challenge, the competitors, Max King, Gabe Harm, Julian Heninger and me. We started by eating a square of coffee cake and drinking 4 oz. of coffee. We proceed to race up to mile one, coffee, coffee cake; then to mile two indulge coffee cake and coffee, mile three stuff the mouth, try not to throw up, then finish. Mile three was an interesting zone because the coffee had hot sauce and we could eat a chorizo sausage cooked the night before to minus 1 minute on our overall time. No one threw up, but I was close, thank you Mike Donaghu for putting together the "meet". You are a mighty fine meet director. Tomorrow we head back into Burns for the night.

7.22.2017
Mileage 6

I am writing an early log today in the hotel next to my coffee cake rival Julian. It's 3:05 PM and I have 13 dollars left in cash and 30 cents to my name in my two bank accounts combined. The joys of being a college student athlete. Tonight's dinner should be covered; a delicious steak feast bought by Harland. I may take a beer, I may take two. Going to lay in bed take a nap and watch cops till dinner time.

7.23.2017
Mileage easy 4

We had a staff meeting today getting everything lined out for another successful week. I apologize if this month is boring to you, August we will start kicking up the good workouts. Today was just an easy 4 mi es with Laney before we part ways for the year. I didn't realize this until now, but I have officially been doing this journal for l ttle over a month now! Pretty crazy it's already been a month! Even crazier we are one week out of August!

Tomorrows run will be a light run of 7 miles with Erin Clark, Div.1 All-American. She is also a coach this week. She runs at Colorado. She is an incredible runne and I am sure we will be running a lot together. Two months till I race in San Francisco!

7.24.2017

Mileage 8

A good 5 miles in the morning with Erin at 7:02s, great relaxing run, really enjoy talking with her. Pretty funny she was telling me her indoor facility is super nice and the biggest hiccup was they only installed one men's and women's restroom. RIP to bathroom breaks. After the run I ate breakfast and watched as the counselors did introductions for the campers. After that ran another 3 miles felt much better on that run, everything started to work right. After dinner right before bed I went to the coach's campfire and Bridget Franek was there and talked with me.

We talked for a good while and she said, forget about what you are doing next year and focus on this year. I think I'll stick with that. she knows what she is talking about.

7.25.2017
Mileage 14

Today was "The Big Day" but not the traditional hike down the canyon for 14 miles, 60/60 for 7 miles up Little Blitzen, climb out the cliffs, and run 7 miles back to camp. Instead; we drove off the mountain and onto a dirt road for two hours, the buses stop as we begin shuff ing kids off into groups. To be honest, I was in the blind today, I didn't know what was going on at the start. Once the groups were divided group one takes off, led by Max King and yours tru y. Our mission? Run the campers to the ground. Make them pay. Just kidding, our mission was run 13.2 miles on a rolling 5000 ft elevated, 98 degree scorched sage brushed dirt road at 6:18 mile pace. At the start, we had 43 campers, at mile three we had 4 campers. Mile 13.2 those same 4 campers finished together beaten and burned.

This was my first real workout since my break and it went pretty well, I think we averaged around 6:40s once it was all said and done. We slowed it down after mile 8 so no one blew up, but it was still a doozy of a day. The four guys had so much grit sticking together and working through the pain together. From small school to big school the campers worked together.

I do feel bad however because I heard a rumor at the start that we were only doing 6 miles, so at mile 3 I told the campers halfway there! I was very wrong. Going to be relatively sore but I am excited to be back in Monmouth putting in the workouts because it's going to be a good year. I know it.

Side note: one month till Olivia is 20!!!!

7.26.2017
Mileage 7

Morning after the big day and I feel good physically. Emotionally I am a little distraught; I'm sitting in the corral and this kid is telling Harland about the trials of his life. He is explaining how his parents are alcoholics, divorced, his mom used to hit him. This kid is explaining his life to Harland and says, "but you know, my life is no different than cross country."

Cross country is the epitome of life. There are hills, rough patches, bad weather, good weather, and how you approach those barriers changes your entire race/life. There are hills of life, storms of years and somehow, we manage to make it through them. After every sunset there is always a sunrise and cross country is a life sport. I didn't want to eavesdrop, so I packed up and left when he said that his life is no different than cross country; but I didn't need to hear more. I heard enough, and he is right, cross country is life. We all have our hills, I surely have mine, you surely have yours.

These last three weeks continuously remind me how important running is to the world. There is no sport like it where you can face your demons and your tribulations. Yesterday the four campers that stuck through the big day took life head on. You know there is a finish line in life, you don't know how far you have till the finish, but you are going to keep fighting. At the finish, you can look back and cherish how great your run at life was.

Ran this morning for 4 miles at 7:15s and a PM 3 mile run at 7:20s for 7 today. This is also my 25th log.

7.27.2017

Mileage 9

3 miles up to the cross canyon start again at 7:20s but trust me it felt like 4:30s, 3 mile run through the canyon, almost rolled my ankle a few times, took a stick in the side and almost punctured my skin; dialed the intensity back a bit through the canyon. After the canyon I ran 3 miles back with the counselors for a good 9 miles on the day. We always race the buses on the way back.

Tomorrow is the last full day at Steens and to be honest I am pretty tired, I love it here, but I am ready to head back, get some good miles in with the guys, kiss Olivia, sleep in my bed. Civilization seems real nice right now. On a different subject, we forged a metal wire into a chevron, and may or may not be getting a brand, (Erin Clark. Piper and Ella Donaghu, Gabe Harm, Julian Heninger, Kyle Thompson, Sam Truax and myself) I am roped in.

7.28.2017
Mileage 8

Today was the last full day up at Steens, great three weeks of training, experience, and memories. Tonight, I got branded with a nice little symbol that looks kind of like ^. Sorry mom if you are reading this, I know I shouldn't announce that I have a brand, but I must document it right? It really did not hurt that bad its right above my left hip, ask me about it next time you see me (or not if we are in public). I was expecting it to hurt a lot more, we will see how it feels for the next two weeks. I still do not have a tattoo so that says something. Never would I think I would be getting a brand before a tattoo.

I have to get up at 5:30 tomorrow so I am going to keep this log short, sooner I go to bed, the sooner I see Olivia. Easy 8 miles throughout the day. We are almost in August folks! We almost have workouts!

7.29/7.30.2017

This is a combined entry from yesterday and today. Yesterday I woke up at 5 and started to unpack camp. Once that was done, we left camp at 8:30, said our goodbyes and I got on the bus to Salem. I thought I would be going to Portland, but Olivia has to work next two days and has a baby shower to attend so I will just head home and catch up on some sleep.

7.31.2017
Mileage 8

Last night I went to bed at 9 PM and I woke up at 9:18am undisturbed it was a great reset. This morning Brady and I ran an easy 3 miles at 6:55s pace. Then he bought me breakfast cause like I said I have 30 cents to my name until I cash this check. I'll pay him back. Going to pack up a lot of clothes I don't need today and donate them. I say that because I looked at the three weeks of clothes I packed, and it did not even look like I dented my dressers and drawers. So, it's time to clear out.

Tonight I doubled with AJ for an easy five miles. Today is already the last day of July! Tomorrow will be a hot day, 100+ so it says. 5 mile AM run 3 mile PM run on deck! Its 12:01 am, officially August!

8.1.2017
Mileage 8.5

First run of August this fine morning. 6 miles with the guys; my training is starting to look a lot more structured training with the guys.

Today: [1 mile warm up on the track consisting of 2 laps 2 laps, first two laps jog, 100m run, 50m walk for 2 laps then into a 4 mile run at 6:32s. then a PM run once the sun went down, 2.5 miles at 6:42s.]

Tomorrow morning will be a good run with Zach Holloway and Brady; both my previous roommates my sophomore year and super fans at USAs.

8.2.2017
Mileage 9

Easy steady miles in Corvallis. 9 miles at 6:45s I feel much better than I thought I would after 18 Buffalo Wild Wings and a beer. Luckily, I dropped the 18 freshly made Ribich chicken nuggets in an outhouse before we ran. Ended up helping Olivia and her family do some yard work at her house. Six hours in 105-degree weather was a doozy but it was well worth it. Olivia and I leave in two days for our annual beach trip and it will be a good weekend before it gets crazy before preseason.

8.3.2017
Mileage 7

Woke up early I guess I am still on Steens Mountain time. It works because I was able to beat the heat. Ran 7 miles in 45 mins whatever that pace equals out to, sub 7 mins per mile for sure, too late for math. Today was a hot day and there is so much smoke in the air from forest fires everywhere. Most of this smoke is coming down from Vancouver. Damn Canadians. I am really excited for the next week! I will finally be able to spend time with Olivia, be home and partake in a wedding. Here is my next week schedule:

August 4-6: At the coast with Olivia
August 7: Pack for home
August 8: Fly home
August 9: BBQ back in the county
August 10: Drive back
August 11: Wedding rehearsal
August 12: Wedding

8.4.2017

Mileage 10

This morning run was my longest run since my 13 miler at Steens. Today was 10 miles in 66 mins so that's what? 6:40s? maybe I should just leave the math to you guys.

After the run at some good lunch and headed to the coast. On the way to Newport Olivia and I pulled over on the side of the road and watched the men's 10,000m race because we must use my data somehow! Also, congrats to Drew Windle on advancing to the next round in the 800m at the World Championships! Go Division 2! After using all my dada, we settled into our Pallet Palace, an Airbnb owned and operated by a man named Guy Faust. Turns out he ran with Prefontaine at Oregon and raced him in high school.

8.5.2017

Mileage 3

Today was my off today but Olivia and I still got a good 3 miles in doing the Amazing Race in Newport. It was fun! We ended up winning it but some of the tasks were like; gutting a fish, chugging a beer, doing a puzzle, paddle boarding. Overall it was really really fun our competitive juices were surely flowing. Then tonight we went to a restaurant in Newport called Clearwater. I got the Dungeness crab, a glass of wine. Olivia got fish and chips and a Spritzer. We spent a fair share amount of money but a dinner like this is something everyone deserves once in a while. Tomorrow is my off day so not sure if I will be running, this week will be low mileage, but I am gearing up for a race or two in November.

8.6.2017

Mileage 2

Well I said I wasn't going to run but Olivia and I ran a solid 2 miles at 7:30s when we got home from the coast and the Timbers game. The Timbers game was so fun! First MLS game I have been to and they won, I must be the lucky charm. Two weeks now till preseason and all you readers won't have to read these boring logs! You can start reading the workouts! Wahoo!

8.7.2017
Mileage 9

Ended up doing 9 miles today in a workout pattern [3 miles at 6:45, 3 miles at 5:55s, 3 miles back to the house at 6:30s, 3x80 stride once I made it to Olivia's].

It is still morning, but I figured I would just do my entry log now because my flight got cancelled tomorrow and has been now switched to today. So, I am hoping my legs don't fall off when I am in the plane. From Portland to Enterprise it is only a 6 hour drive. However, I do not have my car, and my car still does not have updated tags. We chose a flight into Lewiston because it will be a lot easier to pick me up there then Portland. In Lewiston I will be meeting Falk, my German foreign exchange student I hosted my junior year of high school.

If you didn't know this about me, I hosted six foreign exchange students growing up from 8th grade to senior year of high school. I really recommend anyone thinking about hosting a student to go through with it. Looking back at it now I am so blessed that I was able to experience growing up with 5 different countries and experiences. I have family all over the world and seeing them someday will be incredible. Anyways, my flight pattern for tonight is Portland to Salt Lake City then Salt Lake City to Lewiston, why am I flying over Oregon and Idaho to only go back to Idaho? I don't know but it works. I will hopefully be working on my journal tonight on the plane, hoping for a comfy flight.

8.8.2017
Mileage 8

Today's run felt like dog****. After flying yesterday with the 9 miles in my legs I am a little stiff. Feels like I am learning how to run again, maybe even learning how to walk again that's how stiff I felt. I didn't have my GPS watch on today, so I have no idea how slow I was going.

Tonight I will be going out to dinner with my high school coach Dan Moody. I am going to buy him a beer and present him with my 2017 1500m National Champion trophy. What he does with it after I give it to him is up to him. My logic is the trophy is great, but it does me no good sitting on my shelf gathering dust. I have 5 other All-American trophies sitting on the shelf (also gathering dust). With my 1500m being absent from the shelf it must mean I need to get another one. I am giving my trophy to Moody because I would not be where I am today if it wasn't for his patience and mentoring as I developed. I would have not been able to accomplish everything I did in and after high school if it was not for him. He deserves that trophy just as much as I do, if not more. Moody has coached at Enterprise for the last 30+ years. Did you read that right? 30+ years!! If he is not coach of the world, I don't know who is.

Tomorrows run will hopefully be better, I am meeting up with a high school guy Spencer to put some miles in. Spencer is from Central Catholic and here in the county on family vacation, his coach messaged me and asked if I wanted to run with him, of course!

8.9.2017
Mileage 6

Early morning run with Spencer It was nice to run with someone here in the county. Usually when I come to Enterprise, I have to convince one of my friends from high school to ride a bike next to me. Spencer saved me that trouble and we went on a good 6-mile loop on country dirt roads.

After the run, watched a lot of world championship races. My heart is SO BROKEN FOR QUIGLEY OMG! To summarize, she got disqualified for a steeple prelim for "gaining advantage" from stepping on the line. When realistically she had no choice but to step on the line or she would of ran into the girl in front of her. Complete bull. Later, Paul Chelimo went down in the 5000m prelim, got up and still qualified! Like what? He could have easily packed up and called it there, but he rose back to his feet and raced to the finish getting a time qualifying mark.

After watching all the intense races at worlds and getting really jazzed up about it. I went to a BBQ at the lake, it was a BBQ for me, as weird as that sounds. I just wanted to see as many people as possible so if they could all come to my location, I figured that would be great. I saw high school friends, elementary teachers, high school coach, roughly 20 people showed up and it was actually pretty successful! I am glad I did that.

After that Damon. Rocky, Falk and I went to Embers Brew House (a place where I rose the ranks as a kid, dishwasher, cook, server) we had some beer, ate some jalapeno poppers and had a grand ol time. Tomorrow I am meeting back up with Spencer to get some more miles in. We are running up to Slick Rock, one of my all-time favorite spots.

8.10.2017
Mileage 7

Busy day, ran with Spencer up to Slick Rock. We rock climbed to a swimming hole, took a quick dip then ran back towards the car. It is about a 3.5 mile trail from the start to the swimming hole, so 7 on the day? Probably will not run again today, I am happy with that run. Especially happy because I ate it and tripped on a root on the way back. That's what happens when you try and record a video of you running while running.

After that I watched the 1500m prelims, Andrews advanced, Gregorek advanced, and the defending Olympic 1500m champion does not. Now how does that work? Does that mean there are 25 guys better than the Olympic champion? Most likely an off day, off year, a lot of stuff going on for him. It all depends who is good on the day and who is not. A lot of variables are added into the mathematical equation called track and field. I am excited to watch Andrews and Gregorek advance. Gregorek runs his own race which is so cool to see, he ran that prelim just like he ran at USAs. Wait, wait, 300m, go! Pretty incredible patience on his part on a world stage to do that. Crazy to watch these guys on the world stage two months after I ate their dust.

Tonight we are driving to Monmouth, should get in around 1 am. I have to get back for the wedding rehearsal and begin to get situated in Monmouth. It was a short trip home, but it was much needed.

8.11.2017

Mileage 7

Ran in Monmouth this morning with the guys. Felt good to be with them again. Randomly my right ankle started aching, not incredibly bad just weirdly sore, I assume it's just from the travel, so we shall see how it goes on tomorrows run.

Oh yeah, HOLY AMAZE BALL EMMA COBURN AND COURTNEY FRERICHS! 1-2 for steeplechase IN THE WORLD! Just wow...I have never yelled at my phone so much. I was ready to race right then. It was the most inspiring, motivational race I had ever seen. Truly incredible, I am so happy I used all my months data in 10 days to watch worlds and to watch that race.

Tonight we are driving down to Zach and Rachel's wedding rehearsal. I know right now Zach is doing a 20 miler on his wedding day tomorrow so let's see how many miles I do.

8.12.2017
Mileage, any guesses?

Today is the day! Zach and Rachel are getting married! Our bachelor party was a good ol 20 miler. We did 20 miles, when I say we, I mean Zach. Brady did mile 1-8 and 12-20 for a 16 mile day. I did mile 6-20 so quick math 14 miles. Most definitely my longest run of the summer and a pretty big jump in terms of aerobic work. Now, when I say we ran I should say we worked out. It will be split up in terms of Zach's miles because I joined in at mile 6, so these are the miles I ran in association with Zach's workout.

(mile 6)/6:39
7/6:23
8/5:48
9/6:08(big incline)
10/5:46
11/5:45
12/6:42
13/6:36(RECOVER 2 MILES)
14/5:50
15/6:04(STRUG. BUS MILE)
16/6:06
17/6:30 (COOLDOWN)
18/19/20 7:00+
**Overall really satisfied with today, clicked off good splits with a lot of climb involved. Very happy I was able to do this with Zach and Brady.*

Now, Zach's wedding is complete! It was absolutely amazing! Love is in the air! It was so great that I was able to be a part of their special day; as well share a dance with my girlfriend at the wedding. After a long day we are currently just relaxing in the room. One thing Riley (longtime friend of the group) had us do is go around the room and tell each other one thing we love about each other. When it got to me, Sam, Riley and Brady told me I am humble. Now is it humble for me to talk about being told I am humble? I don't know. But what I do know is that I hope I can live by that standard. Being humble is something I hope to carry throughout my entire career.

8.13.2017
Mileage 8

Early morning 6 miles with Josh and Brady, felt heavy, first three miles were rough then opened the stride a bit and I loosened up. The pace was around 6:20s at the end. Today I meant to watch 5k, 800m, and 1500m at worlds but I did bad math and got the times mixed up for when they were racing. Tonight, a group of the guys did a "Firecracker 800m" where Josh won it in 1:53 and I kid you not he walked it in. literally. He is scary fit and so are the rest of the guys. I surely would have done it if I didn't have 14 miles in my legs from the day before. We will have a damn good top 5 this year. Our biggest competitor will be health.

Chico and Alaska are good obviously, but we are more focused on maintaining our health through November, so we can compete with those teams. Tomorrow is an extreme recovery day, after the run it will be 15 mins rolling out, 6 minutes in ice bath, 6 minutes in heat tub, 6 mins in ice, 6 mins in heat, 30 mins in compression boots. I have to make my body fresh before next week.

8.14.2017

Mileage 10

Getting back in the groove and its feeling nice. Today's AM run was a mile warm up.

For future reference we usually do two laps two laps which is two laps jogging then two laps of stride 100m walk 50m. after we went into an easy 5 miles @ 6:50s then this afternoon. Sorry if this is a surprise. We played some dungeons and dragons then did a 3-mile run finishing off with two laps two laps again.

Some drills we did after:
2x20 leg swings
2x5 rocket jumps
3x5 drop squats
6x6 hurdle walkover
2x6 side walk over
4x6 over under hurdle walkovers.

All in all, today was a successful day, tomorrow we are doing a speed workout.

PSA: DON'T EAT CANDY I CHIPPED A PIECE OF MY FILLING OFF BECAUSE OF RUNTS!!!

8.15.2017
Mileage 7

Quick speed test at the track
Two laps two laps into a 20-minute run
3x200s @ 26.5 26.4 26.7
3x120s
Into a campus loop (1.5 miles)

Overall, I felt really good this morning, that is the first time I have spiked up in eight weeks. still feel like my legs have the speed but lost the coordination. I'll find it and be all good to go when I need it. Tonight, I was planning on doubling again, but it got too late from a 4 ½ hour game of risk with Josh AJ and Dustin. Tonight will be roughly 10 ½ hours of sleep, if that is a care to anyone.

12 miles on deck for tomorrow.

8.16.2017
Mileage 13

Good day in the books! Morning was a 10 miler with a solid group of guys. I was a little worried last night going to sleep cause my mind was running risk scenarios and dice rolls till I fell asleep. Todays 10-mile morning was by far the easiest 10 I have done in a while, we did our two laps two laps into just a 9 mile run. After we gathered back at my house, made some breakfast.

After breakfast I went into Coaches office and he told us (the four of us) that we should be leaders by example. That we shouldn't be the ones worrying about the freshman's success. Take care of our business and keep doing what we're doing, they will be alright. After we hung out until we started another game of risk. After that we went back out for 3 mile shakeout. Tomorrow I am hoping for anywhere between 8-10 miles. Five days till preseason!

8.17.2017
mileage 9

In the AM, I ran 5.5 miles, mile warm up (two laps two laps) then 4.5-mile run. Legs feel pretty good after 13 miles yesterday. We did not do anything but hang out today like every day really. We are sort of sloths in human bodies, especially this last week before preseason. I also typed up a lot of entries for my journal, so here I am journaling about my journaling, what does that make then, journal-ception?

After dinner we went back out for 3.5 miles to finish off the day with 9 miles. Tomorrow, I'll be happy with 8-10 again because Saturday we have a 12 mile single run we have to do, then Sunday we help people move in. Holy cow it's almost preseason. This is my last preseason. Are you all excited? I am excited! I can give you more structured days instead of you reading a paragraph of, "We did nothing, we played DnD, I ran miles...blah blah blah." Only 4 days out from preseason and roughly a month and 4 days out till the first race!

8.18.2017
Mileage 10

Only two days till preseason and three days till the eclipse so technically the end of the world, right? The world ends on the eclipse so if you are reading this now, we lived.

This morning's run was an easy 5.5 in the am like yesterdays. And PM was 3.5. both runs averaged around 6:50s, super slow and recovery based. Crosswhite is back in town now and it's good to see him fitter than ever going into this upcoming year. Tomorrow we have 12-mile single run, we will see how the legs feel.

8.19.2017
Mileage 13

First week of real miles done for the year! Wahoo! If I am doing light night math, I think I was at 70 miles for this week on the nose. This morning was a 12-mile run at 6:36s. At 11.5 miles in we stepped on the track and the group of us 8 threw down a 70 second lap, jogging one more lap to finish it at 12. A fast lap at the end of a run like that really wakes up the legs. It sounds painful/difficult and it was but the last 100m felt smoother than ever. Leg swings, strides, and stretching followed.

After rolling out and stretching out the legs I talked a lot with my sister Madison, I haven't talked much about her, but she is an incredible woman! She lives n France and today we agreed Olivia and I will be going to see her December 9th-18th or some days like that. After the planning with her, some of the guys and I played our third game of risk in the last four days. After the game I ran a mile with Brady and AJ, but I stopped after a mile because my right Achilles was being weird. Tomorrow morning going to take off and go out to breakfast with Olivia! Finally! In bed at 9:55

8.20.2017

Mileage 9.5

Looks like I got 9.5 miles in for the day. Probably should have taken it easier but everyone just got here for pre-season, everyone likes to go hard the first few days. The guys team looks good and I think it will be a fun and competitive year. My days runs were like this:

Morning: 2 miles at 6:43s
Afternoon: 2.5 miles at 6:35s
Night: 5 miles at 6:04s

The night run with the team is always faster than it needs to be. It is like all the guys comeback and measure each other. Comparing each other's fitness. I mean I'm sure guilty of it. I like to surge to the front and see where everyone's at. Tomorrow is the eclipse so who knows what kind of mileage will be done.

8.21.2017

Mileage 10-11

MY LAST FIRST DAY OF PRESEASON IS COMPLETE! Started off the day with a 3-mile run before the eclipse. The team all met at 9:30 and we watched the whole event unfold. For the first 30 minutes I was thinking ..what a joke this is so lame. Then totality hit, and I was like OMG IT IS NIGHT TIME 360 DEGREES OF SUNSET O MY GOSH! (20 seconds later) alright this is lame again. But in all seriousness, it was cool! Super happy Johnson made it a big enough deal to bring everyone together for it.

Our PM run was organized, we did:
two laps two laps for warm up,
3x40 side to side,
1x 20 leg swings,
1x20 second Achilles stretch
30-minute run
Back to the track 100,200,300
13.4,28.7,43.2

I felt tired going into the workout and was somewhat nervous, but our big workout is Friday, and this is just what I needed to shake out the legs.

8.22.2017
Mileage 7

Would you look at that! 50 logs in the journal, if you have read each log through and suffered through my summer words thank you! If you are just joining us because you skipped to preseason! Welcome!
Another workout in the legs getting everything fine-tuned for Friday. I am kind of treating this workout coming up like a race. Not saying I want to win it but just this is my first “real” workout since 1500m work this June, I am excited to see where I am at.

Quarter mile warm up
1x20 leg swings
3x40 side to side
2x20 alternating toe touch
1x15 Spiderman
30-minute run
3x80 acceleration
3x2x200
Goal: 30|jog 200| 27
Set 1: 30.3|27.3
Set 2: 29.3|27.7
Set 3: 28.3|27.1
Cooldown
1x3 minutes inverted
5 mins lying quietly

Hit all the times we were supposed to. We kind of red-rovered this workout where we had 3 groups of 6 and 1 or 2 people from a group would swap after each set, so I got to workout with almost all the guys, pretty good day. Tomorrow I will be sleeping in till 8 and will not be talking all day. Why? Because after we played a game of Killer Bunnies I realized how verbally aggressive I can be towards Dustin. He is a backstabbing two timing board game player that is really good and really hard to beat. So, for how harsh I can be I told him I will give the world one full day of silence. Hopefully that will suffice 364 days of aggression. We shall see how tomorrow goes.

8.23.2017

Mileage 10

Slept in till my alarm went off at 8:30 and wow did that feel great. Woke up had a good ol English muffin sandwich and went to our team meeting. At this meeting we wrote down our goals for the year. I drew mine out in a mind map. If you don't know what that is, google it cause its really cool and really efficient.

I try and separate my goals into two categories, abstract and concrete. Abstract are more intrinsic motivators, concrete are extrinsic, tangible results or awards. My abstract goals can be summarized: enjoy the process not the result, love the team, my family and Olivia, enjoy the competitions. Concrete goals: Win DMR title, set the Division II record in the 1500m, sign professional contract.

Those things stated above cannot be achieved without focusing on each day. With that said, today is Wednesday, our circuit days.

Here is our average circuit:

Warm up 2 laps 2 laps

2x 30 turning side to side

1x20 leg swings

1x20 right hand left leg

20 to 25-minute run as assigned

90 second Achilles stretch leg stretch at fence

Circuits 2 sets-4 mins between sets (everything is in meters)

2x10 burpees-30 second break- with pushups

2x10m- 2 float speed skater-30 sec break

4x80m technique

2x50 big skips – 30 sec recovery

1x40 speed skater

2x25 wheelbarrow

1x4 position plank-10 sex hold each position

2x5 rocket jumps with med ball

1x10m md ball overhead lunge

1x10 lateral lunge

1x4 position balance plank

1x15m inch worms

3x80 technique stride

Cooldown

3x200 stride or relaxed cooldown 20-minute run

1x20 supine & prone leg swing

3 minutes inverted

5 minutes peaceful relaxation

There you go, our average circuit written out! Did it hurt your brain reading it as much as it hurt my body doing it? Probably! Chances of me writing that out again for next week are slim so maybe just always refer to this week for circuit work. I'll add drills if anything changes. 2 mile PM run as well to shake out the legs. Although it was only a 10 mile day it could be easily added up in terms of work to a 15 mile day.

8.24.2017

Mileage 10

8 miles with the guys in the morning. Took a while to feel good, adjusting to the big groups. Today's am 8 miles was a good shakeout from yesterday's circuit. Our location today was Saddle, it's a nice forest loop in the McDonald National Forest outside Corvallis. Some people wanted to pull away and really drop the hills, but I am trying to conserve my energy for tomorrow's workout.

For activities outside running today I went to the dentist. I hate it! I mean getting my teeth cleaned is awesome, however I did not get that today. Instead I sat in a chair for two hours while the dentist X-rayed my teeth explaining how expensive my procedures going to be to remove and add a new filling. RIP to my bank account. So, I was kind of upset from that on the drive home, teared up a bit, but held it back because momma didn't raise no *****.

After dinner the guys and I ran 5 mins after getting home so I felt like I was going to throw up all my food, but I held it down nicely. We played some Killer Bunnies then watched a movie. It is a little late right now 10:26 so I'm going to call it a night because tomorrow is going to be a great day! It is my first workout of the year, Olivia's 20th birthday, stellar recruits on campus, and it's our annual MAFIA NIGHT! I did not order those events in order of importance…or did I? Doesn't matter.

8.25.2017

Mileage 10

Today was a solid day!!! Holy crap! First ran to Olivia's house (which is across the street) and shook her awake saying happy birthday! Then she rolled over with her cute little sleepy smile and I went home. After that moment, it was game face time. Turned on Russ, shadow boxed the mirror, and got changed into workout attire. From there I joined the team on the track for an extremely successful workout to start the day off right.

Warm up:

2 laps/2laps

1x20 leg swings

3x40 side to side

3x80 acceleration

Campus loop warm up

Switch shoes into New Balance 5000m flats

3x80 acceleration

1x200 @ 32

Workout goal:

Mile 1 @ 6:10 | Mile 2 @ 5:10 | Mile 3 @ 6:00|Mile 4 @ 5:00 | Mile 5 @ 5:50 | Mile 6 @ 4: 50

So, the workout was designed to be speed change over under work. Slow, fast, slow, fast, slow, fast. Progressing to the last mile being the fastest. At least those times were what we were supposed to do. Here were our actual splits:

Mile 1 @ 6:14 | Mile 2 @ 5:14 | Mile 3 @ 5:52 | Mile 4 @ 5:02 | Mile 5 @ 5:44 | Mile 6 @ 4:39

What can we see with this workout? To start it was tough pacing. We had 7 guys finish the workout strong and everyone alternated leads so overall it was nice not having to do all the work pacing or having one other person do It all. For the last mile, it was split 2:25 and 2:14 for the 800 splits. For the last 400m of the last mile we split 62 seconds. 34,28. It felt so good closing in a 28 after that many laps on the track. What was even better was finishing and looking over my shoulder to see six other bodies finishing strong within 4 seconds of me. (not saying I am surprised I am just so happy we have a deep team.)

The most important competitor we will face this year is injury or illness. We need the team to stay healthy. If we can manage that, we will be big time contenders against the conference and region. Today was also the deciding factor that Tyler Jones, Dustin Nading, Justin Crosswhite, Josh Dempsey and I won't be opening till San Francisco September 23. So a month away. That is currently the top five. Today's workout was 10x better because we had two recruits on campus Hunter and Josh from Bandon. They got to see our first workout of the year crushed in a swarm of seven guys. Today's workout was the biggest group I have ever been a part of finish that strong. Usually it separates thin towards the end but today was tighter than ever.

After the workout I went home, cleaned up and presented Olivia's birthday present. SURPRISE WE ARE GOING TO FRANCE! Olivia and I will be going to visit my sister this December from December 9th-18th (rough dates). I am going to buy the tickets mid-September once we organize everything better.

Looks like you will be getting a bit of winter travel thoughts when I am in France. Maybe I will attempt a whole log in French (probably not). Olivia has taken French classes, so I am banking on her being my translator until we meet up with my French fluent sister.

After the birthday shenanigans, we had our annual MAFIA NIGHT! If you have played the card game version; this should make sense. If you have not played the card game version, I will do my best to explain it even more.

Here is how it works out; tonight's group was a record 46 people. So that was crazy:

1) Everyone wears black and shows up to a house with all its windows covered so no light can come through.
2) Everyone yells over top of each other because they are super excited to play
3) We pass out playing cards to everyone
4) If you drew a numbered card out of the deck you are a CIVILIAN
5) If you drew a King or Queen out of the deck you are a MAFIA
6) Everyone hands back their card to the deck and closes their eyes. The mayor (whoever wants to speak) calls mafia to open their eyes and see who the other mafia members are.
7) The round then starts, and all the lights are shut off into complete darkness.
8) If you are a civilian, you must run around the house in the dark and try not to get killed by the mafia.
9) If you are mafia you should sneak around and try and kill the civilians. How you kill a civilian is you gently (or forcefully if the civilian doesn't want to die) slide your finger across the neck of a civilian killing them.
10) If you are killed by a mafia you collapse on the dark cold floor and say NOTHING!
11) The round is over when someone finds a "dead body" and yells "dead body dead body" for all to hear.
12) After "Dead body" is yelled the lights turn on and if you died you stand up, exit the house/room and don't say a word.

Dead people cannot speak so you should leave without hinting to who killed you.

13) Everyone gathers in a center location for city council.
14) In city council, you argue and discuss who you think killed who, who was being suspicious, who saw who kill who yada yada yada.
15) Two people get placed on trial
16) The two people on trial defend their cases why they are innocent.
17) After each case, the town votes on who they believe is the mafia.
18) Whoever has the most votes after trial gets killed and must say if they were mafia or a civilian. Then, they leave the game and sit in the graveyard. (because we had so many people. The game was played at Olivia's and the graveyard was at my house. But with few people you can totally have the graveyard in a separate room in the house.)
19) After the trial, and execution, a new round begins.
20) The game is played until either only mafia are left, or the civilians vote out all the mafia.
21) The end, game over, conclusion, checkmate.

That is your 20 step guide to play mafia with your team. We had 8 mafia per round just because we had so many people. Usually we try and keep it 1/5 ratio so if there's 25 people playing 5 are mafia so on and so forth.

For tonight, I was mafia first game and was the last mafia alive, all my fellow mafia members were voted out in council. So here I am 50 minutes into the game alone in a dark house with only 4 other civilians. So what did I do? I fake died, slammed the floor like my body collapsed and waited till a civilian came to me to ask if I was dead. Then, I slit their throat with my finger.

I successfully did this trick to Nicole. Once Olivia came to check if I was dead, I attempted to slit her throat in the dark but was unsuccessful after slicing at her arm and her forehead.

Now I am sure you are reading this and are thinking, what a turd! Attempting to kills his own girlfriend on her birthday! How mean! However, last year's game Olivia and I decided to attempt to hide together, I ask her "Are your mafia" she says, "No I swear!" I said, "Okay." We proceed to hide behind the couch until I heard her giggle and felt her soft finger slice across my neck. Trust has been broken since.

After the unsuccessful payback attempt, we go into council because Nicole's body was found and someone says, "I think It was David! I also heard Olivia struggling with someone earlier."

Aaron then said, "David would not kill his girlfriend on her birthday."

Olivia proclaims, "Yes he would!"

I reply, "Hell yeah I would!"

After that I gave away my identity and they voted to killing me off. Civilians won.

We played another game but nothing too eventful happened I died second round. As you can see, we do work on the track, and team bond off the track. Something I really love about Western and Collegiate athletics is everyone is (usually) in it together and in it for the right reasons. Go wolves!

Happy birthday Liv!

8.26.2017

Mileage 9

Good early morning run 7 miles @ 6:27s with Hunter and Josh the recruits. It was not a designated practice, we had the morning off and I have known Hunter since he was in 7th grade so he has been a longtime friend and I am happy I got to go run with him. After yesterday's workout I felt surprisingly good today, Josh (recruit) dropped the last 3 miles and none of us really wanted to respond because of how much speed we did yesterday. After the run I went out to breakfast with the sophomores (Justin, Brennan, Sawyer) and with Hunter, Josh and Hunters dad. We went to the good ol' Starduster Café in Independence. I highly recommend it for breakfasts. Starduster is our teams Sunday breakfast spot after a good long run.

After this morning's meal and run, I went to AJ's house because they were hosting the Mayweather and McGregor fight. I personally was rooting for McGregor because I love his fire and competitiveness. However, you could see he was surely out of his element once the 5th round hit. I won't spoil who won in case you are still waiting to watch it on your DVR or something like that a year after the fight. The real losers are those of us who watched two men beat each other up for half an hour making 200+ million dollars. After the fight two easy miles at seven-minute pace conversating fight scenarios with Dustin.

Tomorrow is our long run so going to try and get some sleep. Early night 9:55pm.

8.27.2017

Mileage 13

Quarter mile warm up
4x40m side to side
1x40m quad stretch
1x20m RHLL (right hand left leg, left hand right leg stretches)
1x20 leg swing
3x80m stride
12.5 mile run at 6:42 miles
5x80m strides

First 55 minutes were 7-minute pace and I can tell you it felt so terrible! I felt like I couldn't find a rhythm or my form at all.

The last 25 mins we picked it up and I was finally able to feel good. From 60 minutes to 70 minutes we had 8x 40/40 tempo 40 seconds on tempo pace (5:00-5:30) to normal pace (6:30s). Something I love about our long runs here is Johnson incorporates these speed changes that really spice up the runs. At 55 minutes into a run you could feel stagnant, just try and pick it up for 30 seconds. While you speed up, stand tall, smile and then back down to the original pace. Guarantee you will feel sharper. I was planning on running again tonight but my stomach hurt pretty bad. Not sure if it was something I ate or what. 10:36PM woohoo! Night owl!

8.28.2017
Mileage 12

This mornings practice looked as followed:
Warm up 2 laps 3 laps
1x20 leg swings
4x30 turning side to side
1x20 way back stretches (reach as far back as you can down and touch your toes)
1x20 RHLL
2x40 big skips
2x20 scissor jumps (jumping jacks)
1x10 lateral lunge
3x5 drop squat
1x10 prone and supine leg swings
2x120
50-minute run @ 6:44s

Today's run was only supposed to be 40 minutes, but we swung back to the track and just asked if we could go extra ten minutes to eliminate going longer tonight. Of course, Papa J (Johnson) said yes. The air quality is starting to get a bit shaky from all the forest fires around, hopefully we don't get any big ones in Oregon. We also hung out and played some Dungeons and Dragons.

On a different note, David Torrence died today. They found him in a southern California swimming pool. He was such an incredible athlete and it is unbelievable he just passed. A healthy, fit, Olympian. Social media and other runners have exploded with the news. Kyle Merber a great friend of his and fellow Hoka Athlete tweeted some deep tweets about him and Torrence. It is so sad. I pray you take each day as it is and forget about the small stuff bothering you. This puts a lot in perspective that anything can happen at any moment. Love, live, and forget about the small pains of the world. When you're driving to the grocery store and someone takes forever to turn. Why get impatient? When your mom calls and you just want to play video games and she is interrupting, pause the damn game, talk to her.

If I die suddenly in my life, I hope I can rest easy knowing I changed lives, helped dreams come true, and inspired. If I die tomorrow, I hope today I loved, lived and enjoyed each breath. My life has been nothing but incredibleness since the day I was born. Sure, I have fought some battles with deaths, heartache, pain, but I am surrounded everyday by people who help me pursue my dream. If I died the day after this book is published and one person reads this journal and is inspired to live or love, I couldn't ask for more.

8.29.2017
Mileage 9

Today was a light day, just went out and ran an easy 9-mile morning at 6:50s and then went to a scary movie with the team. We watched Annabelle. It was pretty scary, so scary Olivia and I stayed with each other not sure who needed who more. (definitely her). Right before she was about to sleep, I pranked her and gasped super loud. She jumped up looked at me and slapped me across the chest. I deserved it. She then crawled away from me on the bed and pinned herself against the wall. Now I am writing this journal entry looking at her tucked as far away as me as possible.

Dustin asked if I was going to run with him and Brady at 9:30 PM but heck no! that's when I brush my teeth for bed!

8.30.2017
Mileage 10

Alright flip back to last week's circuit, that is exactly what we did this week. However, we only did it one time through because today we got here at 8 o clock, half hour earlier than everyone. By we, I mean AJ Dustin Josh and I (DMR team) and the women's 4x4 (Olivia, Suzie, Megan, Greyson). This morning prior to the circuit we did weights. Like we lifted. Today's date marks the first time I have ever been in a weight room for my sport. In high school I would go in a weight room for PE class but never had I actually lifted to benefit my running. Today's weights were not really that crazy.

3x 15 lb. kettlebell hip thrusts
5x3 20 lb. each hand overhead squat jumps (no idea what they are called)
5x5 20 lbs. goblet squats
3x5 full extension pull ups.
4x5 back straightener things. Also have no idea what they are called.

After we did the weights we went for a run and it was miserable. I attempted to take a nap today but was unsuccessful. In the am the mile total was 5 @ 6:50s and this afternoon was 4.5 @ 7:02s I was really hoping for 12 miles today but with the new weights added, I won't be too upset for missing those two miles. Tomorrow I will go for twelve miles.

8.31.2017
Mileage 12

Today's run was a recovery run from yesterday's circuit. One mile warm up of two laps two laps into 8 miles at 6:23 mile pace. It was quicker than I thought it would be but overall felt comfortable. After the run which was at saddle, we drove back and I proceeded to roll out for 5 minutes, stretch on the vibration platform for 10 minutes then get in the compression boots for 20 minutes.

After practice Olivia and I went to lunch in Woodburn. We double dipped to get me some new shoes and to use her free birthday burger with Red Robins. I usually run in Nike Pegasus, and I usually eat a Tavern Double at Red Robins. We treated ourselves with new shoes and a fat dessert too. We ordered the triple layer chocolate ice cream cake and boy was it good! I absolutely love eating dessert and I see nothing wrong with indulging every once in a while. This cake was a celebratory cake, so I mean, it's okay right?

Tomorrow is workout day for the top 5 and race day for the rest of the team. Looking forward to watching the team compete!

Part II: Fall

September: Last First Cross Country Race & School Unfortunetly Starts

October: Conference Race & Halloween

November: Regionals & Nationals

9.1.2017

Mileage 11

Now would you look at that it is already September! The month it all begins once again is here. 3 weeks out from race day! I am getting antsy already; I am just ready to race! Today's workout was a pretty good indicator that the top 5 are ready to race as well!

4 mile warm up @ 6:44s
Leg swings
Warm up drills like we are about to race
Quad stretch
Side to sides
High knees
3x 40 second rhythm strides
Walk to the start line
1x2000m tempo in 6:19 (it was 100m long)
5 min jog
1x1250m in 3:39
8x40sec on/40sec off tempo @ 5:10 pace
2 mile cool down/watch the team compete in the first meet!

The guys and girls both raced well! Our women got 4th and our men got 1st. It is good to see how competitive everyone is. I think the term top five is a bit much for cross country. Everyone on the team has a role and has a specific job to contribute to the team. Top five should never be a solidified group. If you are in the "top 5" don't distant yourself from the rest of the team, don't exclude people who aren't in the imaginary, made up status of "top 5". If you are the 6th 7th 8th runner on your team be confident that you contribute to your team. Challenge your teammates, encourage them and compete WITH them. Your role on the team is just as if not more important because you are what holds the team together. “Top 5” can only go so far before someone gets hurt, sick, or has a bad day. 6-10 must be ready to be the 1 that day if needed.

Bed at 10:30 after swinging by the casino and losing $50. Sorry mom. Sorry dad.

9.2.2017

Mileage 12

Today was a recovery day so not much happened; woke up and calculated I am at 68-ish miles for 6 days, so today my plan was to shoot for 75 and just do 7. Until this morning, I got to 7 miles and felt great! Brady tagged along with me for an extra 2 miles to get to 9 miles at 6:34s. after the run and lunch Josh, Dustin, and I played Dungeons and Dragons for 3 hours. Fought a crazy boss, won some good xp (nerd abbreviation of experience) and items. After the cool nerd stuff, we went 3 miles to top off an 80-mile week. Tomorrow is our long run so chances are I will just do my usual daily miles in an am run. 20 days out till racing and I feel really, really sharp. Excited to get some speed work in.

9.3.2017

Mileage 12.5

Good AM long run with speed change. Averaged 6:38s per mile but it was all over the place. Some miles were at 7:10 some miles dropped to 6:10s it was an inconsistent run, but the speed change felt good. Towards the last 5 mins of the 80-minute run we ran past Oregon's team, Sam Prakel leading the way. Him and I raced down at USAs. He seems super cool and I haven't fully gotten to know him. Hopefully someday we meet up outside of races, so I get the chance to talk with him.

After the long run and lunch, Olivia and I drove to Troutdale for her and her brother's birthday party. Their birthdays are only a week apart, so they just combine the parties. All the relatives can come over just once. I talked with her uncle, Grandpa, dad, all of them said "we are expecting you to go sub 4 so we can tell people we know you." No pressure with her family; if I don't go sub 4 hopefully they still accept me in the family.

After the family left Owen (Olivia's brother), Olivia and I played games like Catan and Exploding kittens. Tomorrow on Labor Day we have our annual team trip to the coast, that will be exciting!

9.4.2017
Mileage 10

Today was a good day! Early morning 10 miler with Brady and Dustin, we ended up doing Shady loop, a famous team loop roughly 9 miles. We just stretched it out to 10 for a total of 67 mins this morning.

No matter the level of the sport, healthy team bonding is important. You must surround yourself with other people that share the same love and passion as you do in order to succeed. For us; our Labor Day weekend always consists of a beach trip. This year was the best year yet. We had a volleyball net set up, footballs, frisbees and a spike ball game going. Only thing we were missing was a cornhole set to top the activities off. All in all, we somehow had 48 people come together for the day and have all sorts of fun. When I was serving the volleyball, my first overhand serve I spike it right into the pole holding the volleyball net, snapping the pole right in two. We fixed it with athletic tape that was wrapped around our random zucchini we brought. Yeah you read that right. We had a zucchini on the beach. I am not sure why we had a zucchini. The team fixed the net and played until the other side was snapped.

After the trip we went to the usual Pig N' Pancakes in Lincoln city where they served all of us together. Crazy to think this was my last trip to the coast with the team. Time flies incredibly fast and I am thankful I get to spend my collegiate years with the people here at WOU.

Tomorrow I believe is a speed workout so that'll be interesting, pretty tired from today, but we won spike ball so the soreness from the sand is worth it. I am lying in bed with my legs throbbing, they are tired from running in the sand all day.

9.5.2017
Mileage 12

We were supposed to have a track day, but the smoke literally smoked us to Corvallis for hills. All the fires in Oregon are taking off and covering the air in a thick blanket of smoke.

Today we had:
10 min warm up
7-mile loop (super hilly)
3x3x30 second hill accelerations
3 cooldown strides on flat part.
PM run 30 minutes @6:45s to make it a 12-mile day

Surprisingly I felt really good today, I thought the sand would have taken a bigger toll on my legs, but I sort of dropped the saddle loop and ran it in 38:04 if you take the hills right you can fly on it. The loop is really 6.75 miles, but we round up. Always round up for effort! Then on the 30 second hills I did most of them solo but would hunt down groups ahead of me so I could try and catch them. Worked for majority of the hills but I was the last one doing them cause everyone had 2x3 hills. Johnson just looked at me and said, today's a day you are doing nine.

Hills hurt like slamming your finger in a door, constant throbbing. They are not easy, and they are a grind but the amount of strength you can gain from hills is incredible. For us, Johnson never focuses on beating people up the hill; we focus on beating people off the hill.

Looking forward to racing, only 16 or so days till we are in San Francisco! 10:18PM, off to bed!

9.6.2017
Mileage 10

Today was the circuit with weights again:
2 laps 2 laps
Leg swings
RHLL
2x40 side to side
Half campus loop (mile)
3x60m acceleration
Into the weight room
3x30m kettlebell overhead swing. Really hard to describe this; but we circled a kettle ball over our head and just walked for 30 meters. It's a lot harder than it sounds.
3x3 each side hip thrust kettlebell swings
3x5 pull ups
3x5 abdominal extensions
Back on the track
1x20 burpees
2x30 wheelbarrow
4 position balance planks: this is where we stand on one foot and put the opposite foot forward for 15 seconds, back for 15 seconds, then to the side for 15 seconds
2x10 split jumps with med ball overhead
2x30 spiderman
3x40 speed skaters
3 miles run after circuit @6:55s
4-mile PM run @7:05s

Circuit days always feel rough on the body but act as a good recovery agent. They are all good healthy exercises, but everything feels sore all day. Tonight's run was super slow but long enough where I still worked the circuit out of the legs. Excited to see what we do tomorrow.

9.7.2017

Mileage 13

Today was a good day! Two weeks till we travel to SF!! Woke up went to the course to set up for our home meet we host. Setting up the flags makes me want to race so bad! I am ready! Two weeks, two weeks, two weeks. It has gotta get here! I am going crazy! After we set up for 3 hours, we took a van out on a dirt road like two miles from campus. We easily could of ran out there but none of us wanted to run on the asphalt roads to get there. Dustin, Tyler, Phil (Justin), Josh and I did 7 miles @6:35s. pretty good pace, but it was sporadic. One mile we would be at 7:20s the next down to 6:40s it all depended on who was leading. Once we all warmed up, we started cruising pretty good, but I feel the sand from Monday, hills from Tuesday, weights from Wednesday and I was happy to hear everyone was tired.

Today I also cleaned my room which was super needed. It got a little out of control, give it two weeks I'll need to clean again. Read some Game of Thrones this afternoon before heading out for a 5 mile run at 6:33s. I feel good, ready for tomorrow's workout. After the afternoon run, I got on the track to do a quick little speed test.

Mostly because our workout tomorrow is going to be pretty rad, I wanted to burn the webs out of my Adidas Avanti spikes.

300-41.7

200-26.4

100-12.3

A good 3,2,1 to set me up for tomorrow's workout, hopefully I didn't go too fast to where I'll feel it, but I think I'll be okay. So far through this week's mileage I'm at 57.5 through 5 days. So being able to hit those times after the last 5 days makes me feel pretty good about my fitness level. After the shakeout went and watched a movie with the team at our neighbors because it's Thriller Thursday and we always watch some sort of thriller that night. 10:13, tucked in ready for bed tomorrow's workout. It will be a doozy.

9.8.2017
Mileage 15

Today might have been my best workout I have ever had here at Western. Usually I put my best workouts on the track, repeat 500s, repeat 1000s. However, today was an 8-mile good day.

This is how today shaped up:
Mile warm up
15 min run
Change shoes into Adidas Avanti
3x75 second tempo at 75 (400 pace) w 90 sec recovery jog
4 min jog
3 x 90 second tempo 72 pace (400) w 2 min recovery jog
4 min jog
3x 75 second tempo at 75 pace 90 second recovery jog
4 min jog
1x 3 min tempo at 72 pace (3:00 for the 1k)
3 min jog
1x90 second tempo 2 mins recovery jog
1x40 sec tempo down finish shoot.

All our times were faster than prescribed and the only rep I really pulled away on was the 3 min tempo. Going into the workout I decided that was the rep I was going to really drop it and try and run fast. Because we did the entire workout on the Ashe Creek course, and the West Regional Course we knew where all the markers were. I went through the 1k at 2:43. How spot on was I? Not sure, give or take a few seconds but I went through the general area at 2:43. I was trying to run a fast 1k and really felt it those last 17 seconds but all in all really pumped with today. For the 90 sec tempo they were supposed to be at 72 pace but we averaged around 4:38 pace for the mile, (72 pace = 4:48 mile pace). The finishing shoot tempo we did the 300m home stretch in 43 seconds All 5 of us fighting to cross the line first. Best workout I have had and have been a part of. Crazy because I said this same thing two weeks ago when we did the track tempo work. This team is shaping up to be pretty damn good and I am excited to singlet up and race with these guys. We have a lot to prove. Two weeks out till we show up in San Francisco.

So the workout was roughly 8.2 miles adding everything else in from the morning we got to about 12. I then ran 3 miles that night with Oliver and Cam. Two guys I have known from my first year here at Western. They are from Simon Fraser, Canadians, Eh?

The team did really good! We raced our 6-back and finished only 36 or so points behind Alaska Anchorage! Seeing how “weak” (still good but in comparison to previous years) the opposing teams are gives us confidence once the race at conference comes around... Alaska always shows up towards the end of the season, so we need to keep training hard if we want to try and overthrow them.

Tomorrow will be a pretty hectic busy day, working the high school meet at 8am-2PM then driving to Portland to go to Olivia’s cousins wedding at 4. Then being there until we drive back to Monmouth tomorrow night. In bed, lights out 10:17.

9.9.2017

Mileage 5

What a long day!
6:50 wake up
7am 5 mile run
8:15 head to XC course
8:15-2 work the meet
2-4 drive to Sandy
4-9:30 enjoy Blake and Casey's wedding
9:30-11:30PM drive to Monmouth

Although today was a long day, it was also an incredible one. Watching some Steen Mountain Warriors crush the high school meet is always fun! It was great seeing all of the campers in their school uniforms competing. I was "start line coordinating official" what that means is I walk down every box and make sure they take two steps back. In reality I took that job so I could say hi to all the coaches and athletes. Given Johnson said I could do any job I wanted I took the easiest one. I hope to work this meet post collegiately too. It's a fun one to just be involved with.

Grant my man, good race in the elite section! 2nd place after riding the pack in 10th the whole time? Not too bad. A little back story on Grant. He is a Jesuit guy that was 1 of 4 that finished the 13.2 mile big day at Steens. I saw him hurting back then, but in this race, he looked calm and collected. The guy that won it I didn't actually know. During Grant's race I yelled, "How many of these guys can do a 13.2 mile day!!?!" he came up after the race and thanked me for the encouragement when he needed it.

All the other Steens teams crushed it, Marshfield, Jesuit, Ashland, the list can go on and on.

At the end of races, I would be in the finishing chute making sure they got water and continued out the corral. Three separate occasions high school kids said things like, “Hey Ribich how is your book going!?” “Small School Big Dreams am I right?” or “hey Ribich if I throw up on you are you going to put it in your book?” the answer would be yes, but he didn’t throw up. I just patted the guys on the back and told them to stop worrying about me and go cool down. I could not help but laugh afterwards because here they are sixty seconds after finishing a hard 5k and they are talking about my book? My purpose for this is to have an impact on lives sure but after a race go cool down! Don’t worry about this book! Really happy that those conversations happened because it reminded me how important this journal is.

Tomorrow will be another light day; congrats to all those that raced and PRed today!

9.10.2017

Mileage 12

Early morning run at Minto Park by Salem, a good 9 miles at 6:42s we had some surges here and there because right before we took off for the run we watched the New York 5th Ave Mile. Crazy watching those and thinking where I will be next year. Who knows, maybe I will be in that race! My left calf was super tight during the run, but all in all not too big of an issue, I guess I will just see if Olivia wants to massage it tomorrow. After the run Olivia and I spent 3 hours fixing her bike tire. May I also say this is the third time this week we have done it. After that fiasco went to dinner, relaxed till 7 and went for a 3-mile run at 6:45s. My mom called me right before the night run so I just decided to put her on speaker and take her on the run too. Easiest way to make time to talk to the mom is taking her on a run.

Tomorrow will most likely be a higher mileage day with our long run.

9.11.2017
Mileage 15

Back to crystal lake 13 miles at 6:33 pace. Spicing up the long run we had 4x40 sec tempo at 30 minutes and 4x40 sec tempo at 60 minutes. Strides to follow.

Something I really enjoy about the long runs we do is the speed change. Never do I feel stagnant on long runs because I have something to look forward to at 30 minutes and 60 minutes. If you are having trouble getting your foot out the door to do a long run add your own little tempos. At 20 minutes just say alright I am going to pick it up for one minute, then again at 30 and 40. Sectioning off long runs makes it easy to focus and enjoy. This tactic can also be used in a race scenario. Sectioning off a race and looking at it in portions can be much easier than the whole race itself. I will try and hold true to those words and section a 10k this fall.

After the long run went back to the house and relaxed for the day until I went back out for a shake out that night. 13 miles is good for one run but I wanted to flush out the legs before rolling out so I could get ready for the next few days. 10 days till we fly out to San Francisco, almost in the range of a single digit countdown. Dustin also scheduled a tattoo appointment for us at 1pm. The DMR team is getting .001 tattooed on our bodies. Not sure where I am going to get it, but I got some time to think. For those of you who don't know, we won the DMR at the Division 2 National Championships by .001. if anything went differently than it did, if Dustin hesitated his move on the 1200m leg, if AJ and Josh's hand off was half a second late, if Josh didn't accelerate to the lead on the home stretch handing off in a slim margin, if I didn't dive for the finish. We would not have won.

Getting the .001 tattoo is a little weird to be honest. I am all for doing whatever the guys want to do but rings would be so cool! When I look at it though I don't want to look at it like HECK YA WE ARE NATIONAL CHAMPIONS!! I want to look at it and be reminded of the dedication, friendship, and sacrifice that took place for all of us to come together and make every 1000th of a second count. Goodnight at 10:33. I hope it doesn't hurt.

9.12.2017

Lost the log for this day, but the skin is tatted now with .001

9.13.2017
Mileage 10

Circuit day, always a doozy. Today Johnson sectioned off the circuit sheet into a few parts: Speed, Strength, Flexibility and Agility. We got there this morning at 8 am and finished around 11:30. Three and half hours of continuous work (this included cooldown and recovery stuff at trainers). The weights we had today were the same as before. I can tell the difference each week, I feel much more stable and stronger as I do each exercise. Today was still tough though because prior to the circuit coach had us do a

100,150,200
100-12.3
150-18.1
200-25.2

This speed usually does not take that big of a toll but after weights, and circuit I was fatigued.
After lunch I went to the dentist and had my tooth worked on once again. It is going to be roughly a 1300-dollar deal to get my mouth all fixed up. Long story short, I had a root canal when I was 14, the previous dentist never properly sealed it, this dentist will. Did a 3-mile run @ 6:55s this afternoon with my face pretty sore and numb. Tomorrow I will be doing an Instagram take over for Citius Mag. Don't know who they are? Follow them on Instagram and Twitter they are a really great information and media source for track and field. Tomorrow is a recovery day, super late tonight 11:14 usually in bed an hour ago.

9.14.2017
Mileage 10

7 miles this AM, nice and easy, then 3 miles again at 9PM with Josh. Pretty lazy day for the most part. Got in the ice bath, boots, did all the proper recovery techniques for tomorrow's workout. Running the social media account was cool because I got a lot of questions from other runners asking about my training, life, what character I would be if I was from twilight, stuff like that.

The main reason I liked it was because a lot of people just messaged me about Division 2 and asked me if I ever got recruited to go D1. Answering questions and talking with other runner's high school, college, pro was so fun! What I think of Division 2 is that everyone is pulling for each other. It is not as cutthroat as Division 1 and you still get to race against them. Coming out of high school I was not fast enough to get recruited by Division 1s. I only got recruited by two NAIA schools and Western Oregon. You could say now that D1 should have given me a chance, but I would have to disagree. I am very thankful for the opportunity to run D2 and for the opportunity to be as successful as I have been here at WOU. When I was at USAs, I got messages about how happy people were to see me representing D2 on the national stage. Messages that said, "you are an inspiration to all D2 and D3 runners! Go get em!" if I would have been at a D1 I surely would not have gotten those messages. The trophies, accolades, titles are nice; however, the best part about this sport is the support and development. Running is a give and take sport, you can't be a taker, you gotta be willing to answer the youth, cheer on the kids, and give. Help the sport grow.

I have been given the opportunity to represent Division 2 and I wouldn't have it any other way. After USAs I got asked if I was going to transfer to a D1 school. That would just be darn right silly. If I did that, I would be going against everything I ever stood for since I started this sport. My identity was representing the little guys. I plan to do that till the end. Small schools, underdeveloped athletes, D2, I want to help encourage and inspire as many athletes as I can. If I would have gone to a D1 out of high school, who knows, maybe I wouldn't be as successful as I am now. Maybe I would have gotten hurt, burnt out, nobody knows. All I know for sure is Western gave me an opportunity and I am thankful.

8 days out till we race in San Francisco, after today I am just excited to put on the big red W and race already. Tomorrow's workout will be just another step for next weekend's race. Also, I darkened my blonde mustache with Just for Men. I am still waiting for the day I can properly grow facial hair.

9.15.2017
Mileage 13.5

Today's workout:
Campus loop to turf
Leg swings
RHLL
4x40 side to sides
6x80 strides
2x40 big skips
---
30 minutes of Xs at 5:14 pace

Think of the turf field as a giant square, we tempo from one corner to the other, jog the end side, and do a diagonal tempo back across the turf to the other corner. Making a tempo X. We did this for 30 minutes straight, our average pace was 5:14, the guys did it together and at minute 22 I started feeling like crap and just thought, well this is the moment I might feel bad in a 10k, so I might as well speed up. I ended up speeding up and dropping the last 8 minutes down to 5:05 pace average (including the jog across the side). It's a running total clock so my guess is its roughly 4:50 for tempo and 5:30 for jog across. The jog across is only about 50 meters so you don't get a whole lot of time to recover. After the Xs we went to the course and did 6x berm hill technique strides. They were roughly 600m reps at just slower than race pace effort.

Cooldown:
Stretch
3 minutes inverted. (where we put our feet in the air and do a shoulder stand.

3 minutes lay quietly and peacefully think about today's workout.
3 mile PM shakeout run @ 6:51 pace.

After this morning's workout I am beyond ready to race. One week out till we dance in San Francisco and I am hoping for a good showing of our team. We looked good today so if we race like we workout we will be golden. Like the Golden Gate Bridge!

Tomorrow will be a full recovery day before a drop down into race week miles. (aiming for 65 for the week coming up).

9.16.2017
Mileage 3.5

Woke up and ran 3.5 miles then drove to Portland with Olivia to get her tattoo done. I was going to run 7 miles but decided to listen to Paul Chelimo's tweet. It said, "you were in the womb for 9 months and couldn't run, you can take one day off." His words are true, so I just called it at 3.5 to get ready for the long run tomorrow. Olivia and I both have tattoos now! Mine took 10 minutes, hers took 3.5 hours and it is half way done!

9.17.2017
Mileage 12

Good long run today at crystal lake once again. First 10 miles of the run at 61:57. At 40 minutes we had our usual speed change 10x40/40 tempo on offs. The sheets said to do them at 50 minutes two sets of 5x 40/40, but I didn't look at the sheet. All I heard was 10 by 40/40 so I just did them straight through. Oh well, it felt good. I finished off the mile and a half pretty easy at 6:40 pace. We had our usual warm up loop and 2x80 strides prior and post run.

We don't have practice till 9 tomorrow, so I am going to try and catch up on sleep. It is currently 9:55pm and I am sleeping in till 8am. 10 hours of sleep sounds pretty nice. 1 hour of sleep for every mile you run that day? Is that a thing?

9.18.2017

Mileage 10

This morning was typical speed development. Started with 2 laps 2 laps into leg swings, campus loop then to the turf for some drills.

4x40 side to side
2x20 high knees
3x30m side shuffle
30-40 minute run (we just did 5 miles)
Onto the track
3x120
3c250 sprint float sprint
33.2, 32.8, 33.1
4x60 acceleration
2x5 drop squats
2x200 jump rope
Half campus

We got 7.5 miles for the morning, setting up my night run for only 2.5 miles at 6:50s. All our runs this week are easy. Real test is in four days so none of us really pound it. At 8PM I tried to get into the Health and Wellness Center to box or I guess hit the bag? I feel like it sounds super lame when I say, "just going in to box/going in to hit the bag." Like I am 130 lbs. of stick and bones, but you know it feels good to workout some energy.

I hope years to follow I could have my own set at my home. I think boxing helps a lot with agility and quickness. After doing it all last spring I could say it made a difference. In bed 10:10

9.19.2017
Mileage 8

Starting to taper some miles for the next three days.

Today's bread and butter was:
Campus loop
3x40 side to side
RHLL
1x20 leg swings
3x10 hurdle walkovers
1x200 at 80% effort (28-30)
40 minute run out then back to the track
3x80m
Stretches upstairs above gym because it got super cold and rainy
15-minute rollout
3x5 ankle stability

Rained all day today so we just hung out inside played some video games, watched tv did what any normal college male would do on a rainy day. Not a whole lot happened today, felt really good, confident going into this weekend for how I feel.

9.20.2017
Mileage 8

Circuit day, met up at the track at 8am
Campus loop
Leg swings
RHLL
3x80 strides
25-minute run
Weight room exact same as two weeks ago

Pull ups were super easy today, stepped up the weight of the dumbbell split jumps, 25lbs in each hand. Felt explosive in those and fresher than I thought I would feel in those exercises. I am really enjoying the work we are doing in the weight room, it's a fun dynamic that's never been incorporated in my training and it's a good mental break from speed or runs. Not sure how I feel about weights in young age runners but in terms of collegiate athletes, I can see how it is beneficial.

Packed my bags tonight! Here we go! It's just about time to fly! After tonight's shakeout I am beyond ready to take flight to San Francisco and race! We will be racing Cal-Baptist and Academy Art. If we can beat both of those DII West Region teams, we will be golden heading into our conference meet in a month. Looking forward to a good next few days in San Francisco with the team. We are bringing 9 guys and 8 girls! Going to be a good weekend

TOMORROW IS PRE-MEET DAY!

9.21.2017
Mileage 8

3 miles nice and easy this morning with Josh and Tyler. Good shakeout before we had to catch the bus for the airport. Crazy how for the last month it has felt like an eternity till we fly but now, now that it is today, it's like whoa. Time flew. Crazy how that works isn't it? We landed, changed at the hotel and drove down to the course. My left arch of my foot hurt bad. I wore dress shoes today because we are supposed to look business professional. I sure looked good, but I sure didn't feel good. That saying is not always true I suppose. My Nike Pegs felt really good on my arch, but I had to stop and stretch in multiple times on our run.

Our premeet was:

Outside loop of course with additions of certain turns and corners for tomorrow (become familiar with the course). 4 miles.
3x80m start strides
Jog down to horse track, it is a massive oval that is half cement half loose dirt. Really weird surface,
On the horse track we did 30/40/30 second tempo faster than race pace. 30 seconds on, 40 off, 30 back on.
Cooldown strides and stretches

Now, let's talk about tomorrow. Tomorrow is my first race since June, since USAs; unless you count the coffee cake 5k you read about in July. What are my expectations for tomorrow? I have none, going into a race you should not throw extra pressure on yourself. There is a big separation between Expectations and race plans. Don't let expectations outweigh your race plans because you never know what can really happen in a race. I am not really sure on what tomorrow will be like, it's an interesting course, deceivingly tough, and many areas where critical race tactics can be made to gain separation on competition.

For my race plan I hope to run WITH the course, let the course carry me, it has a lot of uphill and downhill switches where if I can just lean properly on the downhill, ride the wave of gravity and use the momentum to charge up a hill I should be good. The hardest part about a race is not owning the competition, it is owning the course. You have to act like a roller coaster at an amusement park, be the cart that's attached to the roller coaster and ride it. Another race plan I have is be in CONTROL wherever I am in the front pack I hope to be in a position where I feel like I am the one dictating the race. You can dictate a race from other locations than the front. If you can be behind the competition overlooking their downhill speed you can really pick it up and cruise past them. Forcing them to really surge if they want to try and catch up. I just hope to be in a position where I can control it. My third and final race plan STAY RELAXED. Going into a race be confident that your workouts are harder than the races. If you can do that, every time you step on the line it's a second nature of confidence of "heck yeah I can do this. Last Friday's workout was way harder than this." Last three weeks we have had ball burner workouts where I am confident whatever this race throws at myself and the guys, we can handle it.

Tomorrow is going to be a good day regardless of results. I am just excited to start another year of repping the W. Feels like it's finally Christmas tomorrow.

9.22.2017
Mileage 10

3 miles in the morning to shake out the legs. We did not race till 4:15 PM so we had a lot of time where a shakeout was necessary. After the shakeout we went to a good café for breakfast and hung out in the hotel. At 12:30 we had our athletes meeting where our guys all got together, analyzed the past years results, top returners, top times and our thoughts going into the race.

In the meeting we talked about how we have the best middle-distance team in the country and this course serves in our favor. Downhills are for speed, 500m finish shoots are for speed. We can make up a lot of ground being tactical and staying confident in our speed. This is an incredibly dedicated group of guys and no matter the results of the season, these guys are gold. All their hearts are in the right place and I could not ask for a better team to be with my senior year.

Now, the race, unfortunately I went down 500m into the race and got trampled never to get back up. Just kidding, the race went really smooth. The first part was a joke, I did not go down, however Dustin did almost trip someone at about 500m and he almost went down, not a surprise. Dustin trips everyone. Breaking it down mile by mile, mile 1 the whole front pack was together I could glance over and see 5 W so that was good to see. I also saw a lot of Cal-Baptist jerseys and Academy of Art jerseys. At 1800m I look over at Dustin and said, "Someone is going to be impatient." He looks back immediately and said, "Don't let it be you." Well I have always been bad at listening so 10 meters later I am in the front breaking away with two other guys.

By two miles it was just me and an Academy of Art guy. This same guy edged me out at regionals last year by half a second so I was quite familiar with him. Mile 3 I am alone in the front on the downhill portion where I see Colleen Quigley running up the path we are racing on. I call to her, "Hey Colleen!" she was quite startled and called back, "oh, hey... Hey!" not sure if she remembers talking at USAs but I definitely recognized her from a distance wearing some top of the line Nike gear. 100m later I see Johnson and we exchanged some words about me talking during the race, but I felt relaxed and really good, so I just kept going. This same lap and around mile 3 I had to split two dogs walking on the path. Some owner had his two dogs unleashed walking freely across the course. Not a big deal but I really did not want to steeple. By the time I got to mile 4 I just repeated to myself, "You are miler, you are a miler, you are a miler." In the race I answered the question to the camper at Steens who asked me, "what do you think about when the race starts getting tough?' and to answer you 3 months later. I say, when the race starts getting tough, I focus solely on my strengths and rely on those to carry me to the finish.

With one mile to go when it started to get tough alone in the front, I just repeated I am a miler. This is my race, one mile to go, this is my distance I can do this. Forget about the first four, I am a miler. For the last mile I just kept repeating that to myself because a) I am a miler and b) I really didn't want to get caught after being so far ahead from 2.5 miles in. I won the race in 24:48 nothing too crazy fast but good enough to seal the win. 1 point is 1 point for team scoring. First race in September is not supposed to be an all-out race. As I finished, I sipped on the water cup and started counting. Cal-Baptist got 2nd, 4th,5th,6th, Dustin ran in a solid 7th, and then 8th to round out Cal-

Baptists top 5. I thought well shit we did not beat them. Dustin was in the mix of Cal Baptist, then all of a sudden, I saw 3 Ws race to the line, Tyler, Josh, then Stephen...wait...Stephen!? He was coming in this weekend as our 9th guy! And he ends up scoring for us! Goes to show that whether you are the top runner or 10th, 11th, so on; you have an important role for the team success. After the scoring took place, we finished second as a team. Overall, I would say we are happy but not satisfied, had we beaten Cal Baptist we would have had a much easier year in terms of a national bid. However, I would say we are in a good spot! We are still hunting, and we are now being hunted. Both of those are a good combination going into the next half of the year.

9.23.2017

Mileage: maybe 55 miles (just kidding 8? Maybe 9?)

Today was a fun day of just hanging out in San Francisco with the team. This is the first time EVER at WOU where we got to stay the day after and play. It was so nice to just wake up, shakeout in the morning (easy 6.5 miles @ 7:02s) then enjoy the rest of the day.

To start, we watched a dog parade! Yeah you read it right, a dog parade! So many owners dressed their dogs in cute little costumes and marched them down the street. I wanted to take so many of those doggos home with me, but we can't have pets in our apartment, maybe we will register an emotional support animal. After the parade and after we spent 13$ on a coffee and burrito we drove down to the Golden Gate Bridge. From there we took the typical pictures. We then made a man-bridge of our top seven replicating the real one. A couple tourists hopped in for a picture because they thought it was hilarious.

Then the pursuit across the bridge began, the bridge itself wasn't ever breathtakingly impressive; but running across it sure made it breathtakingly long. After the bridge we drove down to the wharf and walked around there until we ate dinner. Brady and I ate nachos. SO MANY PEOPLE at the wharf. I guarantee the peers had more people in a square mile than the entire population of Enterprise. Shoulder to shoulder the entire way through.

After the wharf we rolled on to the airport where we flew out, drove home and got into Monmouth at 12:00am. Pretty exhausted, but I would not trade today for anything. Team bonding activities are so important in building cohesiveness with the team. Cherish your teammates, my lifelong friends have all came from sport teams. I am so thankful to be on this team; a fun, hardworking group of guys is unbeatable.

I encourage you to cherish the time you spend with your teammates. They are your family and friends. Without teammates it is hard to achieve your maximum potential. Put the track aside, by maximum potential I don't mean just athletically, I mean character wise, socially, morally everything. The people you are around shape who you are as a person. Those people you call teammates are the same ones that struggle with you on the hard workouts, share the passion to achieve all their running dreams. Without my teammates nothing would have ever been possible. I am sure guys (teammates) if you are reading this you are laughing thinking of me complimenting all of you, but I am, thank you for being my best friends.

9.24.2017
Mileage 5

Day after travel and I took it pretty easy. My legs are wrecked. That course was deceivingly difficult, very technical and very uneven. After an early morning five miles, Olivia and I took the rest of the days for ourselves and went out to dinner, dessert and watched a movie. Last night of summer and I get to spend it with the most incredible girl. Tomorrow is my last first day of college (as an undergraduate).

9.25.2017
Mileage 12

AM run on the first day of school, good 9 miles @ 6:35 pace with an upbeat tempo at 48 minutes. The tempo was 5:15 pace with two minutes till we ended the run. After the run we did our usual 4x80 strides. I was out of groceries today except for eggs and English muffins, so I had 5 English muffin egg sandwiches throughout the day. That kind of sucked, going to the grocery store tomorrow.

PM run was easy solo 3 miles at 7-minute pace. At least I believe it was 7-minute pace, I lost my watch last week somewhere in my room and I don't mind not wearing a watch. Sometimes when I wear a watch I feel as though I'm trying to race it to run faster. Today was a good day for not knowing my speed. All the run was about was feeling good. I challenge you to put the watch away sometimes and only base the effort on how you feel. It is currently 11:15 and I can't go to sleep, no idea why, tomorrow is a workout.

9.26.2017
Mileage 13

Starting off the day all the same!
2 laps/2 laps
3x40 side to side
Leg swings
2x30 high knees
2x30 running backwards
3x120 acceleration
Spike up into 10x300 w/ 200m jog 30 min run to follow
The pace for the 300s was supposed to be 52s
However, hitting 52s is like slam dunking when your 4 ft tall.
Nearly impossible
We went 52,51,53,50,54,52,52,53,52,50,

We were over under 52 but relatively on. The 200 jog was on average 38-40 sec pace for 200. Overall the workout felt really good, first workout since the race and it is nice to get a bit of track work in the legs after a tough course like San Francisco. Johnson gave Dustin and I the option to do 2 extras, but I turned it down for multiple reasons; reason 1) josh the roommate just got sick so today is not the day for me to over rev if whatever josh has is contagious. 2) just came off a race, next week will be the time where I can add on 3) maybe most important Dustin and I argued during a 300 rep and he was going to do 2 more and I didn't want to do them with him. We were on rep 4 and Tyler and I were behind getting ready to surge to the front, so we could control a few reps, but every time we surged Dustin and Phil would surge in the lead. Unintentionally blocking us from getting to the front, they were like a two person shield constantly countering our efforts.

Finally, I went into lane 4 and raced to the front. I picture this moment kind of like when two race car drivers drive right next to each other and look at each other through the car windows like, “sup bro ready to race?” Dustin and I exchanged words like, “Yo Dustin you going to let me get to the front or you just going to keep surging?” he replies, “surging? We are slowing down, we are just hitting 52s!” ultimately this was the first time Dustin ever snapped back and I got fired up, for two reps I was pissed, then after I was laughing at myself because I got Dustin to finally raise his voice at me. A task long overdue.

The main reasons I didn’t do extra was because josh was sick, and I didn’t want to over work. The track work rounded out to 5k. After practice raced home for some breakfast where I went to class to learn relatively nothing. First week of school is always a time crunch for no reason. After classes Brady and I went out for a good 4 mile run at 6:40s. Tonight we also had our first study hall, believe it or not I had an assignment from Monday’s class and it was due tomorrow so day two of school and I am already working. Our study hall is something the team organizes so we can stay on task and free up the week for homework. Today was a good day overall and that run was a good shakeout going into the circuit tomorrow.

9.27.2017
Mileage 8.5

3 months till I am feeling 22!!! Thank you, Taylor Swift! Today we went to practice for circuit day like I thought it would be, but Johnson pushed it back to tomorrow, so we could get an extra day of recovery. Something that I am sure I have mentioned, will mention, is we emphasize a lot on recovery, work hard recover harder because it makes the work easier.

With today's morning run usually I would double but my Pokémon Go app calculated I walked 5.5 miles, which is incredibly inaccurate because that GPS robs you for Ks. I would say I walked somewhere between 6-7 miles because I walked from home-track, track-trainers, trainers-home, home-class, class-library, library-home, home-class, class-home. home-park, park-Johnson's office, Papa J office- home, Home-AJ's, and every step sucked. it wasn't bad but by 4PM I knew I wouldn't be doubling.

9.28.2017
Mileage 8

2 mile warm up
Leg swings
RHLL
2x40 side to side
2x40 figure four stretch
Into weight room
5x25lbs split jerks
5x3 kettlebell swings
3x20m walking twisting kettle overhead
3x5 pull ups
5x5 ab/back straighter thing.
Out of weight room
3x8 hurdle walkovers
3x8 side hurdle walkover
80m stride
1x20 speed skaters
2x20 lunges with medball
2x15 sec mountain climber
2x15 side shuffle
REPEAT CIRCUIT
30 minute run

Today was a long day, went for a mile run this afternoon just to work the legs up to stretch and roll out; try not to roll out cold cause sometimes that's a bit painful. My upper left hamstring is sore which got sore from a workout we did in January, roughly 10 months ago. Tomorrow is a big workout, hoping for the best. In bed early, 9:45 gotta get that sleep. I also had school today, but who wants to read about school. NOT ME.

9.29.2017

Mileage 11

Today was a DOOOOZY!!!!

2 laps 2 laps to start

Side to side

Leg swings

RHLL

1x15 spidermans

1x5 burpees

2x5 rocket jumps

Jog to the course

Flat up

5x1 mile temp with 3:30 jog/walk recover.

the purpose is to do the miles at cutdown tempo pace, what we try and do for tempo pace is get a rhythm established with good cadence, heart rate, while breathing is under control. Tempo is a pace where we are relaxed, in control, and capable of going another gear if needed. It was really rainy as well which made the course slippery and cold. I wore gloves and arm sleeves, but by the end everything was ripped off because it was just weighing me down at that point.

Mile one: 5:03

Decent, felt good, was a relatively short warm up so took a while to find the groove in this rep

Mile two: 4:53

Felt better than the first, group of 10 of us doing these so pack felt good

Mile 3: 4:48

Still the group is pretty solid, Tom has led the last three, so I volunteered for the fourth rep

Mile 4: 4:44

Definitely the hardest rep, the second to last one always feels tough right? But once you get on the last rep you feel good again.

Final mile 5: 4:24

How this one worked was we staggered the top 9 so 8,9 took off, 5 second gap, 7,6 took off, 5 second gap, so on and so forth till just I remained, we call this stuff Tigering or Tigers. So how a Tiger works is it is staggered and whoever is in front of you, you are supposed to catch, since I had the whole team in front of me, I really tried to catch the whole team, I ended up catching everyone except Phil who was released as our 4. He had a 10 second head start on me and ran 4:34. He broke away early and it took a lot to close on him, apparently 400m into the last rep he told Tom, "I am going to give David someone to chase." I would say he did a good job of that.

After the morning I had a class from 10-11:50 which obviously sucked because I just wanted to be at home taking a nap or watching a movie with some hot coco. Ate some lunch, a mean plate of nachos and slothed around until I went on a 3-mile shakeout with Tyler.

Tomorrow the team races at Willamette, going into this next week I hope I can just stay healthy, this week last year was when I got sick, then immediately got hurt in the workout that costed me my season.

Goal for this upcoming week? Stay injury free AND illness free!

9.30.2017
Mileage 10

Just like that we are three weeks out from Conference, our guys team is ranked 2nd right now behind Alaska Anchorage and we are ready to rumble, today was the Willamette meet in Salem. All four years we have raced there for cross but I myself never have. I have either been resting for a different weekend or sick on the day. Today was a 7-mile morning running around Bush Park. All the teams were warming up as I was just weaving in and out of spectators by the start line. The nicest thing about running is the community. You hear that all the time and I agree with the statement. Today I saw coaches I haven't seen since track season; they just yell at me as I run by having a 5 second conversation, then on the next lap around the park they pick up the conversation like I hadn't just ran a mile and a half in between sentences. Being in college for the last four years laid some roots with the coaches that I hopefully remain in good contact once I graduate this spring. After this morning's competitions Olivia and I got some breakfast and organized our schedules.

This term will be pretty chaotic I suppose Rhetoric in Civic Life, Motivation and Adherence, Business Communication, Organizational Communication, and last but not least Sports Management. Luckily, I am in my major and minor classes, so I find them somewhat enjoyable. The hardest part will be the reading, I love reading but I would much rather be writing this than reading for a class. This afternoon's run was 3 miles at 6:49 pace nice and easy. My house celebrated the last night of September with a beer and a movie. Tomorrow we will have our first long run of October! Bring on the Halloween month baby!

10.1.2017
Mileage 15.5

Today was our long run and easily the best run I have had up to date this year. We did a mile warm to loosen up the body. It seems a little weird to do a warm up before a long run I agree but stretching and working out the kinks before the run makes the first 8 miles much more enjoyable. After stretching and strides we embarked on a 14.36 mile run averaging 6:16s the entire time! We are 20 days out from Conference and I would say our guys are ready, that was the longest, fastest run I have ever had with that many guys. 9 to be exact. The last 3 miles were solo back at Bush Park. Once I was alone, I sort of picked it up to average 5:52s for my last 3. Felt good to pick up the last bit but once I stopped, I was pretty wrecked.

After stretching and 6 strides I felt good as new. After the run, went out to breakfast with some of the guys to fill up on pancakes, eggs and hash browns. The rest of the day consisted of an hour nap and 2-hour readings for classes. Tomorrows AM run will be 6-8 miles, going for 10 tomorrow to try and put myself back on track with 75-85 miles for the weeks. time for bed 10:02. Side note we are Watching Rick and Morty now, a comedic cartoon show! Hilarious!

10.2.2017
Mileage 10

7-mile morning run with Justin and Tyler then a 3 mile PM run on the treadmills. The morning run was at 7:23s, and the PM run said 8-minute pace, but treadmills lie so I don't know what pace I was going. This morning's run felt like December, super super cold. Hoping for a mild winter after today's weather.

After I froze on my run my day looked like this.
8 AM run
9 shower and breakfast
1030-12 homework with josh
12-2 class
2-5 intern work with Sports Information Director
5-630 shop for groceries, eat dinner
630-730 homework
730-8PM run on treadmills
8-830 box at the gym
9 snacks, and tv with the house
930 shower
10 sleep zzzzzzz

It was a long day, but long days make you stronger! A lot of people are getting sick on the team right now so it's incredibly important to sleep and eat well now more than ever. With our team being as close as it is sickness spreads like butter on a soft served piece of toast. Going to bed so I can continue to feel incredible from yesterday's run. Tomorrow is a workout and rumor has it is hill reps.

10.3.2017

Mileage: 12

Hill repeats. They are the best r ght!?! Eh… sometimes I find myself loving them, and some days I find myself wishing the world was completely flat. However; tcday I loved them. In 18 days, we race in Bellingham Washington for the GNAC Championships. That course is an 8k arɔund the lake style race where the first 5k is flat and the final 3k is rolling hills. We need this kind of work if we want to see any kind of success at GNACs.

Warm up (.5 mile) at Peavey outside Corvallis
Leg Swings
RHLL
2x40 side to side
2x20 speed skaters
1x15 Pogos (a newish exercise where we vertically jump up in small hops like we are on a pogo stick.)

To help with this next part, Peavey is a walking bark chip trial system that encompasses part of the McDonald National Forest. The trails take you around for 8 or so miles. Up, down and around the hills. To start we went onto a trail called Intensive Management (I didn't name them). The team then tempoed Calloway trail, Calloway is an uphill grind of a trail that takes us up to the lake. We tempoed that for 3 minutes until we came back out on the service road that is a straight shot to the lake. Took about 23 minutes to get uɔ here. Once at the lake the workout began with:

2x short hills 1:09, 1:10
2x long hills 3:01, 2:56
2x short hills 1:11, 1:07
15-minute cooldown.

I let my watch run and it was 70 minutes of continuous work. Pretty good Tuesday. I actually feel the boxing in my shoulders, but other than my shoulders and back I felt really good today. Had to poop on the run and if you have ever run hills you know that hill poops are the worst. Luckily a port-o-potty was near.

After the morning went to classes then had a 2 mile PM shakeout with Josh. Today was a busy but good day. Got in the rapid reboots today and let the legs recover a bit. Felt good, overall looking forward to the circuit tomorrow. In bed 10:13.

10.4.2017
Mileage 8

Olivia and I have been dating for 15 months now! Every day I swear I love her more and more, so I have no shame in writing about her. One of the funniest moments I can think of off the top of my head is when she first said she loved me. She says in quotes, “I love you, but I am not like in love with you!” I was not sure how to respond but I think I just kissed her said, “same.”

For today's circuit:
½ campus loop into 2 laps stride walks
1x20 leg swings
3x80 strides 75-80-90% effort
Then into circuit work:
3x3 deep squats
2x100 jump rope
2x30 overhead med ball lunge
3x harness 40m
1x15 box jumps 12”
1x10 lateral lunge
2x30 wheelbarrow
1x15 unbalanced push ups
2x15 pogos
Into the weight room
Kettlebell swings 15 lbs. 5x3 each hand
5x4 split jerks 35 lbs./35/30/30/30
4x3 goblet squat with 3x5 pull ups
The recovery between Goblet sets were pull ups.
GS, PU, GS, PU, GS, PU, GS
Medicine ball ab extension

Back outside for the circuit
1x20 mountain climbers
1x20 spiderman
2x10 over/under hurdles
3x80 strides
30 minute run, stopped at 4 miles

After the circuit I felt really good, didn't feel the hills from yesterday at all which I am pretty surprised about, shoulders loosened up good with all the exercises. Something I really need to work on is posture. My everyday posture is fine but occasionally when I am running my shoulders roll forward a bit. Not a whole lot but enough to where coach says, "shoulders David". This is my typical Wednesday, 8-10 circuit, 12-2 class, 2-4 work, 4-5 study, 5-7 or 5-7:50 class, 8 dinner 830-9 pool stretch. 930 shower and bed. Wednesdays as you can see are pretty rough days.

Balancing being a student athlete is really important when you get into college. Coming out of high school I really wasn't prepared for this kind of schooling. Before, it was always 8-3 Monday through Thursday. In high school I was living in a controlled environment. I would come home from school and practice to a warm home cooked meal waiting for me on the table.

Once I went to college, I realized...wow I was quite spoiled. Freshman year wasn't too rough because I had campus dining but after that, I was responsible for my own meals.
I know a lot of people of D1 programs that have dining options where they could show up to the "athlete lounge." Or "the athlete dining." To get a full meal or just a snack. Here at Western, we are not given that option. That is nothing against the school by any means, we just can't afford it. The athlete

"perks" at a Division 2 school are quite low in comparison to power house Division 1 schools. However, the sport is about a lot more than the food you receive and the gear you get.

I was going to save this rant for another day but today in class a student made the claim that, "student athletes walking around with full rides." HAHAHAHA are you serious? Full rides rarely ever exist at a Division 2 school. Hopefully that's not earth shattering to hear, I myself am working with the Sports Information Director for a few extra bucks and as well I take out a few loans. We are half way done with our cross country season and we are still waiting on our gear to get printed by our print agency. All of collegiate athletics shouldn't be compared to the university empires of the world.

No way in hell am I going to complain that I have to take out loans, cook my own food, buy my own gear, because if my biggest worry in the world right now is "I have to make my own food, or I have to buy my own shoes." Then I am living a good life. When athletes complain about the microscopic aspects of the sport like gear it somewhat ticks me off. Like sure I would love more gear but it's not a priority, it's not going to make or break my collegiate experience.

Here we are sponsored by Adidas but rarely ever get orders, after this year I received my first pair of spikes Adidas Avantis and Adidas MDs. Johnson gave me those spikes based of the performances I had throughout the year. That's realistic, you shouldn't wake up as an athlete and expect to receive anything. You should wake up and feel the drive to work for another shirt, work for a pair of spikes. My point is this, I wake up every single day to live my dream of being an athlete, after college I hope this dream continues. I cannot complain about my life if there are people who live in Houston who are unsure on what to do now that their house is flooded. People that are getting hit by hurricanes and storms trying to comprehend if they will have a home tomorrow. People that live in poverty and hunger that are never sure if they will make it another week.

If you are an athlete, and are pursuing athletics, cherish every aspect of it. You are the 1% of the world that gets to wake up and compete. Compete with a full heart and never take anything for granted. Goodnight after a long day. I also made myself nachos and they were DELICIOUS.

10.5.2017
Mileage 11

7 mile AM run with Brady and Zach Holloway on the bike! Remember Zach?! He is the fool that ran 20+ miles on his wedding day! Anyhow, he is a little banged up right now and was supposed to race this weekend in a 50k down on the coast. His plane tickets were nonrefundable, so he decided to still fly out and make a trip out of it. We talked a good amount about post collegiate stuff and It is so exciting/nerve racking to talk about. I am excited to see what the future holds, but then I am nervous about the whole thing. 4 mile run this afternoon with the boys @ 6:45 pace. Nice and easy, getting ready for tomorrow's workout, should be a speedy one. In bed 10:02

10.6.2017
Mileage 11

Workout day! Two weeks and one day till its race day baby! Today got me very excited to race again:

2 laps 2 laps
Warm up drills as if we are racing
15 min run
Change into flats, head to the regional course (at this point it started raining)
First 5k of the regional course tempo!
5:18, 4:48, 4:55/ 15:28
Jog from course to track switched to a dry shirt, and switched to spikes
3x600 broken 30/40/30 goal pace, 800m jog in between each rep. always continuous.
30/39/31, 30/40/29, 29/40/29, we had an optional 4th rep so we all did it 28/36/27.

I AM READY TO RACE! Very happy I took that last rep alone, we all decided to do the optional 600 because think of it like this, today we had 3x600 and 1x600 for fun. Always treat your last rep as fun. You have 8 hill reps? No, you have 7 and 1 for fun! Brad Barton taught me that back when I was in high school, but I still think about it all the time now.

2 mile cooldown, went to class, then hung out the rest of the day. It's a great day when everyone has a solid workout. Judging by today I would say we are all ready to put on our super suits and race. Later this afternoon I did not run again, well I did not intentionally run. I ended up running on and off in a haunted corn maze at 8pm. It is all fun and games until a 10

year old girl in a wedding dress chases you through a maze. We had a group of 12 or so go tonight from the team and activities like this are so fun together. I have seen a lot of these guys and girls run pretty fast, but everyone showed an extra gear when the chainsaw man fired up right next to us (unchained saw of course).

There was one point where Tom, Olivia and I got separated from the group. Then two baseball bat wielding creatures, I don't even think they were human, started chasing us through the corn. We ended up juking the guys and I look at Tom and say, "Aw crap I have to go back and get my girlfriend!!!" I puff up my chest and raced back into the scary guys to find Olivia corned. As heroic as I am, I dashed left, uppercut, Karate kick! Dashed right, elbow to the head, punch to the balls! I then blink to see the men still standing and I only envisioned kicking their butts. I then girlishly screamed, "Olivia!!! Run! Hurry!!!!" she never thanked me, but I saved the day and we escaped no harm done. After the corn maze fiasco, we went to Sheri's and had milkshakes and pie. Tonight almost sounds like a classic horror film. Group of people meet up and share laughs and conversations. Then suddenly it turns dark and monsters fill the air. After some time, problem resolved with minor casualties and they celebrate with some treats. The end. It was a later night than usual but nights like this I would lose a few hours of sleep to gain a lifetime of memory (cliché but whatever).

10.7.2017
Mileage 7.5

Super easy day slept in and did not wake up to an alarm. Crazy how refreshed I feel after sleeping in till 9:45. Went out to breakfast with Olivia and then went to the pumpkin patch with pretty much the same crew as last night. This time of year is so special because the trees are turning colors, the air is crisp, and pumpkin spice lattes are in!

After the pumpkin patch, Oliva biked with a speaker as I went for a run. Sometimes music runs are okay as long as you are not plugged in. my favorite night runs are when one person is on a bike with a speaker and 10 guys are just mobbin through the dark. You never feel so fast. Today was a good recovery run going into tomorrow's long run. Rarely ever are our long runs slow so we shall see what tomorrow holds.

10.8.2017
Mileage 14

I know one thing for sure. I am NOT running this fast next Sunday, 13.56 miles in 80 mins, roughly 6:06 pace. 11 guys tightly packed together the whole time, we hit some surges here and there but overall kept it pretty consistent. Typical 3x40/40 speed change at 30 minutes and 50 minutes. Kept the long run interesting and got everything working well. Dustin broke away from us at 7 miles because I challenged him and told him to slow down. So, what does he do, speed up! Gotta love Dustin. he wanted me to write, "Make sure you tell the world I averaged 5:55s this run."

These runs are funny to me because at mile 6-9 I felt like complete crap. I wanted to slow down the pace, but then I think well shoot if 10 other guys are chilling, having conversations, who am I to complain that it is too fast, I was the one that lead the first two miles in the first place. Overall good team run. Spent the rest of the day with my feet up writing and reading. We are just 13 days out till conference, with a team like this I know we are more than capable to pull out the win.

10.9.2017
Mileage 7

Pretty low mileage day but after yesterday I decided it would be best to double in the pool. This morning was a good Monday run we call Mindis. Easy rolling 7-mile pavement loop. After the run, Monday was definitely Monday, I like the classes I am taking this term but I really don't like the schedule throughout the week. Thankfully Monday only consists of 1 class at noon but still. Mondays always suck, right? Anyways, after the day was completed went to the gym for some boxing.

Went in to this 5'3 ginger guy round housing the dummy. No joke, it looked like he was mixing jujitsu and karate. I felt so intimidated, so I faked a phone call and walked out of the room, peaking through the window to see when he was going to finish. After I thought he was done I went back in and started softly punching the bag like I was warming up. Him and I chatted for a bit, turns out he has a black belt in karate. He helped me with my boxing stance and punch. After he left, I felt like Rocky and turned on some Eye of the Tiger tunes.

To top off the night Dustin, Josh, Tyler and I played horse in the pool and did some aqua jogging and stretches, somehow the most uncoordinated guy out of the group wins horse.... Dustin.... what. the. heck. I guess the saying is confirmed that just cause you're not the favorite doesn't mean you can't win.

10.10.2017
Mileage 12

We are in double digit days for October which means we are 11 days out from racing! Today was once again the difficult workout at Peavey, tempo to the lake then run hills. Thankfully we ran them correctly this week, but they still hurt.

Here is how today shaped up:
½ mile warm up
Side to side
Leg swings
Toe touches

This week we made it to the lake in 18:42 whereas last week we got there in 20:32. Roughly 3 min tempo on Calloway trail and 90 second tempo from Bonzai to the lake. Much faster than last week.

For the hill reps:
1xlong hill 2:43
1xshort hill 1:09
1xlong hill 2:45
1xshort hill 1:07

Best part of today was Phil throwing up going into the second long hill. He pulls off to the side of the trial as he spits a nasty red liquid. All the other guys gagged from just seeing the sight of it spray out.
Compared to last week these hills were far more successful. On each hill Johnson had us run off the top, more and more each rep. by the last rep, we were 20 seconds off the top. That is so

critical because you never want to beat someone up a hill, all you do with that is beat yourself up. Beat them off the hill, after you crest one you always take a deep breath to establish a rhythm. That's when you pounce! In that gasping moment of deprivation. It's a hard move to pull because you too will be gasping but after a big hill if you can keep momentum off the hill, they will break I can promise you that.

We are 11 days out till conference and if I can, I hope I can try and break off the top of every hill at Conference. Usually those hills are pretty difficult, but after these two Peavey trips they will feel like a piece of freshly baked pumpkin pie.

10.11.2017
Mileage 10

Another Wednesday, another circuit however today was a tad bit different. With the pouring rain we turned the first half of the circuit inside.

This is what we did today:
Campus loop
into the upstairs part of the gym
Leg swings
RHLL
Sideway twisties, I have no idea what these are called…
4x15s one legged balance plank
1x10 burpees
4x5 clapping push ups
1x10 burpees
4x bridge single leg
2x20 spiderman
2x20 prone & supine leg swings
into the weight room
4x4 30lbs split jerks
4x3 35 lb. goblet squats
3x5 pull ups
3x5 med ball back extensions
back outside, rain stopped, circuit continues
2x80 stride
3x50 second jump rope
3x40 harness
3x50 second jump rope
3x40 shoulder harness
30 minute run

Today's work was incredibly hard, the burpees and clapping pushups made the weight room far more difficult. During the day I was wrecked, I really didn't want to sit in class and wanted to stay home in bed but, I am a STUDENT athlete....

After class ran for a good 2 miles. During the run I began thinking about racing, the book, the team and got excited. 11:34 for 2 mile shakeout before getting in the pool. I guess that circuit was not as draining as I thought. I was in the pool for 30 mins to stretch and massage out the legs on the warm tub jets. When we wake up tomorrow, we will be single digit days out from racing. 10:22 in bed ready for tomorrow.

10.12.2017
Mileage 8

Today was on our own so I had 5 easy am miles at 7 min pace. Then 3 solo miles this fine night. The temperature is starting to turn to fall weather. Nothing really crazy happened today just a boring Thursday at school. Feeling a bit stuffed up oddly, so I am going to bed early.

My mom also arrived today for a few days as she runs some errands on the west side of the state. She is staying at my place instead of buying a hotel. It does not make much sense to have my mom spend 80+ dollars for a bed when I have one available. I just crashed at Olivia's for the night. Problem solved, hopefully a pizza will be exchanged for her stay.

10.13.2017
Mileage 10

Friday the 13th!!! Sppoooookkkyy. Early morning workout with the crew, very similar to last week's tempo and 600s except we shortened it up a bit.

Campus loop warm up
Leg swings
RHLL
Side to side
2x80m stride
2x5 squats
1x200 in trainers @ 31 pace
Change into flats
1x3k tempo on the course 8:55 for me, 9:05-9:20 for the crew, jog back to the track
3x600 30/40/30
600 jog in between
1x200 @ 25.1
15 minute run
Cooldown stride

This morning's workout was great because when we read the sheet this morning, we saw 3 600s, 4th one optional. Of course, all of us kind of got the memo that we will be doing 4 600s. After the third rep, I felt so good that I was ready to rock the last one, we gear up for the last rep and ask Johnson if he wants to time the 4th 600 and he says, "you guys look so damn pretty in the first 3 600s, call it there and do a 200, quit while we are ahead." Everyone solo'd the 200 at the end and no one was slower than 27.5. It gives me great confidence in myself, and the team that after a 45 minute workout we can close in a 25-27. This team is 10k ready and in less than a month I am excited to see this team show up at the regional meet. Our first focus is conference considering It is in 8 days, but these workouts are very exciting for 10k.

After the workout I went out to lunch with my mom before she went down south for the night to visit family. After lunch, took an incredible 40 minute nap. I walked over to Olivia's and crashed in her bed as she did homework. I told her to slap my face to wake me up when she gets bored. I woke up to a heart attack as she shook me awake. Thankful she didn't slap me, but I was scared when I woke up; but was immediately wide awake.

PM 2-mile shakeout with the house, ready for tomorrow's easy day.

10.14.2017
Mileage 8

One week till conference! Looking forward to racing, woke up this morning feeling physically great, but my nose was a tad bit stuffy. Made today a low mileage day, five for the first run.

The house ran three easy miles together before our team pictures and football game, so I did an early double. Olivia and I worked the football game and I failed to introduce her to some of the basketball players, I suck at introductions. Like I just always forget, they should know who she is though right? She was third in the nation last year for Division 2 in the 800m. A lot of them are my neighbor as well so they should see Olivia walking to our house.

4 mile PM run and I am actually plugged up, hoping this cold rolls over fast but it is just going to take dedication to get it out of the system. I am confident however this won't affect me in a week.

10.15.2017
Mileage 11

Church of the Sunday, long run, they always say. Good relaxing 11 miles with the guys at 6:40 pace. Felt so refreshing to relax and actually be able to talk through a long run. Occasionally we would dip down to 6:15 pace but for the most part we kept it moderate because it is officially race week. Usual speed changes at 30 and 40 minutes made this run perfect.

Let me tell you about something we have in our house. It is a mini roulette table that I got for my 21st birthday last year from our good friend Sam Naff. Whenever we want to dare someone, or whenever we think of doing something ridiculous we say, "if it is black 18, I will ____" or "if it is double zero you have to ____" so for today, I said, "Josh if it is Red 32 I will give you 20 dollars to gamble at spirit mountain casino and we leave in the next hour."

Well folks...it was red 32. As a house, Tyler Josh and I already planned on hitting some golf balls on the driving range today, we were going to be in that general area anyway. After some good Happy Gilmore swings at Cross Creek golf course we drove west a bit to Spirit Mountain Casino. Tyler is only 20 and his birthday is not till mid-November, so he wasn't able to gamble. However, Josh and I played for a good hour making 80 dollars profit each! Walked out with 108 dollars all before 3PM.

I won't tell you if I am positive or negative in my entire life at the casino, but I will tell you blackjack treated me well today. Once I got back to Monmouth I went and played some Dungeons & Dragons at Dustin's. Yeah, yeah call me a nerd but don't knock it till you try it. A little stuffed up still, casino probably was not the best idea. In bed 9:45 going to try and sleep this stuff out.

10.16.2017
Mileage 9

Monday is DONE! It is officially conference week so what does that mean? A slight head cold…always during a conference meet I come down with something, or a small ache pops up. That is all part of the game. The team has been sick periodically the entire, I am actually surprised I got a stuffy nose now. Illness rolls through our team like a flood because as of right now there are nine relationships on the team. Each one of those relationships ties the houses together.

For instance, I am dating Olivia Woods who lives with Grace who is dating Matt. Matt lives with Parker who is dating Megan. Megan lives with Felicia, Sara and Suzie. Suzie is dating Hunter, Sara is dating Aaron, Felicia is dating Josh. Josh lives with me. Aaron lives with Cody. Hunter lives with Stephen. Stephen is dating Booey, who lives with Isabelle. As you can see, our dating tree is more so a forest, and when one tree gets sick, the forest goes down with a plague. I approach colds competitively not like it's a competition of who can get unsick the fastest, but how fast can I get rid of it. You cannot get worked up about a cold because you never know what your competition is dealing with. Who knows, maybe they have a cold too. Just do what you can do! Sleep, eat, and wash your hands.

This morning was a 6.5 mile run with Thomas and Zach Mindis Monday once again. Afternoon practice was campus loop and 10x120 strides w 80m walk. Felt great to just open up the stride and fly in a controlled environment. Some little kid maybe 4 years old wanted to race me, so I got on the line and lost. Hopefully this will be my only loss of the week. In bed 10:04 time to sleep this cold, 7:30 AM practice tomorrow.

10.17.2017

Mileage 8.5

Last big workout before conference, who is ready?!?!?! Not sure If I am... nose was super runny all day and I went through 43 tissues. Not that I was counting or anything. It felt like I had to sneeze from 3pm-bedtime. Those tissues weren't a onetime use blow either. They were used till they seeped...TMI?

Anyway, today's workout was campus loop into 20 minute run on the course
Back to track
2x80 strides
1x200 @ 31.2
Then 1x2000m 30/40 broken pace
38/31/44/30/41/30/41/30/40/29
Jog 800m
1x1200 broken
40/31/40/30/40/30
Jog 800m
1x300 @ 42.3
Cooldown 15 minutes

Overall felt really good and in control. This group of guys is fit, last spring only Dustin, Josh and I could do more than a mile of this work, today we had 8 guys finish it together. I feel confident in this group going into this weekend.

Tonight, our entire Men's team listened in to the GNAC Insider, a weekly radio show that takes place every Tuesday featuring athletes and coaches throughout the conference. Tonight, an athlete from Western Washington spoke and our team couldn't have been more pumped. To start, earlier today the GNAC released an article about the upcoming weekend and it gave all credit to Simon Fraser and Western Washington saying, “Simon Fraser and Western Washington stand the best chance to end UAA’s string of team titles.” Our mention in the article: “Western Oregon has run its top runners just once this season but cannot be discounted in the title chase.” How can we not be mentioned more than that? We are ranked 4th in the region and 13th nationally. We are ranked the highest out of all GNAC teams so why are we not credited for having “the best chance”.

All the guys screenshotted the article and sent it to each other, we are all fired up. What this means is we are still the hunters, we are in the dark, GNAC does not know what we are capable of and that is just fine. If we lose, this article stands corrected and I am wrong, if we win, well then, the wolves are out to hunt and are ready to eat. The runner from Western Washington mentioned my “killer 3:39 speed.” And that my speed will be something to, “watch for the final 2k”. This makes me reevaluate my race plan. If the competition is expecting a kick at the finish, why not make the move early when no one will expect it? I will sleep on it, but I may have a new race plan. Two days till we travel, four days till we race. Currently having a nice cup of tea before bed at 9:30

10.18.2017
Mileage 7

I think this will be the first meet where I legitimately taper, I am 35.5 miles through 4 days. Feels good! The cold also has transitioned to minor stuffiness. Last night's sleep was good I think I am on the upswing of this bad boy. It will have zero effect come Saturday. For today's circuit it was pretty great. The most refreshing circuit I have had all year.

Here it is:
2 laps
30 minute run
RHLL
Leg swings
Into the weight room (same exercises as last week):
4x4 30lbs split jerks
4x3 35 lb. goblet squats
3x5 pull ups
3x5 med ball back extensions
Back outside
3x 100m running jump rope
2x10 burpees
2x20 mountain climbers
1x15 second single leg bridge extensions
Stride 80m
1x20 spiderman
Jog two laps
3 minutes inverted
Relax and stretch

Today's circuit was refreshing, I think it has something to do with the speed work we did yesterday. Instead of doing hills again, this made the recovery really nice. We handed out our gear for cross country today it is pretty cool! One cross country Jacket, One cross country Sweatshirt, and two short sleeve cross country t-shirts. Pretty nice Adidas products, excited to see what is in store for track season. Tomorrow we load the bus and travel up to Bellingham Washington for the meet. Crazy, we are so close to racing, I am starting to get nervous.

10.19.2017
Mileage 10

Good 3 mile morning shakeout prior to the bus departing, then made a delicious egg sandwich, I realized I as well haven't really included anything I have eaten in this journal, so don't think for the last 100 logs I haven't eaten! I eat! Food is important!!! Eat lots of food!!

After we arrived here in Bellingham we went straight to the course and felt confident in it being a fine course for this fine weekend. Dustin and I ran around the lake twice, attacking the back side of the hills and conversing about the race.

I will do my best to give you a visual representation of this 8k GNAC Championship course preview, are you ready? The breeze blows ever so slightly from the northwest, a cold Canadian breeze that rolls over the tree covered hills on this rainy October day. Rain skydives from the dark clouds above, dive bombing into absorption of the earth. Foot strikes on gravel rhythmically in between back and forth banter as a pack of Wolves run along the bike path. These Wolves came from the start line, a soggy green grass field one hundred meters long that in two days due time will carry the weight of runners from five states and two countries. These wolves' stride off the grass into the initial two mile teardrop portion of the course. Down a mile long path along the scenic Lake Padden; the Wolves break into smaller packs to analyze the course with their own company.

After the two miles the wolves' sort of regather with their packmates and turn back in which the start directed them. Encompassing the entire lake as if drawing a lasso with their run. The wolves complete a loop around to the finish. Standing on a hill the wolves analyze Saturday's hunting grounds. The start side of the lake is a calm collection of grass and gravel path harvesting the potential for a speedy race. The back side of the course, a dark and terrible rolling thunder of hills. These hills would take the breath away from giants and suffice as a mountain to a mouse. As you loop around the northernmost part of the lake, you find yourself facing the hills that will be the friends for some and the foes for others. Making your way up and over and down the other side of the hills you weave yourself a blanket tying in 5k-7k of the race. As you crest the final hill you take a hard hairpin; leaving you one final turn before the finish, back on the beloved bike path you turn right and make a home free finish on the slick grass. Crossing the line first, you crown yourself the GNAC Champ.

Now hopefully that helped, in summary the first 4k of the race is super flat and speedy, the back half is atrociously hilly, however; with the work we have done at Peavey I am sure those hills will be a cold Canadian breeze. Today I also messaged Drew Windle and told him about the race this Saturday, I follow the Brook Beasts on Instagram and saw that they were in Bellingham so thought it seemed fit to invite them/him to the meet. The Beasts will be leaving tomorrow but he said he will for sure be there! Pretty cool guy if you ask me, postpones heading home to Seattle to stand in the rain and watch a cross country race that is really only visible for 20% of the race. Looking forward to seeing him!

In bed at 10:45 late night talking with the team. My cold feels great, unfortunately Dustin is a bit stuffed up now.

10.20.2017
Mileage 7

Premeet complete. At the course we did:
Mile warm up
Lap around the lake
300/600/300 tempo work on parts of the course we wanted to work on.

I jogged back to the hills and did a 300m tempo coming off one of the hills and into another. I think finding the flow of the course is important in staying relaxed and comfortable. My 600 tempo was off the final hill and around a hairpin turn. Then finally my last 300 tempo was the final 350 to the finish, I stopped 50m from the finish and just mean mugged the faint spray-paint line in the grass, like "I am coming for you." I then did two good strides off the start line to find a good start path. I am excited for tomorrow race, racing only once in the season before this meet is kind of scary because we are towards the end of the season and it feels like we are just getting started. I am confident in the guys for how fit everyone is, but who knows what tomorrow will hold.

After the premeet we went back to hotel showered and went out for some food and to catch some Bellingham Pokémon on PokemonGo. Like I know it's a nerdy game don't judge me, but it is sort of fun. After we "caught them all." We went back to the hotel and I went 4-0 in chess against Dustin. Dustin you are reading this I am sure, sorry I had to include your massive defeats, but I did whoop you in those speed rounds. We had our team meeting at 9pm, just an athlete meeting ran and organized by us. We all gathered in the hotel conference room and circled up the chairs. I will fill you in on the meeting because it was a pivotal talk that really prepared us for tomorrow. We talked about the season, each other and our expectations. Earlier Johnson told us, "If you are struggling in the race picture your favorite runner and run like them, think about them and race like/for them." In the meeting one of the guys said what gets him through the tough parts of the race is thinking about us. He thinks about us and knows he needs to run like us, run for us.

We had a serious talk for 15 minutes about what we need to do, what our job is, and if we go out and do our job we will win. This is my last conference cross country race and I am confident it will be the best, I told the guys I am going to do my job as best as I can to win, not for me, but to deliver 1 point to our team total. If I get second giving my all for the team score and we win I will be happy. I am far beyond the individual title aspect, I would much rather get first as a team, and second as an individual than win as an individual and get second as a team. This team is beyond what it was last year, and these guys DESERVE and WORKED for this title. It won't come easy but these guys grinded all summer for when we showed up for pre-season everyone was on the same page and we were ready to accomplish whatever we believed.

After the serious talk we hung out for another half hour and just talked and laughed, we talked about stories of when we had to poop on a run. I told the story that one time I full on cupped my shorts and held poop in my hand as I raced to the bathroom after a run, after dropping it in the toilet I jumped in the shower in my shorts. We are all friends, we all laugh, work, and sweat together. I have never been this close to a group of guys and tomorrow all I am going to tell myself is "Do it for the nine." Do it for the nine guys behind me I am busting my ass for.

They are my favorite runners tomorrow; these clowns are the ones I will be thinking of when I start to hurt. Do it for the nine.

This season has been such a different season than anything in this past. Last year, we didn't lose anyone from the cross team, I think we finished 12th or 13th at regionals. Tonight we talked about winning the conference and qualifying for nationals in two weeks. Crazy what can happen when everyone buys in to each other and believes.

What I did next doesn't mean I condone this behavior. I really had to pee, so I peed in an Odwalla bottle. That is not all, I was not paying attention and it sort of overflowed, all over me, and I sat soaked in pee for the last twenty minutes of the meeting. Johnson even came by and joined the meeting; I covered myself with a sweatshirt. I made sure to clean up the mess I made (which was very little). The team loved it, I thought it was funny too and hey, if we do good tomorrow maybe this will be a new team meeting tradition I do the night before the race. If we win tomorrow, I will pee myself in the regional meeting.

After the meeting Dustin and I went back to our room and talked about the race; after thirty minutes of race analysis I decided if I feel good at 4k I am going to take it out and test the waters. Far enough in the race where I think our team won't be affected by the move, but others will attempt to go with. I think when I made the move to early at San Francisco all the guys got excited and sort of picked it up too, messing up their rhythm. Tomorrow is going to be a good day, I am incredibly grateful to be with this group of guys and I am just excited. This year has been a trip and a half, and I am excited to get this championship season started tomorrow.

Doing it for the nine!!

10.21.2017
Mileage 9

What a day, I woke up and immediately rolled out. I slept like crap and I thought today is the day I fall off the face of the earth and get DNF. After I rolled out, I felt a bit better, but my legs still felt wrecked. It felt like I slept in the same position all night. I didn't want to make it a big deal, so I only told Dustin, but I felt like crap. Heading to the course, the guys were cheery and ready, their spirits lifted me immediately. After we got the course, I was good to go. I said screw the leg, the Big Dawgs (team) are ready which means so am I! It is race day, this season has gone too smooth to feel like crap today! Warming up I warmed up solo after getting dropped by the guys when I had to tie my shoe. That is when I saw Drew Windle, his girlfriend, and their cute dog. Gave them a hug and I felt a new burst of energy. As I continued to warm up, I ran past my dad, gave him a hug and again felt a newer burst. After hugging my dad, I just felt so cheery all I could think was, today is going to be a good day.

We get to the start line and roughly 5 minutes till the start, I really had to pee, so I ran behind some trees right off the start and let out maybe a capsize amount of water. Just nervous I suppose. Ran back to the start line and was ready to go. The race went out as expected, Alaska in the front with Wise from WWU and Jorgenson from SFU. I sat closely behind just measuring out the field seeing how all our guys got out. I peeked over my shoulder to just see Dustin but was quickly brought back to looking forward as I almost tripped on a root.

One mile in everything still tightly packed. I thought about how this was when I made move in San Francisco; in this race it felt far too early.

Coming back around the start we were roughly at 3.5k-4k when I heard the announcer say, “it is a tight team battle right now between Alaska Anchorage and Western Oregon, all five runners from each team within striking distance of each other! It is too close to call!” At that moment I knew what I had to do, hearing that we were in the hunt gave me the adrenaline to literally take my gloves off, toss them to my coach and go. When I made the move at 3.5k Dustin, some Alaska, Wise, and Jorgenson were all packed up. When I got through 5k I gapped Dustin and the group by anywhere between 15-23 seconds, now I don’t say that in a bragging fashion I say that in the fact that when I heard we were in the team title hunt I felt like the race starts now, so I went. Once I was on the back hills, I was definitely feeling it, the first big hill was really good, I felt great climbing up it and as I crested the hill, I strode off and told myself, “Go, Go, Go for the nine!” My breathing felt great, but my arms felt like they were working super hard driving up the hills.

Once I crested the last hill and took the turn into the last 600m I knew I had it. I did not want to slow down however because in two weeks at regionals, I won't be able to relax a finish. With 500m to go I heard someone say, “Be you David! Be you!” I am not sure if I was imagining it, however whoever’s voice I heard gave me a second wind to finish faster than I was going. I came off with 300m to go I drove around the corner to see the finish, as I closed the final meters, I heard the announcer say, “David Ribich wins the individual GNAC title in just under 25 minutes.” I thought about celebrating all week if I won because I was fully confident in myself and the team in getting the job done.

I decided to grab my jersey and pull out the red W. showing off the W. this was the first time I ever premeditated a celebration or fully celebrated across a finish line. For some reason I just knew, I knew that we were going to win and that the nine guys behind me were going to do all they could to bring home the title. I pulled the jersey for them, not for me. This season has been incredible, the process of this year has been incomparable. Usually in years past, once school starts everyone kind of loses focus. This year, it seems like we didn't miss a beat.

After I crossed the line, I had to get my chips off, but I just pulled my shoes off and ran out of the corral in soggy socks (it was a bit rainy and wet throughout the race). I ran down the side of the homestretch in my socks and cheered as I saw Dustin come in at 8th, Tyler come in at 13th, Parker come in at 14th, Justin come in at 15th, and Josh come in at 18th! Six guys in the top 20! The MVP goes to Parker Marson holy cats! Two years ago, as a sophomore we ran here in the Lake Padden 10k. Parker ran 36:20. Today, he finished 14th in the entire conference and scored as our 4th runner. I raced back to the corral and gave hugs all around because I saw our first 5 runners come in before any other teams. I was sure we got it, after a couple minutes of calculations we figured we won by eight or so points, but it was still close and unofficial. We walked back to our stuff to put on more layers to hear, "Western Oregon University wins the men's team title!"

All season we have talked about this, every day, every practice. You could say we were focused on the prize, but we fell in love with the process and the prize was a byproduct. We bought in and believed we could. It was a great cooldown and bus ride home. I was honored as GNAC Male Cross-Country athlete of the year; personally, I think this award should be honored after regionals and nationals because who knows, some other GNAC athlete might race out of their minds finish top 5 at either race and deserve this award far more than me after winning the conference meet. I talked with Windle after the race and he said "I saw you in the front group I figured, oh he has the best speed in the group if he hangs on he will get them at the end....then I saw you again at 4k and you had a 25 second gap on everyone and I thought what is he doing!!" it made me think, why is cross country a grueling all out race? I wonder what it would be like If I didn't go all out half way through the race, maybe my plan at regionals will be sit sit sit sit, go at 9500m or who knows maybe I will go at a mile in, I am not a very patient guy.

Tomorrow will be a good recovery run where we remind Parker that he said on our first long run of the season, "if we make it to nationals, I will shave my head bald and only have my beard as hair for nationals."

10.22.2017
Mileage 8.5

Full day after the race, still working out the legs, overall the run felt great until a bug flew into my mouth and hung on my uvula for dear life until I threw up. No joke. I haven't thrown up on a run in years until today. Given it wasn't pain or exhaustion induced I still threw up. So much for the breakfast burrito I had. Only parts of my body that are feeling a bit abused from yesterday are my left knee and my left calf. Other than that, I feel really good.

After the run coach called me and passed some news along that a competitor said, "I am not worried about David at Regionals he is just a 1500m runner." Now I really don't care much for what people say and given I have known this guy for a while, so I take it as a joke, but never discredit competition. I am not looking that far into this because talk is cheap and people handle race stress differently. Going into a race I would never jokingly discredit or push aside someone's skills. Thankfully Johnson has embedded confidence in our minds that we do not categorize ourselves as event groups, we categorize ourselves as racers. Give us a distance and we will race it. From 400m-10,000m we are ready to go.

Tomorrow is a long run substitution since we raced on Saturday, hopefully the left knee feels a bit better, I have been icing it and resting it appropriately today when I watched Gladiator, all-time favorite movie!

10.23.2017
Mileage 10

AM miles 15.5k in 68 minutes, just under 7 minute pace, a good substitute for a long run, no bugs today so no throw up. Overall everything but my knee seems to be recovered. After the run at 11 I went into the trainers and got a good leg massage from Kurtis (one of the athletic trainers.) I make sure to go into the trainers every day to roll out, boot, ice, just recovery stuff but today I wanted to get on a table and get my legs worked on. After the massage I found out my left pinky toe is a bit sore too, my guess is that it is just from the impact of the minimal flats I was racing in. Tomorrow I may just throw a cushion pad in my shoe to give it a little pillow for impact.

After the run and massage, I had class and work. I was planning on running two miles before the pool tonight, but my foot and knee felt a bit more sore than this morning. 10 in on the day is on track for 70 miles this week so I am not too worried. Swam around in the pool and it felt great, sometimes I like to just push all the air out of my lungs and sink to the bottom of the pool where it is completely silent. After the swim I came back home and watched Gladiator for the second day in a row. Tomorrow we go back to Peavey for hills to flush out the race! 10:21 good night!

10.24.2017

Mileage 10.5

Early morning hill workout once again at Peavey, similar to last week's reps but a tad fewer.

After the warm up:

2x40m side to sides

2x15 leg swings

We made it to the lake with the Calloway portion tempo again in 19:45

1 short shill in 71 seconds

1 long hill in 3:47

The cool part about the long rep was Coach had us run 50 seconds off the top where its flat to re-establish a rhythm, it hurt, and it wasn't fun but definitely needed to get the legs turning.

1 short hill in 66 seconds

This rep cracked me up because Parker dropped the hell out of us going up and I settled for second on the rep. As we crested, he sort of lost momentum and I said oh baby I could win it so I barely got him at the finish. I don't have to win every rep, I don't want to make it seem that way, but it is hard to explain. Sometimes I just treat a random rep like a race, I treat it like the finish, and sometimes those reps are the best ones for race preparation. Kudos once again for Parker, he is killing it.

After cooldown we did some strides and everything feels good, knee, foot, all of it working back in order. Once I got home, I cooked up a mean spinach, tomato, bell pepper, cheese, sausage omelet and went to class. My favorite meal to cook is breakfast. Breakfast foods are the best. Afternoon shakeout was just us guys talking about the game FortNite. I played a few hours today and it's a pretty fun video game, I haven't been big into games for a while but this one is fun. I always feel guilty when I play video games though like I could be doing something more productive, reading, writing, sleeping.

Tomorrow is circuit day, should be a long, but good recovery day. (day three in a row watching Gladiator.)

10.25.2017
Mileage 9

Circuit day! Today was relatively a good day, long circuit but needed. My left knee is still sore, it honestly just feels like a bruise. Tender to touch and a little stiff to move.

Today's Circuit
2 laps 2 laps
2x 40 side to side
RHLL
30 minute run at 6:36 pace
weight room
3x5 15 kilo hip thrust kettlebell swings
3x5 medicine ball ab/back extensions
3x2 split jerks each leg with 30lbs
3x2 split jerks each leg with 35lbs
4x5 pullups and 4x4 drop squat 35lbs
back on track
3x80 stride
1x20 spiderman
1x20 jumping jack
2x10 inverted hip extensions
3x40m relaxed acceleration
3x6 point plank
2x10 burpees
1x15 med ball overhead lunge forward
1x15 med ball overhead lunge backward
Stride 100m
3x12 hurdle over under
Stride 100,
2x10 unbalanced med ball push ups

Achilles stretch

5 minutes relaxed stretching.

Afternoon 28 minute run exactly 4 miles

Tomorrow we are on our own. I am going to try and sleep in and rest a bit. My knee still a bit tender, but better than yesterday. Olivia is also a bit stuffed up, so I am thinking I got her a bit sick. Looking forward to Friday's workout.

10.26.2017
Mileage 8.5

Woke up and decided to postpone today's run until midafternoon let my body wake up a bit before heading out the door. I went into the trainers and iced before class at 11 then ran 7 miles at 12:30, then iced again before class at 2. It feels better today that I ran mid-day instead of early morning. I was in the library for a good 3 hours today working on homework getting everything done before the weekend. I really don't want homework, so I just busted it all out today. Came home, ate some nachos and iced my knee before shaking out for a mile and a half tonight. I'll be ready for tomorrow's workout, not sure what it is going to be, but I am excited. It is also Coach's birthday, I can imagine he will be pretty excited. In bed 9:58.

10.27.2017
Mileage 13

Today was a good work day none the least! Just a good day overall! 8 days out from regionals and this was the first practice since conference where everyone's minds shifted for next weekend. The workout lasted from 7:30-10:00 so I ended up being 15 minutes late to class cause I had to grab some food.

Today we conquered:
2 laps 2 laps
RHLL
Leg swings
2x40 side to side
2x30m big skips
Campus loop into 3k upbeat (5:50s) on the course
3x berm hills (550m) of work each rep
Jog back to track into 5x600m broken once again aiming for 30/40/30 (2 lap jog in between each rep.)
We hit:
31/40/30, 29/37/30, 30/40/30, 30/37/26, 30/40/29

The workout sheet actually had 4-5 but after the fourth rep we decided to dial it back for a recovery rep and end on pace for the workout and really try to do a 30/40/30.

Parker is doing Lactate testing for a final this term and group of us are his subjects prior to the workout my lactate was at 2.8 before the workout. After workout it was 6.2 and after the cooldown it was 1.8. I felt really good today and those are extremely low levels, it was cool to see my feeling in a tangible number. How we test it is with a lactate reader, we prick our fingers with a onetime use needle, draw some blood and send it into a lactate reader giving us our result.

Today's workout gave me confidence for next weekend that after all that work, I still have some freshness in my legs.

After practice the D1 conference meets were going on so I tuned in on my phone in class...I mean, not in class. *Cough* and watched some conference races. After class, I went to Parker's house where we aired the Pac12s and we watched it as a team. One thing I learned from that race is patience, if you watched the race you know Grant Fisher won. He won because he is a great athlete but also by waiting till 100m to go and making his move, he didn't lead a single step until he exploded his kick and won by 50m.

After seeing that finish, I know exactly how I am going to run regionals, wait until the last 200m and make my move. It is going to be extremely difficult to be patient, but I am confident I can close fast because these first two races I had such a lead where kicking wasn't really an option, I also depleted my energy throughout the race to where I really couldn't kick at all. If I hold back and let others make the move, I wonder how fast I can finish. So, we have 8 days to muster up the confidence to be patient. Let's see if it works. Not setting an alarm for tomorrow just going to wake up and run when I feel like it. Knee felt great today!

10.28.2017
Mileage 11

8 miles in the morning with some of the guys as we went to go watch some of the Wolves race in an OSU meet. After that, came home and played some good games of FortNite before heading to the course to tour the Jr High State Cross Country Course. We are hosting the PDX Jr High State meet tomorrow and there's a band of Enterprise runners racing in it! I was really excited when I heard my high school coach was bringing a group of guys over because this group is good! 3 of the JR high athletes are faster or as fast as my JR high times! They are killing it! They have a good chance of winning the meet tomorrow so that would be great to see if their hard work pays off!

I ran the course with them, hung out with them at the hotel, and went to dinner with them all. What a talented, fun group of guys! A team this young is awesome! Great to see the sport blossoming at such a young age in Enterprise, I am happily worried my high school records are in jeopardy!

One of the kids wears size 11.5 shoe which is what I wear, and he doesn't have a pair of spikes, I gave him a New Balance pair I never wear. I asked him how they felt and he said, "I feel so fast! You've ran in them?!? They feel like magic!" I told him he could keep them, his eyes just lit up. It was really great to see. They all asked me if I could sign their spikes and shirts tomorrow and I told them I would only do that if they had a good race. I feel weird doing autographs because I don't see myself as a high enough status to do that. like I still have people in my mind I want autographs from. However, if that's what they want, I'll surely do it. Tomorrow will be an 11 mile single run

10.29.2017
Mileage 11

I just realized Halloween is in two days!! What the heck?!? Do I wear a costume, do I not? I don't know!! Today was a rough run however, I felt really bad during it and never really felt comfortable. Given I had Olive Garden at 9 o'clock last night, my legs just felt super heavy. We did a half mile warm up stretched and did some warm up strides than went out for 10 miles in 68 minutes. 3x40 second upbeat at 30 minutes, usually I feel really good after these upbeats, but they really didn't help today. We finally got back to the school where we could not find josh's car keys. We looked for a good 20 minutes until I opened my backpack and pulled out my sweats to put on. Turns out they were Josh's sweats and his keys were in the pocket. Josh must of put on my pants thinking they were his, there was our mishap.

Once we finally got home, we raced to shower, get a breakfast burrito, and make it back to the course for the Jr High race. My job was pretty fun, cheer on Enterprise and hang out with my family and high school coach The Jr High boys ended up winning the state title and ran to me with sharpies to sign their shirts, bibs, and shoes. I agreed to do it, but I also had them sign my volunteer shirt. They deserve to sign something too! All of them ran incredibly well and that excites me for Enterprise athletics. Next weekend, my high school coach takes his girls team to state after they won their district. They have a good chance to win the state title for 1A/2A/3A.

Running is such an exciting sport to see grow. I challenge you to try and inspire the youth, if you currently "the youth" inspire the youth when you are older. This sport can't grow without you. After the race I got a picture with Colleen Quigley, I felt super weird because we have talked before, but I sort of fangirled and asked for a photo. Hopefully she does not think I am weird.

Today was such a good day and I am beyond ready to race next weekend. Seeing these young guys and hearing them tell me, "I look up to you." Gives me the courage going into this week. I can't let them down. Going to bed tonight with an extremely full heart and a steady head. Tomorrow officially starts the week of regionals, ready for a good next few days to gear me up for the race. In bed 10:02.

10.30.2017
Mileage 8.5

Mondays are always on our own. I did the typical 6.5 mile loop this morning with some of the guys, hard to believe last year at this time we were going into our final week of cross country, given that can still be the case, we feel like we are just getting started. After the run I went into the trainers to do some recovery work 12 minute ice bath into 8 minute warm tub into 40 minute boot session. I don't consider myself a recovery expert, but this feels pretty good. After the trainers went to class then work to follow right after, my school days are so boring I get bored writing about it.

After the day I went out for a good 2 mile shakeout alone, I just needed some time to think. Usually I don't get bothered by what people say about upcoming meets, but someone said, "if we lose, but still qualify I will be disappointed." Now that is a hard sentence to swallow because our entire mission this year is to qualify, of course we will be battling for a team victory but chances of that are less likely than qualifying. We are going into this weekend ranked 4th in the region and it would be a pretty big upset if we beat Chico for the team title. The word disappointed is not my favorite word either. When I hear disappointed, I think of lack of effort, fell short, we could have done better, etc. I know for a fact that the effort the guys team puts in this weekend will be far from a disappointment. They are going to give their all to qualify as a team, we know that every position matters and we will be fighting for every point to qualify. I am proud right now of this team for how they have trained through this summer, came in hungry and now are ready to race. Never will I be disappointed in this team or in my teammates.

When I got back from the run, I was still lost in thought about the disappointment sentence and began to clean, we currently have a fruit fly problem and I felt like I needed to be productive, so I cleaned the bathroom. We have such a bad fruit fly problem they were on the bathroom mirror. After the deep clean and scrubbing, no flies remained in the bathroom. Tomorrow is Halloween and its workout day, so I guess we have a Halloworkout. Are you supposed to dress up for those workouts? Not sure but I am going to wear my Luigi hat and Mario kart the workout, hopefully turtle shells will be implemented this weekend and hopefully they don't test for power up mushrooms.

In bed 10:45, late night.

10.31.2017
Mileage 10.5

Happy Halloween! I hope you have a spooky day full of candy and treats! I still wish I could go trick-o-treating because that was so much fun as a kid. Give me a piece of candy and I'll hand you back an empty wrapper, I don't care what time of day it is candy is delicious.

Today's Luigi hat workout was:
2 laps 2 laps
Campus loop
2k tempo on the course 6:10
2k broken by 400s on the track
68/78/68/78/68
First two laps were on pace, after that I had to stop and tie my shoe, I also wasn't wearing a watch, so I have no idea what my last 1200 was but I caught back up to the group and I know our last lap was a 64.
After the broken 2k we jogged two laps then went into a broken mile
Goal pace was 78/68/78/68
Everyone must have been feeling good because we did 75/65/75/64
Running a 4:40 mile straight out 70,70,70,70 sounds doable but more difficult than a 4:40 broken. Our program if you haven't noticed is all about speed and speed change. This is the first year we have done consistent broken work through cross country season, last spring my workout days were 5x600 30/40/30 now, we are doing that after a 5k tempo on the course, so it will be interesting what our track workouts look like this year.
Jog two laps

1200 broken
66/75/64

Overall everything felt really great! I did not lead a single rep just what I wanted, going into this weekend I don't plan on leading a step of the race until I want to with 800m remaining. It is also comforting knowing that I don't have to lead any reps to get the right workout for me. This team is light years ahead of last year and we will only get better and better.

When we traveled to Conference, we were hyped that Monday because we were leaving on Wednesday so for that whole week we were hyped. With hosting the regional meet, I have yet to really feel the hype of the regional meet, tomorrow I will round of the team and get a good break, everyone is calm right now but I want to add a little bit of excitement.

11.1.2017

Mileage 8.5

Sweet lordy it is November, this month is going to go by crazy fast! We have tomorrow, tomorrow's tomorrow, and then we race. This season has flown by and today was the first day the team felt hyped for the meet, given I was pretty hyper and got a wild team break prior to practice, the guys are ready to race. Today was circuit day and we really didn't back off the workload.

2 laps 2 laps
1x20 leg swings
1x20 walking high knee with twist
1x20 alternating toe touch
2x40 turning side to side
25 minute run plus a lap on the course
3x120 acceleration
Weight room (exact same as conference week)

*The only thing different in the weight room was the pull ups, during the pull ups we would juice each other up by saying "Chico closing in 200 to go? Do you drop?" or "the pack breaks at 2k you going to let it slip away?!?" It's always fun to get in each other's faces when we are lifting or doing pull ups because I mean, we are skinny runners screaming in each other's faces I feel like it looks pretty ridiculous. It probably looks a lot less natural than two linemen yelling back and forth lifting 300+ lbs. but I need that motivation in a 25 lb. goblet squat.

Back on track to continue circuit.
3x100 running jump rope

1x15 unbalanced push ups
1x20 mountain climbers
1x20 six count burpees
1x10 V-ups
2x5 rocket jump
2x10 hurdle walk-over
½ campus loop
3x200 fast and relaxed 32,34,34

That wraps up the circuit, I got in the boots at 11:30 and shook out for 20 mins at 6:30 with Dustin.

After tonight's run, I am getting really amped for regionals. This weekend marks my last school associated cross country race in the state of Oregon. Hopefully this will not be my last cross race entirely. It is funny how my last cross-country race in Oregon falls on the same weekend as the Oregon State Cross Country meet. It is like the chapter book of running cross country finally closes, finishing on the same day it all really started. All those high school athletes beginning their journey as mine in Oregon ends. This gives me a good idea of who I am running for this Saturday. Good luck to all those who will be competing at state!

A high schooler messaged me and asked me for advice going into his first state meet this upcoming weekend I said, "relax and enjoy the next few days. This is your first state experience so test the waters and enjoy every moment, don't overwork yourself early and be confident people are going to fall apart after the big hill." I would tell anyone this that the state course is always over complicated, people look at the hill of the start and off mile two and think it's a giant, in reality give it a good 10 second climb and you are home free for downhill and speed. The state course is all about finding a rhythm and staying relaxed, after I gave him advice, I asked him for some thoughts on what I should do and what he said was, "Make sure they realize why they didn't make it to a USA final."

I guess that is all I needed to hear. Your words gave me a lot of confidence today, I am ready for Saturday! In bed 9:59, just squeaked in before 10!

11.2.2017

Mileage 9

Easy day in the books, 6 mile AM run and 3 mile PM run, today was designed to shakeout the legs from the workout on Tuesday and the circuit yesterday. My morning run was spectacular I felt bouncy, fluid and ready to run fast, my PM run felt a bit sluggish, I will hopefully be ready for a good pre meet tomorrow.

After today's runs the team had a team dinner at the Italian restaurant in town. Any other competition we would be eating out right now with the team. We figured we might as well keep the schedule the same. Getting everyone together tonight was great because we got a lot of what we wanted to talk about out of the way. The restaurants power was out for the first half of dinner, so we sat in the dark only being able to see each other through dimly lit candle light. Tonight, we went around the room and everyone talked about each individual person and what they bring to the team. It was great because it showed everyone's hearts are completely devoted to each other's success. After dinner we sat there and talked till 9:20, everything that needed to be said was said, tomorrow we will have another team meeting where we strictly talk about our jobs. Tonight, was the mushy motivation part of team talk, tomorrow night's meeting will be when I surprise the guys and pee myself for the sake of our conference success, and when we talk about our jobs. In bed 10:30. Tonight's sleep is the most important! Time to get good rest for tomorrow's premeet...it is already time to race.

11.3.2017

Mileage: unsure, maybe 8?

Premeet

Race drills

25 min run

Jog to course

1x300 start

1x600 berms tempo

1x200 finish

For the start, I focused on getting out quick but not going directly to the front of the team, I imagined the guys as other competitors and I just tucked right in behind them. For the berms I focused on staying smooth over them and not letting the berms ruin my rhythm. If I can relax and flow with the berms, I will be fine. For the finish I focused on coming off the fence and dropping it, I plan on making this a 300m-600m race. I focused on fast arms and driving the legs around the final turn to carry me to the finish.

Today I also worked on smiling through the premeet, not showing a huge smile as if I was taking a picture, but a little smirk in the corners of my mouth because Eluid Kipchoge said "the mind is the one thing that controls the body.... the best remedy or medication for the mind is to be happy." I agree completely and after today I felt great enjoying and smiling, kept me relaxed throughout the premeet. To be totally honest I am not very nervous I was far more nervous for conference than I am this race. I am excited to just race fast and enjoy each step. If I can stay relaxed and happy, I am sure I can accomplish whatever I see fit.

Tonight's meeting was very hyped. We went through, everyone shared their jobs, we know what we got to do to qualify and we are ready to fight for every point. Dustin is the book worm and pulled up all regional meets in the last 5 years and averaged out the team score and average time. We need to have everyone under 31:00 mins, place all 5 in top 40 and race. This is going to be a crazy race, the top 6 teams in our region are ranked in the top 25 nationally

Chico State 1st in region 4th nationally
Cal Baptist 2nd in region 6th or 7th nationally
Cal-Poly-Pomona 3rd in region 9th nationally
Western Oregon 4th in region 13th nationally
Alaska Anchorage 5th in region 16th nationally
Simon Fraser 6th in region 21st or 23rd nationally
All in all, we must fight for the top 3 automatic bids.

If you are unfamiliar with the qualifying criteria for the national meet it is a new system this year. The NCAA takes the top 3 finishing teams at the regional meet automatically to nationals. (8 regions, 24 teams automatically in). They then choose 8 at large bids for teams throughout the nation depending on depth, performance, ranking etc. (32 teams selected for national meet.) I suspect we will get at least 5 teams out of our region because of the depth we show. However, we need to fight for an automatic bid because this system could easily go wrong during the at large selection. For an individual, top 5 finishers qualify no matter what, they then take the next two individuals from each region not associated with a championship team.

After that, they announce 8 at large individuals selected for the national meet the same day they announce the team selection (Monday.) If we want to guarantee our spot in Indiana, we are going to have to finish 3rd or better. Time to spike up and race like this is our last meet of the year.

(I also peed myself in the garage during this meeting, wore short shorts so it was an easy clean up but definitely an uncomfortable race tradition. The guys laughed and it was pretty funny, if we qualify tomorrow, we also get to shave parkers head.)

11.4.2017

Mileage: 11

Woke up this morning pretty annoyed because one of our neighbors loves playing video games and always wakes me up throughout the night. I messaged him this week and told him I have regionals so Thursday and Friday night are important, but he didn't seem to remember come Friday, didn't sleep soundly till 11:45. Nevertheless, smile it is race day.

Warm up campus loop

Leg swings

3x80m stride

Stretches

Walk back to course, Russ songs stuck in my head. On the starting line, the gun goes off. Bang.

No clocks, splits were heard for me throughout the entire race, through the first kilometer I was tucked right where I wanted to be 5th maybe 6th place right in line with the lead group, people were chatting in the front joking back and forth. I wanted to join in. I got up on the shoulder of the lead and looked around analyzing where everyone was at, Dustin right behind me so I go back towards him and we run together for a few meters, I then weave back through the group and tuck right behind the lead. This feels like a sit and kick. Going through the first two kilometers I thought no way is this faster than 5:00 pace. I felt good, relaxed, smiling the whole time. I accidently bumped a Chico guy and he said, "cool it man." I just laughed because I lightly touched his arm when I got clipped, we go through 3k and the pack was still tight, no significant moves were being made and I was getting really impatient. The race felt far too easy till this point and I just wanted to drop it. Remembering my plan, I stayed patient and remained tucked in on shoulders. At four kilometers I look over at Dustin and I say, “Man this is slow I need to take this.” His reply, “No David, stay patient you’re fine, keep to the plan.” He gave me an unreal amount of confidence because he is right, who says this race needs to be won in a blazing fast time. Winners are winners in cross country. Time does not matter at all. I didn’t hear any splits the entire race until 5k. I remember briefly hearing 18,19,20 so I assume that is 15:20? I just laughed and thought how slow this race is going and how perfect it feels for me.

We get to 6k and I glance over to see Medina (guy who was second in the 1500m outdoor at nationals) without any gloves on. I knew a speed change was about to be made because he had gloves on at the start, I slip closer towards the front and keep an eye out over my left for Medina to swing up to the front. He makes an aggressive move and I immediately follow. It was not a massive speed change, but it definitely stirred the pot a bit. I tucked in and everyone on the sidelines that knew my race plan kept saying, “good spot David.” Or “stay patient” or “look great, keep it up” every loop I passed coach and he would just give me a thumbs up and I would give him a grinning nod back. So far so good. We get to 7k and another little surge hit, I was actually caught off guard by this one, but I covered it and remained in arm reach of the lead making sure I still never made the move to the front.

Once we got to 7k the racers were becoming fewer and fewer. I occasionally would be one step in the lead here and there, shoulder to shoulder leading it because it is a wide course, no need to tuck behind one person. We get to 8k and everyone was still yelling “be patient” it was getting tough though because I was just waiting for a move to be made, I was waiting for that massive surge from Medina or the Cal Baptist guy. We get just beyond 8k and the Cal Baptist guy takes the lead, I remember hearing the announcer say, "freshman from Cal Baptist." And mid race I thought, damn this guy is a freshman? Let's go! That is awesome, this guy is going to be good. He leads till about 9k where Medina threw down a massive surge. I covered it stride for stride and refrained from taking it another gear further. At this point of the race we only have two berms and 600m to the finish, time felt really crunched to make the move. We cross over the berms and from here I knew with 700m remaining it was going to be a two man race. Down to the speed.

With 500m remaining, I remember still sitting in 1st/2nd neck and neck until the Chico coach yelled, "Kyle, remember how that 1500m felt! Go now! Go Go drop him!" Now, this is nothing against the Chico coach, team or Kyle, they are great competitors and what this coach said was all I needed to hear. I heard that sentence and thought, wait, I know what the 1500m felt too, I remember that feeling of coming down the homestretch in the lead. I felt a sudden surge of energy and said screw it and took off. I felt so good flying off the corner and driving the arms I could not help but smile more because for the last week the exact race plan. I had mustered up in my mind is panning out EXACTLY as I expected.

I come off the final turn and see the finish, I just told myself, "go go go!" I could not hear anyone screaming all I could hear was the roaring of the wind. It was like the entire crowd was on mute and all I had was static. My legs still felt great with 50m to go so I glanced back, I wish I wouldn't of but I saw Medina was a good 40m back, I coasted in the final meters running 29:49. First thing I thought of was the fact that that time is faster than my 5k PR. Up to today my 5k PR is 15:02, I have still never broken 15 minutes! I stand and wait in the shoot to see how the team battle was playing. I saw three Chico, two Cal Baptist, a Cal-Poly… okay here is Dustin in 13th great race! Then more people came in, I lost track of which team had how many runners in. All I knew this was going to be incredibly close for third, Chico and Cal Baptist surely got first and second.

Parker came flying in as our third! He ran 31:04! What the heck? Two years ago, this guy's 10k PR was 36 minutes! Shortly after came in Tyler and Josh. This was going to be so close…I got escorted out for an interview and I just wanted to get it over with to go back with the team and wait for the team scores. Finished the interview and ran back to the group to see 3. Western Oregon 121 4. Simon Fraser 121

What? We tied?! I run back to the team to hear we got third and won the tie breaker because of head to head scoring Dustin and I were both ahead of their 1 and 2 and our team average was faster than theirs. WE GOT AN AUTOMATIC BID!!!!! Everyone hugged, jumped, high fived and I just couldn't believe we did it. I knew we were capable of it, but I just wanted to know how everyone's races went and where we made the moves. We tied…. holy moly… for an automatic bid…we tied. Given I assume both Simon Fraser and Alaska will get at large bids on Monday it is still crazy to think it came down to a tie.
We all cooled down together and were all ecstatic that we get to shave Parkers head tonight!

On the women's side, Olivia ran a PR and finished up her cross country season. She looked good the whole time and used her 800m speed to track down a lot of girls the last 500m. Kennedy Rufener our led woman got 12th and will be on the bubble for qualifying. I really hope she gets a spot because she deserves it and works so hard! She was 7th at conference and was the 3rd GNAC girl today! She had a great race!

After the race I went out to pizza with Olivia's and my family. This is the first time both hers and my parents have eaten together. I got a beer with my pizza and half way through drinking it realized this was my first real liquid after the race, I had some Gatorade and water but yeah, I sort of got a headache. Went home after pizza and rolled out, then showered and went to Olivia's to take a nap. Never ended up falling asleep but her bed is far comfier than mine. I just relaxed there before going to Parkers for his head shave. Overall my legs feel good! My back is the sorest part on my body, my knee is little stiff but nothing too bad. Tomorrow I plan on taking the day off and going to the pool at noon for some recovery. 10:30 in bed.

11.5.2017
Mileage 3

My knee is wrecked, I was planning on going to the pool at noon, but they were closed till 6 so I ran 3 miles instead and went back on the course with Josh and Tyler. I found a pair of gloves so that's cool but my knee hurts. I have no idea what's going on, I stopped and walked for a bit during the run because it did not feel good. It hurts as if I bruised it or smacked it on something. I'll get it checked out in the trainers this week to see if we can identify anything. Today I caught up on homework and played more FortNite. Still haven't won a game.

After that went to the pool. Most of the team went and we played horse water basketball and aqua jogged. after the pool we went to Dairy Queen where I got chicken strips and a small double fudge cookie dough blizzard. My favorite. Blizzards are my weakness too. I love me a good blizzard. After nationals I'm surely getting a large, I'll spend 6 bucks for one.

The team came over to my house for some team bonding. We hooked up a karaoke machine with two microphones, had two people vs each other reading off corny jokes back and forth. If you laughed at the joke told to you the opponent gets a point. Some of them were super funny and I thought I would be much better at reading and hearing jokes, but I laughed a lot. I consider myself a funny guy but quickly learned I laugh way to easy. During this I Iced and heated up my knee going to take it easy again tomorrow to try and make this thing go away, I guess it's been flared for the last 3 weeks. About time I get something done about it.

11.6.2017
Mileage 8

AM practice as a team, official practice will be weird for the next weeks because only eight of us will be on a cross country schedule. For practice today, it was a pretty light day:

Campus loop
Leg swings
1x20 toe touches
1x40 turning side to side
1x30 big skips
3x120 strides

After the warm up exercises the guys team just went out and ran the entire 10k course again. It is crazy how fast that race went because today, the course felt like it took forever! However, it was really cool running on that course again right after regionals because the flagging was still up, and no one was there. It was so empty. Today was the first time I heard how everyone else's races went. People were pointing out what happened here, what happened there, it was cool. It was like returning to the scene of the crime.

After practice went to the trainers to get my knee worked on, not much help but I'll try again tomorrow, no one was really there. I rolled out got in the boots and made sure not to stretch out my knee. It's weird, I have pinpointed the pain to the tip of my knee cap, it hurts the worse when I pull my heel to my butt and stretch out my quad. Maybe it is an IT band issue? Not sure, it is still healthy enough to run on. I am thankful for that. I also let Coach know my knee is sore so hopefully we can figure something out.

From the trainers went to class where Josh and I read the NCAA announcement on who qualified for nationals! We first read Kennedys name, so she is in! that is great, and then we scrolled down to see the men's team qualifier, hmmm, must have been a typo we didn't see Simon Fraser, we read it again, still no Simon Fraser. Wait are you kidding me? Simon Fraser did not get in? which means no Alaska or Cal-Poly Pomona, are you serious? We tie Simon Fraser for an automatic bid, we get in and they don't? How can that be, teams were selected out of regions that were not even ranked going into the regional meet. Let me add some speculation, if we tied Simon Fraser for an automatic bid, and they were not selected does that mean we are the 32 team in and they are the 33rd? are we the last team in to the national meet? I am confused on their selection criteria because any given day Simon would beat some of those teams that qualified. It is sad to see especially because we can't do anything about. I know a lot of guys on that team and they deserve to go just as much as any team going. Just a shame...

In bed at 9:26 tonight, I am pretty tired, the race is just now catching up to me. I think we have a long run tomorrow, I am excited for that. Hopefully shake out the body and get the regional weekend completely out of my legs.

11.7.2017
Mileage 11.5

This morning's run was a single longer run to substitute for missing a long run on Sunday. 11 miles, 6:36 pace. Pickups as usual at 40, 50, and 65 mins. Overall felt really good, first day where my legs felt under me again. Taking the last few days easy was a good call.

Dustin ended up running into a pole and hit his leg pretty hard. Luckily, he hit his quad and not his knee. A loud ding echoed, and we all turned around to see Dustin crawling across the road, no joke. I thought his season was over from how loud the ding was on what I thought was his knee. Luckily, he got up and walked it off.

I was actually planning on doubling, but my knee is still really sore, it might actually be worse today than yesterday. The rankings came out today for Flotrack and they ranked me at 3rd, hopefully I can live up to that expectation, but rankings are over hyped. I am less than two weeks out till my final cross race and I don't want to end my career on a "what if" note so I am giving my all no matter what. Tomorrow is circuit day, we will focus on one day at a time.

11.8.2017
Mileage 8

Early morning circuit and weight room
2 laps 2 laps
RHLL
side to side
Campus loop- 25 mins on the course
2xberm tempos
Circuit weights-
3x5 15 kilo hip thrust kettlebell swings
3x5 medicine ball ab/back extensions
3x2 split jerks each leg with 30lbs
3x2 split jerks each leg with 35lbs
4x5 pullups and 4x4 drop squat 35lbs
1x10 burpees
1x30 mountain climber
1x20 jumping jack
2x30 speed skater
1x10 unbalanced push ups
4 position planks
4 position balancing planks
repeat from burpees to planks twice
3x40 harness
Stride 100
3x12 hurdle walkover
Jog 2 laps

This morning felt decent, my knee is aching of course, but the pain is over my entire knee cap. Not a specific location.

I went to the trainers before class and iced. After icing I went to class read of my coaching philosophy to the class as one of our projects. In my paper I turned the word coach into an acronym Communicator, Overseer, Admirer, Counselor, Hero. I believe a good coach is a communicator, if the coach can't communicate his/her message then nothing will be accomplished. They need to be able to communicate to their athletes appropriately and effectively. Not all athletes need the same communication either. Every athlete needs to hear specific things at practice and or competition.

A coach is an overseer, you need to be able to establish yourself as authority but maintain a friendship. So often, (young) coaches find themselves in predicaments of are they a friend or the coach. Athletes should respect their coaches as coaches while still maintaining a friendship or acquaintance. In my opinion Admirer and Counselor are the most important, but the coach needs to admirer the athletes and their accomplishments. If the coach is too hard, sometimes the athletes may think their work is going unnoticed or not good enough. Telling your athletes good job, or great race is critical in their mental development in the sport. Good coaches say good things to their athletes. Counselor, a lot of issues arise in athletes lives inside and outside the sport. Being there for them when they need someone is critical.

Now I am not saying as a coach you should dive into your athletes lives and work out every problem going on. You should be there for them if they come to your office, sad, mad or upset. Shoot even be there for them if they are having a great day and just want to tell you about something exciting. Having someone to talk to outside of family is so important. As a coach, your athletes will have problems out of your control, but how you control yourself regarding their problem will make you a good coach. Finally, a hero. The athlete must look up to you as a person. Someone they want to be like and or aspire to be. What you say, how you act, is a mirror image of your character in which your athletes see and hear. It's like parenting I suppose, although I am also not a parent.

However, I am an athlete so that response is what I believe a coach should be, hopefully I can live up to my own expectations if I am ever a coach. Back to my training! I was planning on doubling tonight, tried a treadmill to see if that would feel any better and I stopped after .8 mile because it hurt too bad to run. 10 more days, after that I can recover. Going to bed 9:45, we have another 7:30 practice so it is time to get to bed.

11.9.2017
Mileage 11

One more month till Olivia and I fly out to France! I am so ready to see my sister and see France once again.

However, today I woke up and could barely bend my knee, I rolled out and it felt better right after that, I have a feeling it is something going on with my IT band, pulling on something in my knee. That makes sense, right? Any readers out there want to tell me what's going on? Today we went to peavey where we had another hill workout. Once we pulled into the parking lot after the short drive there I told Johnson the status of my knee. He massaged out my IT band and it felt a lot better, we decided to take it easy today, do the hills but not to stress anything too much. Due to the rain that poured we opted off the trail warm up and took a 2 mile warm up on the road to the base of the service road and did our tempo up the gravel. Once we got to the lake, we did a short hill 71 sec

Long hill 3:03 at end of hill, 3:46 at the end of the lake
Short hill 66 sec

In between the first short hill I really had to poop so I went in the bathroom at the base of the long hill and did the long rep alone. I thought I was going so slow on the long hill but in reality, I was hitting the time I hit a couple weeks ago, it definitely hurt worse alone but that's the pain of hearing only your breath and steps climbing for 3 minutes. After the 3 hills we added 3x40 sec speed strides on a flattish service road up on the hill. These felt really good to get some speed in the legs after the hills. Instead of doing 3x40 sec speed strides I did 1 speed stride at 40 seconds, threw a stick down, did the next rep getting to the stick in 36, then again in 33. Those felt very good, well over 200m and just what I needed in my legs, surprisingly my knee didn't hurt at all after the workout. After practice we made breakfast as a house, we had pancakes and omelets. Then unfortunately went to class.

My schedule from 10am-8PM looked like this class-trainers-work-class-run-eat-library. This term has been pretty crazy, 17 credits and working 8 hours a week. Next term will be far easier as I turn down the job for winter term.

11.10.2017
Mileage 8

Another low mileage day but my knee felt great, after yesterday being so crappy I am happy today was a relatively pain free day, tomorrow is seven days out till race day. I am scared, my volume has fallen a bit, but I am trusting the training and the recovery. Convincing myself that the training is exactly what we need going into the national meet.

After my run this morning I went and got some treatment in the training room and it seemed to of worked. We added some stim pads to my IT band and then wrapped it up in heat as Kurtis the trainer ultrasounds where my knee connects to my IT band. If it didn't work, it sure felt good. We will be doing that every other day for a while to see if it knocks some of the tension away on my knee. Dustin met up with me following the treatment and we did 8 miles in 55:40 nice and easy.

After the run I got in the boots for 20 minutes. Sometimes I think I overuse the boots; other times I think no way I need those! Fun fact when I was in the boots I was on twitter and saw that Evan Jager plays FortNite. Post class, I went home cleaned my room and played FortNite for a bit. Tonight's dinner was cooked by the ever so beautiful Olivia, she made me shrimp tacos before we went to the men's basketball game.

Our guys team is very good, they were in final four two years ago and should be pretty damn good this year. Olivia makes such good dinners and I make such good breakfasts that our days are covered for food. However, both of us could possibly work on our lunch game. Tomorrow our cross country team is getting honored at half court during halftime of the men's game so that will be pretty neat. In bed 10:36

11.11.2017
Mileage: 11

Eleven miles on 11.11 make a wish! The run was a good, decided to run with Kennedy our individual women's qualifier, we still clicked off 6:43s with conversation so it was a much-needed run. My knee also feels wonderful so that makes me happy. After the run, got my usual long run breakfast burrito from Muchas and enjoyed it before a couple more games of FortNite. Luckily, I got all my homework done prior to this weekend and I am halfway done with homework for next week. I should be golden to play a few games, right?

Pretty boring day for a Saturday except for the basketball game. Getting honored at half time was cool because it gave recognition to all the hard work the men and Kennedy put in for the season. Of course, everyone on our team worked hard this season even those who didn't qualify for nationals but tonight was cool because the community/school got to see the success our program had this year.

We are a week out and I am getting not nervous, not excited, but antsy? I think that is the word that describes how I am feeling. I know James Ngandu from Tiffin is going to take it out from the gun. He has been second to Vincent Kiprop multiple times and is hungry for a title I have decided that I am going to go with him, I want to taste a sense of gold for as long as I can. If I am in a pack of guys letting Ngandu escape at free will, I will always wonder what I could have done had I gone with. So, let it be known I am going to give it my all and go for it. Who knows what the pay out or punishment may be. Tomorrow's practice was supposed to be optional however Johnson texted us and told us to show up, we will see what's going on with that on the morning. 10:22 in bed.

11.12.2017
Mileage 12

Showed up to 9 o clock practice, for what? A stick! Johnson brought me a stick! This stick was from his yard and he said I would love it, given I do love it, the stick has a backstory. So, last august (14 months ago) Josh my roommate snapped a really cool stick I found on a run. Johnson still remembering this act of cruelty brought me a new stick. What? That was over a year ago (insert cry laughing emoji).

In terms of training I will be completely honest, for some reason I am lost in my training. Should I be doubling? Should I be tapering? Should I be doing speed? I am so lost on my fitness I don't know why. I don't know why today I am questioning my abilities, but I am, I know I am fit but what am I supposed to be doing going into the national meet. We are now six days out and I am ready to fly already. Let's get this show on the road (or sky I suppose.)

Watched the movie Allied with Brad Pitt, super good movie! 7/10 on my ranking.

11.13.2017
Mileage 10

Another magical Monday down, five days till race day, today's run was with Brady and Josh. We clicked off 7 min miles for the first few then dropped down to 5:40s because we started sharing information that is so dark, not even the dark web would want it. Just kidding, it wasn't that dark, but it was enough info to drop the run. Funny how conversation can power your runs. I feel like I haven't worked out in forever, Thursday's workout at peavey wasn't anything close to threshold so maybe that is why I am so antsy to race because I want that grind feeling again. After the run Brady and I went out to eat breakfast and I enjoy his company a lot. He is our assistant coach and he is a good one. He knows workouts, athletes and training. I hope he gets more freedom and athletes this year because he is good. I updated his coaching bio on the roster because it said he was in his first year of coaching for the entire time I have been here at Western.

I failed to mention, today started out as a great day because, MY ONLY CLASS OF THE DAY GOT CANCELLED! Week 8 and I finally got a cancelled class. Crazy, for a while there I was thinking I would never get a break. Today was good though, took the opportunity to go in the trainers and get worked on again. Knee once again feeling good. on the healing process now that we figured out what to work with.

Once I finished work from 2-5, I went for a run and attempted a quad stretch as a test to see if I could do it.

Nope, pain shot up and from there on my knee hurt the rest of the night. After this weekend I must take time to heal, last thing I want is for this pain to carry onto track. For tonight, I have all my clothes lined out for packing except my socks. When someone asks me “what is your biggest regret in life?” I can confidently say, “not matching my socks after I wash them.” Like, how do they get so mismatched! I wear matching socks all the time, but I usually have to dig through my drawer for a while before I find any. Tomorrow is workout day, excited to get this one under the belt before the dance on Saturday! 9:48 bedtime!

11.14.2017
Mileage 9

6 mile morning workout
2 laps 2 laps
RHLL
Leg swings
Campus loop to the course
5xberm tempos anywhere from 1:35-1:50 depending on if we had the wind in our face or back, the wind was brutal for this workout.
After the berms we got back on the track for a broken 2k, because of the wind we changed it up a bit. First 800m was 400m/400m then we went into the usual 200 broken work 68/78/33/43/33/43/33/43

I don't know how fast I could run a 10k right now, but I know for dang sure I could run a good 3k. After the 2k we all soloed a 300m, 44 finishing off with some good rhythm.

I felt comfortable in this workout too, so I am not sure if it was too little or I am really fit, maybe we are just building up for a barn burner this weekend and I need all the energy I could get. After school some of us did a 3 mile shake out before we fly out tomorrow. Packed and ready to fly. Bring on the weekend! Tomorrow will be a long day but after that, all easy. In bed 10:22; wake up at 5:30

11.15.2017

Mileage 6

Traveling from 6 AM pacific time to 5 PM pacific time. We finally made it to our hotel at 7 PM so we just ran for 40 right when we got in. 5 asphalt laps around all the hotels. I felt really good and my knee felt fine, not sure if I really have to worry about my knee much this weekend, given I raced through regionals, I would surely race through nationals too. The day started out in traffic outside Wilsonville where we had to get through security and to our gate in 30 mins upon arriving because of how late we were.

Our morning started rushed, then we flew straight to St. Louis where we got in a rental car for 3 hours. It should have been a 2 ½ hour drive but google gave me wrong directions, so we took a good 30 min detour through the country farms in Indiana. Once we made it to the hotel I was really burnt out from the travel and just wanted to run. We had dinner at Mod pizza and it was free milkshake night so that was a good start to the trip. Tomorrow we preview the course, I am excited to see what this place looks like in the day time.

11.16.2017
Mileage 8

The course is going to be fast, wow, it is a four loop course, 2k, 3k, 2k, 3k. the weather is supposed to be pretty wild, we will see if that plays into anything, I highly doubt it. Before you know it, I will be going into the last lap, just a 3k! sounds easy enough right? For the preview today, we ran the whole course and picked it up to tempo when it seemed right to do so, we averaged 6:36s everyone seemed to be feeling really good. The weather is shaping up to be pretty crazy, potential thunderstorms which means the race time may be delayed.

For tonight's dinner we met up with Simon Fraser women, our teams ate Italian together and it was quite nice. It was cool to join teams for a dinner and learn new names and faces. I have a photo of Olivia and I kissing in my wallet and one of the Simon girls saw it and I totally blushed, I got really red, really fast. She asked me about Olivia and I talked about her for a bit. After the conversation I really missed Olivia, on Monday we have less than three weeks till France! In bed at 10:40, pretty tired tonight excited to get some sleep. Tomorrow we pre-meet and have the banquet.

11.17.2017
Mileage 5

Morning shakeout around the hotel at 9:45 with the team, felt really good, did some strides and was ready to get after it. Roughly 24 hours till the gun goes off. Talking with everyone, they all seem to be ready. Later we went to the course to do our final premeet

2 mile warm up
Strides and stretches
30 sec race tempo
60 sec race tempo
30 sec race tempo
3x20 sec strides
80-90% mile effort on strides

Cooldown

The banquet was really cool, got an Autograph from Billy Mills, American and Olympic gold medalist in the 1964 games (10,000m). he spoke about his life story, and his days leading up to the Olympic games, absolutely inspiring. My favorite story he told was on his way to the track he sat next to a European woman who asked him what event he was in, he replied 10k, and she asked, "o wow who do you think will win the defending champion or the world record holder?" He hesitated and responded, "Me, Billy Mills."

Who knows what happens tomorrow, I know I want to go for gold, try to, Ngandu is good and I want to try to race. This has been my plan all along. It is my final cross country race tomorrow. I do not want to live my life with the thought of "what if" I want to race and hope for the best, try and smile through it all. There are so many good competitors in tomorrow's race, I hope someone tries to go with Ngandu as well. If I slip off hopefully, I have someone to catch if they slip off too or vice versa. Tonight, I was honored with the West Regional Athlete of the Year award, using that as motivation for tomorrow. Tomorrow we go out with a bang. Races have been moved earlier due to weather. Let the Big Dawgs EAT!

11.18.2017
Mileage 10

Well, you could say I went for it. I can live my life knowing I tried at some point of the race to go for gold. However, at 4k I fell back, and never moved up again. We went out the first kilometer just Ngandu and I in 2:44. A pretty brisk pace I would say.... The pack was behind by a large margin by the time we got to 2k, I still felt great. I was like wow this isn't so bad, 8k to go, you can stay on, stay on, stay on! teams from all over were cheering me on and telling me to stay on him and stay relaxed, they carried me through. However, by 4k, I was so far gone that I forgot to smile, forgot to think, forgot to straighten up I sort of lost control. My side began to ache worse than I have ever experienced around 6k, by this time of the race I was in a good 14th or so place. I kept falling back as though I was the only one running through sand. Every Adam State guy that passed me told me, "let's go David, let's go." I tried with every effort to respond but couldn't, my legs were moving fine but my breathing was not rhythmic at all. I thought okay David, top 15 stay on this group, this is podium finish, but by 8k I was telling myself okay David you are in 20th final 2k you are a miler, a miler! I rallied for a bit when Sydney from Adams passed me and pointed at his legs telling me to stay on him. We have become friends through the sport and I tried to go with but truly couldn't go, at this point multiple west region guys were ahead of me. Coming around with 300m to go I just said kick damnit. I dug a bit and finished with the group I was with, claiming 30th.

In this race, to me 30th is gold. I tried for gold, I went out with all I had, I didn't have any left when I finished. All season I was in my comfort zone when racing, I wanted to break out of that comfort and that's what I did. Going into this race I was fully confident in my abilities to be top 15, top 10, top 5 even, but that wasn't my focus going into the race. My focus was trying to accumulate all the cross races I have ever raced before and give it my all one last time. Unfortunately, today was not my best day, given I went out hard I still think other things were going on, a side ache in the race? I never get side aches. 8k vurping (vomit-burping) in my mouth and almost throwing up? I never throw up in a race. However today I did; I was not 100% but that's no excuse, race day is race day and I came to race. I knew today was going to be a long shot for a victory, but I didn't care, the little devil on my shoulder kept shouting at me "get dropped" but I had an angel of encouragement outweighing those remarks. It didn't go to plan, but I tasted the front and the thrill for victory. I think I was the 5th athlete from the west region, and the 2nd GNAC athlete. Not saying the placing matters because I don't think a race defies someone. I think HOW they race defies them. I wanted that to be known so I walked up to a Flotrack interviewer and requested an interview. He was probably caught off guard interviewing someone in 30th place but I wanted to say what I said. Never told anyone that so this is a journal exclusive, I walked up and requested an interview.... To summarize I said, "we are all dreaming of victory, dreaming of achievement, there are moments in our lives where we can wake up and achieve those dreams or we can hit the snooze and wait for another day. Today I am proud to get out of bed and pursue something I have been dreaming of."

I don't want people to look at my performance negatively and think less of me for finishing 30th, I am sure no one will but as I sit in this airplane on the flight back home, I feel defeated. Not defeated in the sense of the race but defeated that I let people down. That I blew up, that people think I gave up, that I potentially gave people too big of expectations for my finish. I mean shoot I agree with the last one, I gave myself bigger expectations. I figured if I went out hot, I could still finish top 15 no doubt. But pain settled in and not once did I smile after 6k. It was like I was outside my body just watching my body crumble. This sounds like a depressing post, and in the moment right after the race I was fired up like, "man, I tried, I really did." and now I think after the adrenaline is gone, I am left here with my thoughts just me, my pen and the recent taste of disappointment. Should I have done more? Should I have tried to stick with more people as they passed? Should I have just stayed put in 8th place or so and moved with the pack?

All I hear right now is "should haves" and I don't know why, I raced the way I raced to eliminate the should haves and the what ifs. However here they are; those thoughts are the ones you have to fight.

I do wonder, what if my journal logs leading up to today said things like, "when I pass him." Opposed to, "if I get dropped or if I fall back." I wonder if I gave myself a predetermined mindset of difficulty before the race even began. Maybe I lost the race the minute I wrote that with my pen.

Self-confidence is the most important element someone can have. I was not in control today. With that experience I know what it feels like to have the wheels fall off, I know what it feels like to bonk. Hard. My sophomore year at nationals my silly self led the first 5k of the race and finished 67th, at a time where I didn't know any of the competition. This year my confidence led the race and it hurt far worse than two years ago. I still walked out of today a Cross Country All-American, which is great, the accolade is great, but I won't look at that medal as an All-American medal, I will look at it as the hurt locker medallion forged in the hottest flames of the darkest pain I have ever experienced in a race. I will wear confidently knowing I put myself in a position to try. As always, coming off this race I am happy, but not satisfied.

Dustin had a rough race, Parker had a rough race. Josh, Tyler, Justin and Hunter had good races, but we surely placed farther back than we wanted. That being said, it does not take away the accomplishments that were achieved this season. Crazy to think I am flying home writing this final chapter of my cross country season. For the last 9 years I have raced in the fall, after this year it will be an off season period. Focusing in the near future I am going to try and contact some agents and chit chat with them about the future. Hopefully they see my 30th place finish as an opportunity not an opposition.

We transition to track now, it is time for speed and miles. No mile will hurt as bad as this 10k today and for that I am thankful. I have been blessed with an incredible support system; family, friends, teammates, coaches everyone. They allow me to live my dream, and If you are reading this journal than thank you. Thank you for believing in me and listening to my rants, thoughts and workouts.

This season was an incredible journey. First GNAC title ever for the Men's Program, 3rd in the west region, and 21st in the nation.

11.19.2017
Mileage 3

Finally got in at 3am. In bed at 3:30am…woke up at 11:30am. Pretty exhausted and slept terrible, I couldn't sleep on my right side at all, the abdominal muscle on that side is so sore it feels like I pulled or strained something. Same side as the race. When I woke up at 11:30 Olivia and I went out to go get our classic breakfast burritos. We talked briefly about the race, but I didn't really want to talk about it. After the high has worn down from racing I feel pretty defeated. Mentally and physically, I am still getting flooded with messages from people telling me how "great" and "ballsy" of a race I ran and how it was so good to see. Those messages definitely help in my post-race feelings but 30th still hurts.

However, if the gun was to go off today, I would do the same damn thing. If I had a 5% chance of winning a race and 95% chance of losing, I would fight for that 5% till I couldn't breathe, till I was throwing up and until I faded to 30th. Going to take the next few days really easy to try and get my body back in order before I start any speed work. It is officially track season starting today so it is time to sharpen up and gear up for a good season indoor.

Today was my vegetable day, everyone needs a day where they can be a vegetable and not worry about a thing. Today was my day, I watched Netflix, played FortNite, and tried to just decompress from the weekend even though I am in bed at 9:30. Like I said back in June focus on every aspect of a race until you find some good. In this race, my knee didn't hurt, and my knee still does not hurt. Maybe that is the blessing in all of this, my knee is healthy, let's see if the next few days continue this pain free streak.

11.20.2017

Mileage 4

28 minute run was quite painful. I feel like a baby writing this. For the last few weeks I talk about my knee, now my ab hurts...when will I be pain freeeeee!!!! Luckily none of these issues are halting to my training, just annoyances. I went into Kurtis today and he ultra-sounded my side a bit, felt around in there and confirmed something is a bit off. He thinks it is just hyper fatigued and or strained. He said that I just need to give it some rest before doing any strenuous work. Something I have noticed is after a championship race or after a national meet usually I need a quick break; a mental and physical reset. However, after this weekend I am ready for track, ready to race, and ready for a speed workout. This week is on our own for the most part, I will listen and relax for a bit, but I'll be doing everything I can to get this healed fast. On the bright side my knee pain is gone, weirdest thing.

Today I also watched Dillon Maggard run a 4:11 blue jean mile, maybe that is the race I'm more excited for. I really wonder how fast I can run one. Maggard and Linkletter, two guys that have done it, our PRs are around the same. I hope I could run as fast as them. With my little waist chances are I will need a belt. I also got a call from the Tillamook coach, we are guaranteed for me speaking to his team in December. This is my first speaking gig where I travel to a high school. Really really excited for that. Finished today with a FortNite win, so it's a good day.

11.21.2017
Mileage 5

Today's workout was a long list of circuit exercises and 300s. I skipped the 300s because my side was really rocked this morning. It is a strange soreness because it pulls randomly, one moment it is fine than the next feels like someone is twisting my side with a corkscrew. Maybe it is just a really bad side ache, I have gotten side aches before but never to this magnitude.

Prior to the exercises we had 2 laps 2 laps, 25 minute run into:
3x5 drop squats
2x80 stride
2x15 lunges
1x300 @ 80 percent (skipped)
2x10 speed skaters
1x10 quick jumps
2x12 hurdle walkovers
2x12 side straddle hurdle walkovers
1x300 @ 90 percent (skipped)
2x10 burpees
1x10 med ball push ups
2x40 side to side
1x 300 @ 70 percent (I actually did this one in 48!)
Stretch
Cooldown

After the workout I went into the trainers and got some treatment done again, so far the best feeling for the side is electronic stim packs and heat, after that Kurtis ultrasounds with a high frequency wand over my abductors. All in all, it feels really good. When he goes over the exact spot on my side with the ultrasound it grabs pretty good but after the treatment my ab felt far better. Tonight, we stayed at Olivia's house in Troutdale and watched Justice League with her family, I could easily say I am a DC guy, I really like the way they film, do character depth, and tell the story in a darker world. Tomorrow will be a day off.

11.22.2017
Mileage: 1

Woke up, did some homework, played some games of cribbage with Olivia then some games of Catan with her and her brother. After that, embarked on a 6 hour drive from Portland to Enterprise for Thanksgiving. Once I was home, I decided to walk to my Dads house from my moms, they live across town, but the town is only about a mile long so after 100m of walking I got bored and decided to just run there.

Once I was at my dad's I started petting my high school dog Neko. Neko is Japanese for cat if you wanted to know, that's why I named him Neko. As I was petting him, I noticed some white fir peeking out around his eyes and it really showed me how old he was. I just remember getting him from the humane society and now he has white fur? I immediately got sad and realized I was very homesick. It is going to be a good relaxing weekend in Enterprise, happy to be home for a bit.

11.23.2017

Mileage 5

First day no pain anywhere, pretty quick healing really. Today was thanksgiving, I kicked off the day with a run, now I don't feel guilty eating everything I see. I decided to leave my watch at home, I know these distances and routes like the back of my hand, I knew today's run was going to be 5 miles with or without a watch. I left it at home because especially being a bit beat up, I didn't want to race the watch. It is also a down period where it is nice to just relax on runs. So often I find myself glancing down at my watch and seeing 6:31 average, or 6:06 average that I think, might as well get it under 6:30 or might us well get it under 6:00. Today was about just running. Once I got back to the house, I did some basic drills like burpees, side to side, strides, RHLL. After the basic drills I grabbed my mom's weight set and did some goblet squats, split jerks, and extensions before calling it a day. The real workout today is filling my belly with as much food as I possibly can.

I always ask my mom if she needs help cooking and every time she says no. I then went down to my dad's again and walked in on him watching my national cross country race, he said, "Wanna watch?" I replied, "I will be in the car." Still too soon for me to watch the race, I like to give it some time. Once at my mom's house him and I played some chess and I lost two games in a row. That never happens, he absolutely destroyed me. After the games, my high school coach came up to the house for Thanksgiving. Him and my family are obviously close, so it was nice to have him at the table. To finish off the table we had Falk (German exchange student from high school) My high school coach Dan Moody, my mom, and dad.

I have a lot to be thankful for, especially to the three adults sitting at this table. My parents got a divorce when I was in the 4th grade but still promised us that they would stay close and connected for us kids. They live a mile apart and travel together for all of my sister and I's events. In December they will sit side by side for 13 hour flight to France to visit their daughter, so hopefully that works out. My high school coach gave me the opportunity to improve in college and never got caught up in high school accolades to ruin my career or burn me out. Falk acted/acts like a brother I never had/have and is truly a part of the family. They allow me to have the biggest worry in life be running. I have clothes on my back, food on the table, and money in my pocket. So often people complain about what they don't have instead of looking at what they do have. What you have can always outweigh what you don't. Like I said in my interview post-race at nationals. "If your biggest worry in life is running or a race than you are living a pretty good life." With that said, life is good.

After loads of food and pie I called it a day and am in bed at 8:56, early night but that just means I did everything I wanted to do today and gave myself a real chance to get some sleep. Tomorrow night is the day I visit some high school friends.

11.24.2017
Mileage 7

Day after Thanksgiving and I feel pretty good, surprisingly because I ate my body weight in pumpkin pie. What is your favorite pie? That is an important question to know in your life so take some time right now and answer that to yourself so the next time someone asks you, you can say pumpkin pie, I mean, you can say your favorite pie. For today's run I put my phone in my arm sleeve and listened to music as I went. I listened to music straight out of the phone because I can't stand running with headphones in. Isn't running a methodical rhythm in itself? The greatest tune to hear is the repetition of your foot strikes in correlation to your breathing. Now I don't mean to sound so poetic but seriously that is the greatest sound in the world, don't drown it out by plugging in headphones. Maybe I am just in a weird mood post turkey feast. To be honest, the only reason I brought my phone was to take pictures, however like usual I packed my phone on a run, got some cool photos, but never posted anything.

It was 36 degrees on the run and like all iPhones my phone went from 22% to dead. The run itself was good however, 50 minutes averaging 6:55s. It was rolling hills; some parts were faster, and some parts were slower. Running out here on the lonely long gravel roads makes me excited to spike up and just rip a speed workout. At one point today my side started to ache a bit, so I backed off. Once home I did the same drills as yesterday and 3x80 strides on our street.

Today I went out to get coffee at our local coffee shop Arrowhead Chocolate in Joseph. It is SO GOOD I HIGHLY RECOMMEND (this was not a paid advertisement). At Arrowhead I met up with Amy and Callyn two girls I graduated high school with and we just caught up. Always nice catching up with old friends. Then tonight went out to the local tavern, or bar or saloon? I think it is a saloon because it is very cowboy themed. So there, caught up with some more old friends and finally got home around midnight, pretty late night for me.

11.25.2017
Mileage 5

Getting back into the rhythm of running after this last week's hiccups. Crazy it has been a week since nationals. It feels like it has been years since. Today's run was the same run I did two days ago, just a nice and easy five-mile loop. For dinner we went to Terminal Gravity, a local brewery where we met back up with my high school coach for dinner. Tomorrow I head back to Monmouth, this was a quick trip.

11.26.2017
Mileage 5

Woke up at 6:30 and began the commute back to the west side, it was a pretty good drive for the most part, I rode in the back seat with a French Bulldog puppy that belonged to the drivers, that was fun. Holding that dog all day made me go into a puppy craze, I googled dogs again, looked up breeders, looked up humane societies. After research I found a dog called a Vizsla, look it up such a cool dog! I texted Drew Windle because it looked oddly familiar and confirming my hunch that he has a Vizsla, after his and my dog talk, we talked about my post collegiate search.

Two days ago I wrote down all the agents, teams, coaches that I am really interested in I had contact info and addresses for all the agents and was planning on calling some to just meet and greet with them. However; Drew said to just be patient and know that I am on the radar and that I shouldn't call. He said come late January if no one has talked to you, then maybe make some phone calls but for now just relax and not stress about it. Hearing that really reassured me and gave me confidence that this should not be a stressful process.

Once I got to Monmouth I went for a run with Josh and Sawyer we went 30 minutes but at minute 9 I had to stop and stretch my side because it was the worst pain I have ever felt in that spot. I honestly think it is something going on with my back because I was sitting for the whole drive and tightened up. After the stretch it felt fine and I was good to go. Also, my homework for the term is mostly done for this upcoming week. I did a lot of it in the car and at home because I want to finish this term off strong. Gunning for a 4.0 again and it is not the easiest term either. In bed at 9:47, hopefully ready for tomorrow.

11.27.2017
Mileage 6

Today was the first workout back, my side was pretty sore yesterday. I figured today was going to be a little rough, then through the warm up it ached a bit. I probably looked ridiculous for how I stretched it but after the warmups, no more pain. So, I carried on my way to the workout:

Warm up 2 laps 2 laps
1x20 leg swings
1x20 jumping jacks
2x40 side to side
1x10 lateral lunges
Campus loop
3x120
1x1000 50s 50s @ 2:55
(50s 50s work like this: accelerate for 50m bring back to tempo for 50m, accelerate for 50m bring back to tempo for 50m. so on and so forth)
1x800 40/30/40/29
3x200 25.4 25.6 26.1
1x20 leg swings
Stretch
Cooldown
Relaxed 20 min run tonight.

We are just two days away from our annual nutcracker (800m race where we dress up in Christmas clothes and have a fast time trial.) In bed at 9:30 PM super tired...

11.28.2017

Mileage 5

Woke up to a text from Danny Mackey today, know who he is? Remember USAs? He is the coach for Brooks Beasts in Seattle, he said he would like to organize a call in the next few days to talk. What a way to start the day! I sat there for 10 minutes looking at my phone making sure my reply had no errors and sounded good. Around 3 o'clock today he called, so I guess the call was happening sooner than I thought which is fine by me! We talked on the phone for a good 40 minutes about anything and everything! It felt conversation based, not like I was talking to a professional coach of an incredible team. I liked that. We talked about workouts, plans, school, everything. The conversation got me really excited for the future, we planned on me coming up to visit on the 13th but I will be in France, so we settled for the 20th, the day after I get back. Hopefully I won't be too jet lagged.

I went to talk to Johnson right after the phone call and he was ecstatic about the visit which is great, I was a little nervous talking to him about it because we haven't really talked fully about both of our expectations for me next year, where I'll train, who I'll be coached by etc. After both talks with both coaches I went and did my premeet because tomorrow is The Nutcracker!!!!

20 minute run

300 39.6

200 27.4

120 16.2

I was really surprised with today's times I just ran them and didn't focus on running anything fast, I thought eh, I'll just go fast and relaxed and save the speed for tomorrow. But 39.6 is fast, usually, I would have been content with a 42 or 41 but if 39.6 feels that good than I have a lot more speed right now than I thought.

In bed 10:12 because tomorrow is a.... race?

11.29.2017
Mileage 7

Woke up to a 20 minute run nice and easy to shake out the legs for tonight. Ate a good breakfast, went to an advisor meeting at 9, from 9:30-11:00 homework, 11:00-12:00 treatment, 12:00-2:00 class. 2-3:30 work. 4:00-5:00 nutcracker, 5:00-6:30 class, 7:00 dinner, 7:30-9:00 PM Library, 9:30 blizzard from DQ. 10:23 lights out.

So today as you can see was extremely busy, and in this journal, I don't want to just give you the workouts because a lot of what happens in our lives is off the track, think about it. If I only gave you the workouts, I did than I would only be giving you 2 out of the 14 hours I am awake, that is 1/7th of my daily life. Sure, that is what you are most interested in but being a student athlete Is about having a life in the balance.

For this next part, I really want you to visualize this:

Now, The Nutcracker *Que Christmas themed intro* November 29th, 2017 *Que bass drop and bells jingling* a day where no man on the Western Oregon University track team wanted to run super fast. *Bass drop, jingling bells, Santa's laugh, ho ho ho, * The night was calm and cold. The Christmas outfits worn were jingling and jolly. Not a frown was in sight for this night is truly magical. The men's team warmed up as they conversated. Giggles and whispers spread through the group that someone was going to GO. The head elves AJ, Dustin and David talked back and forth clarifying that off the turn they are going to finish strong together.

BANG

The race is off, the pace setter josh jingles his way to the front, 26 through 200, the rest of the group jollies their time through in 27, they snowflake dance around the turn as Josh comes through 400 in 54, the main group 57,58. The pace surely slowed as the jingle jangler Josh steps of the track. In lead now is a green elf named David, his bare chest green elf hat and shorts whistle through the cold air as the belled necklace echoes Christmas cheer with each step. Dustin along his shoulder sits cozily in his fireplace warm stocking red tights. With hints of red and green he festively represents those Christmas costumed lovers. AJ shadowed silently behind the two as they come around the final turn, 1:53,1:54,1:54. The group comfortably flies through the finish knowing in the back of their mind that 1:55 was a cold winter breeze. Now the question displays, how fast could they of ran? The world may never know....

The cookie dough blizzard was the best part of the day delicious and rewarding.

In bed at 10:05 Olivia and I leave for France in 10 days! Let's gooooo!

11.30.2017

Mileage 5

Easy morning miles with Tyler. It is going to be a busy day once again. First run in a long time where neither my side or knee hurt. After the run I went to the trainers to keep consistent therapy.

Today was class from 11-12:30 then worked on essay from 12:30-2:00 then took a final from 2:00-3:20, 3:20-4:30 more essay work. Came home after dinner and won a game of FortNite. Today was a good day. This was a great Fall.

Part III: Winter

December: France & Winter Training

February: Indoor Continued

March: Indoor Nationals & Start of Outdoor

12.1.2017
Mileage 9

It is December 1st baby!!! This is my favorite month of the year! Why you ask? Christmas, my birthday, new year's, snow, pre-season to indoor, and usually everyone is a tad jollier this month because they feel obligated. So how did I kick off December? With a circuit...

Relaxed 2 laps 2 laps
1x20 leg swings
1x40 side to side
1x20 rhll
30 minute run with the team 6:27 pace
15 minutes of Xs on the turf
1x300,200,100 @ 52,33,17
Strength and circuit time
2x40 light skipping
2x40 power skips
3x80 stride
2x20 overhead med ball lunges
2x10 pogos
3x5 drop squats
1x40 skipping backwards
1x40 running backwards
1x300 @ 80% 50
2x5 single leg hops each leg
2x40 speed skaters
1x300 @ 75% 55
1x20 spiderman
1x20 inchworm
1x10 lateral lunge each direction
1x300 @ 70% 58

Tomorrow will be an easy day, Sunday will be a long run. Shooting for 55-60 miles next week even though its finals it should be doable. My body feels surprisingly great and today was no problem. Today was my last day of class too, to celebrate I worked on my final essay for 3 hours and got home around 3pm. Hopefully I can get this essay done on Sunday, so the rest of the week is a breeze. Shooting for a 4.0 again, I got one last spring and really surprised myself so now I need to try and do it again. Tonight, we went to the casino for Tyler's 21st birthday. we all lost money and we all tried Appletinis. The appletinis were not too bad. In bed 11:45

12.2.2017
Mileage 7

Nice and easy 7 mile run, went out at 2PM because it was the only window in the clouds that looked clear. On the run, it was weird. I mentally spaced out for 2 miles thinking about speaking on Monday. I will be at Tillamook High School doing a speaking gig, I think I said that already, but I'll just say it again for my sake. I am really looking forward to speaking and I think I have the speech all polished up. I will talk about my development, USAs and this last cross country season. Hoping for the best, Olivia is joining me so that will be nice.

12.3.2017
Mileage 11

Getting back in the groove again today, these miles were nice and easy. 11 miles in 70 minutes. I ran with Thomas today and it is always nice running with him. we talked about a lot of stuff which made the run go by fast, we mostly talked about FortNite. After the run I finished up my fifteen page rhetorical analysis essay so now all I have left is other class assignments and I will be DONE with the term! Olivia and I fly out to France in 6 days! So crazy, we talked about this in August and now 4 months later here we are. Time flies.

For finals week we do not have regular scheduled class times so my schedule is really opening to just run and do homework. Tomorrow I am going to the library to start the day, practice at noon before traveling to Tillamook. In bed at 11:05

Tonight we weighed ourselves, I weigh 140.5

12.4.2017
Mileage 8

Woke up at 8 and started the day with some homework in the library. After finishing that up I jotted down some notes for tonight's speech before heading to the track for a quick workout.

Campus loop
1x20 leg swings
4x100 jumping rope
4x20 running high knees
2x40 side to side
2x40 skipping
2x40 speed skaters
1x200 fast and relaxed 28
5x300 100/100/100 sprint/float/sprint
43.7, 43.2, 42.3, 42.8, 40.2

These felt tremendous! Never this early could I really conquer a speed workout like this without throwing up. Tyler threw up today. That is okay though! He did every rep at these speeds and crushed it! He deserves a good puke!

After practice Olivia and I drove to Tillamook, we step out of the car and sweet lord it smells like dairy. It was a manure slap in the face.

For the speaking engagement, I learned a lot, I learned that I fidget with my hands a lot, and I also learned I need to adjust my speech in accordance with the audience. For instance, tonight there were a lot of parents in the crowd too. I never really targeted them with anything, it was all on the kids. If I could go back now, I would say things like, "and parents, thank you so much for the support and influence you have on your kids. This sport is far more than about running, and I am sure you have seen your kids change and develop into incredible people. Because from what I have seen here today they are incredible." Something like that...At the end of my talk I asked for questions and no one raised their hands, which makes sense I guess because this really isn't the time or place to ask questions, it's a sports banquet not a Ted Talk.

Overall though it was a great first high school speaking gig. Parents afterwards came up and shook my hand, talked to me and thanked me. Some parents said that my story was perfect for their kid who is slowly developing and needed to hear what I had to say. For that I am grateful. If one kid in that cafeteria was changed and has a positive outlook than it was a successful talk.

In closing for today, they had dessert and I had cinnamon rolls that were by far the best cinnamon rolls I have ever had. Dexter, you make a mighty fine cinnamon roll.

12.5.2017

Mileage 10

Last day of fall term!!! Practice today at 2:40 included an unreal amount of happiness being done with the term. Today's workout was also very very good. After doing finals from 10-2:30 I did not think I had the mental capacity to blast a workout,

2 laps 2 laps

1x20 leg swings

3x10 hurdle walkovers

2x20 hurdle skips

2x80 stride

2x40 running high knees

Campus loop (15 mins) into 5x3 min tempos 2 min recovery.

I did all of these on the road except the last one, once I got back on the track I did the final rep in lane two and got 2:58 for the kilometer so I am not sure how fast I was running them, I just went on how I felt but they didn't seem too far off pace from the last one.

After the tempos I spiked up and did 2x80 stride. Originally, we were going to do cutdown 500s at 68,64,60 through 400 but Johnson switched my work out because it was getting a bit too cold for that also because I went through 400 on my first 500 rep in 61 so he knew I needed something different.

I wasn't trying to go that fast he just said fast and relaxed don't look at your watch, so that's what I did. After the first 500 he had me jog a lap and tempo a 300. After the 300 tempo he wanted me to do another 500 this time just try and be as smooth as I can. I felt like I was flying, just slicing through the air. Everyone was off the track except the three coaches and so it felt perfect. I went through 400 in 56 and finished the 500 at 69.8. I cooled down then went to the trainers to roll out and work out the workout.

Topped off today with some pizza and a blizzard while I played FortNite. The term is over, and I should be pretty darn close to getting a 4.0

12.6.2017

Mileage 10

Mileage 6.5 @6:43s with Dustin. First time I have ran with him since nationals. Then later ran again with him and AJ for 25 mins before watching "The Room." May be one of the most interesting movies ever created. Nothing too interesting happened today, so now it is a waiting game till we leave for France.

12.7.2017
Mileage 5

Mile warm up
22 min run
Weight room
5x3 12kg kettlebell swing
5x2 27.5lb split jerks
3x5 back ab extension
3x5 med ball twist throw abs
1x3 30lb goblet squat
5 pull ups
Goblet squat
5 pull ups
Goblet squat
5 pull up
Goblet squat
Then to the circuit
2x50 side to side
1x10 burpees
2x100 jumping rope
2x20 overhead lunges
2x10 pogo jumps
4 position planks
Standing plank
side to sides

We had decided to include ab exercises because our abs may be the weakest part of our body. Dustin and I talked on a run that maybe all of us experienced side aches during nationals happened because we haven't done enough abs this year It makes sense partially but then at the same time, why did it just hurt at nationals and not anywhere else? Anyhow abs are a must because it takes 5 minutes a day minimum to make a difference.

In 48 hours, I will be in France. Crazy

12.8.2017
Mileage 4

Easy day with Olivia, we leave tomorrow and she wanted to get some work in, so I joined her. We did a 10 minute warm up then 1-1 ratio tempos. 1 minute, 2, 3,2,1 felt good not sure exactly what the pace was but overall felt good for her. I slept like crap last night due to the wind so that's sucky, but if I sleep like that again I will just sleep on the plane.

12.9-10.2017
Mileage none!!

Today was pretty much two days because of time change, (9 hours) so I have no idea what day it is. However, we traveled for 25 hrs. and 52 minutes. I started a stopwatch when we began moving out of Olivia's driveway, and stopped it when we got to Madison's in France. It was a long trip, but Olivia and I never fought and still love each other so that's a good sign. Looking forward to seeing this part of France. Tomorrow we will do a little bit of traveling but for the most part just adjust.

12.11.2017
Mileage 5

First day in France, easy 20 minute run with Olivia then ran another 16 minutes alone. Just kind of scoping out around my sister's house trying to find good running spots, nothing really that I could see unfortunately but there is a lake close to her house, I will explore there tomorrow. Today we went into Bordeaux and saw a Cathedral, visited shops and spoke really bad French. I tried to order a croissant and it was terrible. The French that is, the croissant was delicious, my French is what's terrible. Apparently 22% on Duolingo isn't sufficient enough to be fluent.

12.12.2017
Mileage 10

10 mile workout/run this morning and a six mile walk through the city later today
The workout was a good 20 minute warm up then
1:1 tempo
1 min, 2 min (4:30 pace mile pace), 3 min (4:40), 4 min (4:40), 3 min (4:35), 2 min (4:30), 1 min. each tempo had its exact time for recovery (1:1 2:2 3:3 etc..)

At first it was really nice, I was tempoing on this long service road until a man stopped me in a service vehicle and spoke French to me. I did not understand a thing he said. I just kept nodding and finally said, "Merci" as he drove off. For all I know he could have said, "Awesome job out here running and doing a workout you are an inspiration man! Keep it up!" or he could have said, "This is for service vehicles only, please do not run out here, but you can run on the road closer to town, just not past that sign." I think he said the second option. It was flattering he spoke French to me. I must look French myself.

Overall though the tempo felt great, a little surprised I was able to do this just two days after landing, but I got bored and wanted to just get my heart rate up. I have a bad feeling this is going to be my only real workout option for the next week, I doubt we will be able to get on a track. The best thing however that happened today was I got a fluffy coat! One of the ones with the furred hoods. The ones that are totally "in" in France and the same ones that are totally "out" in United States. It is so warm and so fuzzy. Tomorrow Olivia and I are going to attempt a circuit before we head to a sand dune along the Atlantic Ocean.

12.13.2017
Mileage 5

Today was a low mileage day for me. I woke up at 8:05 and snoozed till 8:40. I was really tired, luckily, I have an Olivia that literally pulled me out of bed. We ran 30 minutes and did a circuit:

2x80 stride
2x40 side to side
2x20 lunges
2x20 high knees
2x15 second standing plank
1x10 burpee
1x80 stride
1x10 pogo
1x10 lateral lunges
2x20 skips
1x30 running backwards
1x80 stride

The greatest thing about a circuit is you can do it anywhere. Given this circuit is far shorter than the usual one we were still able to get basic drills done. After the circuit we got in the car and drove to the Atlantic Ocean, on the shore of the ocean was a mountain of sand! It literally took me two minutes to run down. Once down at the ocean my dad and I walked the shore before we tried to take some steps back up, however the steps did not lead where we thought they would. They led us into a neighborhood and we were far too deep in our problem, so we walked for half a mile through the city and finally made it to the sand dune.

12.14.2017

Mileage 8.5

This was a funny run, I averaged 6:35s but the first 30 minutes were with Olivia at 7:43s, who knows what the last half of the run was at. I felt pretty good, the travel didn't take as big as a toll on my body as I thought. However, I did nap today. After the naps, we went to the Christmas market in Bordeaux but on the way there we had to wait an extra hour because suddenly, the train honked, the train slowed down, then thud. A conductor walked through our cart and said, "so that was either a person or just a big rock; we have to double check to make sure." She said it in French so Madison translated and we sat there for a full hour or more. Once the train started moving again, we passed ambulances and police cars, we all assumed it was not just a big rock.

12.15.2017
Mileage 5

Today was a relatively easy day, 35 mins at 6:43 pace with the last 10 mins holding my sisters' dog by a leash. After the run, we went and toured a wine castle and it was really cool. The culture, the history, the architecture makes Europe so much cooler than United States (in those aspects). I'm not usually a white wine guy but the white wine here was super super good. The red wine was also great, but I usually like red wine anyway.

The story behind the white wine is the Duke who owned the property originally had a wife. He went to war and died, so after that she only wore white dresses in his memory. Rumor has it that when mist rolls over the vineyards, the white lady has returned to care for the vines like she once did.

12.16.2017
Mileage 0

Woke up and cooked breakfast for my sister and mom as we went into town early with Madison. Madison works at a children's school that teaches English as the primary language. My mom and I just hung out around town for two hours waiting for Madison. It was a good alone time for the two of us where we could just talk and relax. After Madison's work we went back and had a huge lunch with Victor's family and our family. His family came into town to meet us and we had huge lunch.

After that, we got on a train to Paris for the last part of our trip. We could not get into our Airbnb till 10:30 and we didn't eat dinner till 11:00pm. Strangely enough that is a common time for French people to go out and eat. The restaurants were all packed by the time we got out. Once back at the Airbnb sat awake till 3 o'clock because of how loud the people were in the apartment. This is going to be a long few days if they act like that every night.

12.17.2017
Mileage 0 but walked 13 miles

Today was a busy touristy day in Paris. We got breakfast than right after went to the Louvre for 4 hours. We all split up to cover what we each wanted to see. We saw a mummy, hieroglyphics, old vases, the Mona Lisa, hundreds of paintings, statues. We were in there for four hours and we didn't see all of it. After the Louvre we toured the Notre Dame, then Eiffel Tower, then the Arc De Triumph. It was a crazy busy day but great. My parents fly out tomorrow, so this was a perfect last day together.

12.18.2017

Mileage 0

Hard to come by places to run in Paris. However, Olivia and I walked for a good 10 miles around the city. We went to a ferris wheel, put a lock on love lock bridge, avoided a street painter, and enjoyed our last night here with pristine French wine. The story behind the street painter was we were walking across a bridge and a guy stopped us and said, "ah you have a beautiful smile let me paint you," I said we didn't have any money and he says, "no no no free of charge just please you are perfect both of you." We sat down knowing this guy was going to ask for money.

He asked my name, I said John and Olivia said Sarah, so he puts a J and an S in a heart as a final touch. Olivia and I tried our hardest not to laugh. He then said, "perfect now 35 euros" we look at the picture and laugh, I mean it somewhat looked like us, but it wasn't incredible. Definitely not 35 euro worth. We said sorry and just left. John and Sarah escape. Looking back, I wish I would have tried to swindle him to sell it to us for five euros that would be such a funny framed photo. Tomorrow we fly out back home, our flight has been so jumbled with cancellations and delays that I am not sure what time we are actually flying out. Thanks a million, if you are still reading through France. It wasn't too running related, so I apologize for that, you are true fans if you made it through this trip!

12.19.2017

Mileage 7

I think it is still the 19th, we landed in Seattle and I have no idea what day it is, it was only 20 hours of travel but easily the hardest 20 hours of travel I have experienced.

4am wake up to the roommates singing and dancing in the Airbnb

7am wake up and check phone

7:04am kick Olivia in the shin and say that our flight has been re-assigned to 10:45 (and it's about a 2 hour commute to airport.

7:30am rush from apartment to metro

8:00am accidently buy the wrong metro ticket

8:40am be fined 70 euros for buying the wrong metro ticket

9:10am check in to find out we have been re-assigned to a 10:10 departing flight

9:17am stand in line of 300 people for passport check, look down at the boarding ticket and see that our plane starts boarding in 1 minute.

9:30am cut through the line as far as possible, make it 5 people before a lady said, "I am on the same flight too you can't cut." However, she never looked at my ticket, so I doubt she was.

9:47 jump out of passport line and run to a priority window and beg to be let through

9:48 call over Olivia to the window

9:49 Olivia gets stopped by officer saying she can't get out of line, after yelling back and forth the lady let her through and as Olivia gets to the window, the man stands up and leaves the check in stand.

10:02 make it through security and run to the gate, plane departs at 10:10

10:08 make it to the gate

11:55am (after 9hr time change) make it to Seattle to find out our bags are not there

So long story short, everything you could think of for a rough flight we had it, delayed, cancelled, missing bags, it was incredible.... I ran 7 miles once we got to our friends' home, but it was a wobbly painful run. I will be borrowing clothes tonight and visiting Brooks Headquarters tomorrow, hopefully I am not too jet-lagged but I am ready, very excited to visit.

12.20.2017
Mileage 8

Woke up at 5 am, I guess I will blame jet lag. While I sat awake, I read Game of Thrones before heading to Brooks at 10. Once there I met Bryce and Izaic Yorks. Izaic introduced himself and I couldn't help but laugh inside because any American distance runner knows who he is. Absolute animal, and a really great guy. He told me he went to the University of Washington and I couldn't help but chuckle at his humbling attitude. I mean technically we are complete strangers, but I knew so much about him since his days at UW.

After the run Coach Danny Mackey talked with me about our upcoming day. We started the day with an 8-mile run before going to lunch with some of the athletes, a lot of the athletes are away due to Christmas. The athletes I met with Hannah, Izaic, Baylee. I really loved the company and the team, and their overall joy seemed surreal. We ate at the headquarters because the athletes receive meal stipend for lunches at the HQ. In all honesty I was blown away with the HQ right when I walked in. The pros of Brooks, as in the positives, seem to be that all the athletes are happy and feel appreciated. Hannah said she can have a conversation with the CEO of the company and he knows they are human.

So often it seems that athletes are devalued used just as advertising and propaganda robots. So, hearing this made me feel really great about Brooks. They only have a handful of athletes as well. Handpicked and thoroughly thought about to see if they are a good fit with the team dynamic. The size of the company to me is a positive because it gives the athletes direct say in products, advertising and the company itself. I can see myself learning a lot here and being able to voice my thoughts a lot easier than if I was with a different company. I was mind blown about the presentation of the company as well, in all honesty my whole life I had the interpretation that all companies were envious of Nike. A cool thing about what I learned today is Brooks is in such a Niche, and such a keen part of the sport that they are who they are. They are who they want to be, and everyone is incredibly proud of the company and what they stand for.

After lunch Danny and I traveled through Seattle and looked at facilities and their doctors' offices. Everything is already paid for by the company so that is not taken out of the athlete's contract. A HUGE BONUS. I really liked their training staff and facilities. The doctor's office, InHealth, has a jacket from Michael Phelps's Rio games. The head doctor here helped Phelps in Rio. If that's not a stamp of approval and professionalism I don't know what is. After that we went back to the HQ where Danny took me over a contract, not my contract, a generic blank contract. His purpose was not to get me to sign or look into Brooks, it was how to read a contract. It was a massive help because he didn't say if you signed with Brooks...he left it open and said whoever you sign with this is what you should read and look in to, Danny is a genuine guy and as an athlete having him as a coach would be an incredible. I was really impressed and felt really connected.

After that we went over training logs for Izaic and looked at what a basic schedule looks like for specific athletes. He writes the workout and weight plans himself so seeing the time he puts into the schedules shows how much he cares about the individual growth for the athletes. After leaving and driving back to Portland I can confidently say they are THE REAL DEAL. They are the first group to contact me and from what I

saw they drive a hard bargain. I could see myself there and I could see myself happy.
After the visit we traveled to Troutdale where we immediately went to sleep because wow, we were tired. Olivia also liked Brooks after I told her about my day, so that's a bonus. Tomorrow I will be back with the boys in Monmouth. Flotrack predicted who will be the 500th US sub 4 miler. They made a big article on it, I was on the list, but they didn't rank me being before or at 500. When I get my shot at the end of January, I bet I will be the 501st, just my luck.

12.21.2017
Mileage 9

Here we go, now we are back in the land of the living! We are ready to get workouts and training in… you no longer have to read about wine, travel, museums. You get to read about workouts! Pain! Agony! Maybe not the last two but surely workouts. However, I am sore today, like painful sore. I feel like I will be crawling tomorrow for how bad my glutes and back hurt after today.

2 laps 2 laps
Leg swings
Rhll
30 min run @ 6:42s
2x40 skips
2x40 big skips
3x80 stride
2x40 backwards running
2x20 lunges
2x10 pogos
3x3 drop squats
1x10 burpees
1x120 stride
2x10 hurdle walkovers
2x10 side step overs
1x20 inchworm and pushup
2x40 speed skater
1x80 stride

After the circuit I got a classic breakfast burrito from Muchas and went home and took a 2-hour nap. Holy crap I am tired, and

I am sore, I have a bad feeling that I will be wrecked for a few days.

Woke up at 4PM and played some FortNite. I will be getting an Xbox One soon, so I am excited for that no doubt. Watched Peaky Blinders on Netflix before a 30 min shakeout run @ 7:15s....in bed at 8. 8...going to be a hard adjustment.

12.22.2017
Mileage 6

Sweet misery I will never walk again!!!! My days, my life, my career is over...I am so sore. Today I ran 40 minutes but took occasional walk breaks and stretches. My body is shot. My body feels shocked from travel and the circuit, if I could replay the last 48 hours, I would run a little slower and a little less. Nothing really to report today but I am tired, and my body hurts over every inch and in every crevasse. In bed at 8:30

12.23.207
Mileage 7

Awake at 5 am. Why!!! Why is this happening, read some more in Game of Thrones so it wasn't a total loss, but my sleep is ridiculous. Today I took a smarter approach. Rolled and stretched 30 minutes prior to the run, once we started running my body felt terrible at seven-minute pace, so I decided to just tempo. For some reason the faster I went the less my back hurt. so, once we got to the base of cemetery hill, AJ and I did 4x40 second hill accelerations. Once I started working hard my body loosened itself up and it wasn't so bad. After the run back, I called it at my house, 5 easy mile morning then doubled for 2 easy miles. Unsure what the Christmas plans are, pretty sure I will be going to Olivia's. First Christmas away from the family.

12.24.2017

Mileage 7

Woke up today and decided that it's going to be a good day for some speed. Woke up feeling far less sore in my back so I figured it's safe to say I can train normally. Still did a good 30 minutes of rolling out and stretching before heading to the track. Once there:

2 laps 2 laps
Rhll
Leg swings
2x40 side to side
35 minute run @ 6:30s
1x300 @ 44
2x200 @ 27, 27
3x120 @17,17,16

It was cold today, 29 degrees, so I really didn't want to get up and go. Looking forward to getting back on the track soon, but first, Christmas.

12.25.2017

Mileage 6

Merry Christmas, 6 mile run at 70 minutes. Yeah, you read that right, I ran 6 miles in 70 minutes laugh all you want but it was icy, cold and it took me a good ten minutes to make it up a hill. I was ice skating the whole time. Overall though I can live with a recovery day. These last days have been rough on the bod. Once I come back from Christmas though its foot on the peddle no interruptions.

12.26.2017
Mileage 4

Due to not having my own car still...aka I haven't gotten the tags renewed since June, I wasn't on my own schedule so I thought we were leaving early morning today to go to Monmouth but Josh and I didn't leave till like 7PM and that's fine, however I didn't run today for the weather was far too violent and the roads were still too icy to get any benefit out of it. Once I got back to Monmouth just an easy 4 mile run @ 7:00. Tomorrow is my birthday, I am looking forward to a track workout because all I want for my birthday is to be fast.

12.27.2017
Mileage 12

HAPPY BIRTHDAY TO ME! 22 *Que T-Swizzle song* what a time to be alive. For the birthday gift I got a workout in:

2 laps 2 laps
30 minute run
15 minute Xs on the Turf (Diagonals)
Jog to the track/spike up
2x500 going through 400 in 58
2x200 at 31

Breakfast burritos and a birthday coffee followed the morning festivities. The rest of the day consisted of more Peaky Blinders before running 3 miles in the PM at 6:43s. I am feeling fresh again and ready to roll. Tomorrow, no longer a day about me...just another day. Until next year birthday.

12.28.2017
Mileage 7

2 laps 2 laps
Leg swings
Rhll
25 min run
Prior to circuit, 2x200s @ 27, 27.4
2x40 skips
2x40 big skips
3x80 stride
2x40 backwards running
2x20 lunges
2x10 pogos
3x3 drop squats
1x10 burpees
1x120 stride
2x10 hurdle walkovers
2x10 side step overs
1x20 inchworm and pushup
2x40 speed skater
1x80 stride
Cooldown mile

After the circuit went over to AJ's and again watched Peaky Blinders. Tomorrow I am getting an Xbox One so hopefully my training, journal and girlfriend stay in place after this purchase.

12.29.2017
Mileage 7

Good easy seven mile single at 6:44 pace with a 40,30,20 sec pick up at 30 minutes. Just brought the speed up to tempo pace to work out the circuit. Tomorrow is the last big workout of 2017, let's see if we can grind out a good one and prove to myself, I'm not out of shape. Also, my Xbox is AWESOME!!!!!

12.30.2017
Mileage 11

Here we are, the end of 2017, well we still have tomorrow but enjoy this intense intro….
Que dramatic music
The end of 2017 just a man, his men and the track. Ready for another incredible workout.
Overall it was AWESOME
Que light show and guitar solo

Campus loop
2x200 @ 27, 27
Walk 200 recovery
5 broken 600 30/40/30 goal
Jog 600 recovery
30/39/30, 29/41/30, 29/39/30, 30/40/30, 29/38/28
2x200 28.4, 26.2
PM, 5 mile run @ 6:52s shakeout the legs and gear up for speed workout on January 1st.

Overall this workout felt pretty good, the speed change was harder than I remember. During cross season these seemed far smoother but overall, I'd say it was a 7/10 on how I felt. Maybe I will start rating workouts off a scale, I don't know, what do you think? Should I? just kidding your vote means nothing because this book is already written, and your input cannot be heard. I am excited for the season to get going however I need some more workouts to dictate what I will be doing on January 13th for the indoor meet. Do I do the 3k or do I do the 1k…not sure. Tomorrow night I plan on going to Dustin's for New Year's should be a good time.

12.31.2017
Mileage 8

Today was an easy 8 mile run to run 2017, nothing too crazy to report other than the fact that I feel great and ready to race. I am leaning towards a 1000m opener opposed to a 3k just because it seems up my alley a bit more with how my fitness feels. Now that it's December 31st it is time to summarize the year and what to expect and dream for 2018

A lot of great stuff happened this year only great things happened this year never was there a bad moment. As I am writing this I can't think of any major hiccups in training, deaths, illnesses or anything. So far, this year has been all positives. Going into 2018 I have a lot of goals in mind and I have a lot of work to do to achieve those goals. If I was a senior last year, and I graduated with no more eligibility you could have said my collegiate career was successful. Thankfully I am back another year with still a lot more to do. Going into 2018 my tangible goals are: Sub 4 in the mile, win an indoor national title, defend DMR national title, defend 1500m national title, set new Division 2 national record in the 1500m, and sign a professional contract. Now all those things would be great, but more importantly my biggest goal for 2018 is to blur the line of Division 1,2,3 and just race.

So often it seems as though Division 2 and 3 get brushed under the rug but in reality, great talents come out of Division 2. Going into 2018 I want to just be able to race, inspire, and challenge the predetermined thought that smaller schools are going to bow a knee to power houses.

Any school is a school to run at and pursue your dream. If you are given the opportunity at a school to run, dream and achieve than do it! My last upcoming year I want it to be memorable not only for me, but for Division 2 entirely. At this moment I am unsure how this year will go; but you as a reader are reading this after the year has been completed. So, how did I do?

HAPPY NEW YEAR!

1.1.2018
Mileage 7

Wow it feels weird to write/type 1.1 and 2018. Feels just like yesterday it was 2017...old joke? Sorry. Today was just another day of improvement. It felt and went exceptional considering this same workout almost took me out a full season with a hamstring tweak.

Today was speed development:
Mile warm up
Campus loop
2x3x250s (broken Sprint 75, float 75, sprint 100)
33.2, 33.7, 32.5, 33.8, 33.5, 33.2
20 minute cooldown

In between each rep we just walked 150 and went right into it. Between the first three and last three we took a 4 minute recovery walk, jog, stretch. The sprint portions at the end felt incredibly fast and I felt really good, so I think I have a bit more speed than I thought. A year ago, we averaged 34 and 35s on all of them so seeing these times consistently shows we have a good amount of improvement since last year.

3 mile PM run after watching more Peaky Blinders, I would say this is my favorite show. You should watch it! Tomorrow is a circuit then we have a workout on Wednesday, recovery on Thursday, workout on Friday.

Today is also the first day of the new year. Do you have any New Year resolutions? My New Year's resolution is "inspire more." Track and field is such a personable sport that I want to be able to help others more. With track season rolling around I'm not sure what the seasons will hold but I am confident that with a clear mind and a full heart I can accomplish anything. I encourage you readers to do nice things. Like, hold open doors for little old ladies, this new year I want to try and be the best version of me I can possibly be.

1.2.2018

Mileage 7

2 laps 2 laps

20 minute run

Weight room

3x5 kettlebell thrusts 15kg

3x5 back extensions on ball

4x4 split jerk 35lbs each hand

3x5 pull ups

4x4 drop squats 40lbs

on the track

1x40 big skips

1x40 small skips

2x40 side to side

3x4 drop squats

1x40 speed skaters

Stride 100

2x10 hurdle walkovers

2x10 hurdle side steps

1x10 inchworms

Stride 80

Cooldown

After the workout we watched more Peaky Blinders and ran 2 miles for a PM shake out. Tomorrow's workout is a doozy, in bed at 10:30 trying to get back on a normal sleeping schedule.

1.3.2018

Mileage 12

The group was working out at noon, but I decided to go a little earlier. Sometimes hard workouts are best done alone where you have only yourself to push you and drive you through a rep. Solo workouts allow you to find your own rhythm and flow within the exercise. In a race, when the race gets tough, no one is going to save you put yourself. Dig deep and be confident that this race is yours to control. Controlling the race mentally more than anything else. Today, I somewhat did that until I hopped on board the pain train.

Mile warm up
Leg swings
Side to side
15 minute run straight into 5k tempo @ 15:38
7x40 sec hills with minute jog down recovery
Back to the track, spike up
1x800 at 80-90% 62/59 for a 2:01
Cooldown

Collectively the workout went really well, I wanted the tempo to be the hardest efforted part because that's where I feel like I need the most work. Once I got to the hills, I did 7x hills. I was supposed to do 8 but on my way down I literally...I mean literally almost crapped my pants and I was a good quarter mile away from the nearest bathroom. I was in the neighborhoods too so it's not like I could just pop a poop on a lawn. I waddled back to the track and dropped the extra weight before the 800. Once on the track my plan was to just run 1:58-2:00 however the first lap made that plan very difficult and I thought I went through 400 in 60 until I looked down and saw 62. That was a very hard 2:01 and I do not recommend.

After the workout I jogged around campus for my cooldown and saw that the training room was open. I did what any sore man would do, I rolled out, iced and got in the boots. A really great 45 minute recovery process to where I am sure tomorrow and Friday workout I will feel just fine. I went to sushi for a mid-dinner meal. If brunch is breakfast-lunch what is between lunch and dinner? Dunch? Linner? Dinch? Long story short I had sushi and burped it up quite frequently on my 3 mile shakeout run at 6:34s. Today was a great training day.

1.4.2018
Mileage 11

Tyler the roommate is back so it was nice to have him on the run today, the team just did a 7 mile loop. Once the loop got to my house, Tyler and I went an extra 2 miles to call the morning run at 9. Overall feel a lot better than I thought I would. I woke up pretty sore but by mile 3 I was back to normal. At 30 minutes we did 40,30,20 pickups again just to get the legs moving.

After a day of rolling out and playing FortNite I went to coach's office and talked about France, Brooks and the season. We have agreed I will be opening the season in the 1000m. We also talked about an interview I am getting tomorrow with Flotrack. It's supposed to be 15-20 minutes over the phone, I hope I can represent and say what I want to say about my upcoming year. After the meeting I ran 2 miles in the pm. Feeling ready to roll tomorrow.

1.5.2018

Mileage 9

First workout back with Johnson and boy did he not mess around. It was good, really good. Got to the track at noon to see the team somewhat assembled. Still missing some people but a good enough group was back for the guys.

2 laps 2 laps

Rhll

Leg swings

1x40 side to side

3x3 drop squats

1x15 jumping jacks

20 minute run straight into 1200m on the track doing 50/50s

How 50/50s work if I have not explained yet, is you get tempo rhythm for 50m then accelerate to race pace for 50m, then back to tempo, then accelerate. It is constant speed change and constant agony of rhythm breaking. Our 1200 was 71/71/70 so a 3:32

After that we spiked up for 3x120 accelerations 17,16,16 (they weren't supposed to be timed but I did anyway)

After that we went into 3x500 59-63 was the target time going through 400m

Our reps through 400 59,59,57

Our reps at 500 73,73,70

In between each 500 we had a 600m jog and a 100m walk.

After the 500s we went right into 3x200s fast and relaxed target times 26-28

26.4,25.2,27.4

The last rep I was trying to hit a 30, just to feel what 4 flat pace felt like and I went through in 27 so I guess that's a good sign. These 200s felt great and I feel as though we are gearing up for a good opening meet because everyone was able to handle this workout. Tyler, Dustin, Phil, Parker and I

No PM run tonight however; ended up going to Portland to visit friends. Great to see them, but a bit bummed I couldn't double. This workout made me very very excited for the 1k race. Also, today I had the interview with Flotrack and it ended up being a 40 minute conversation. Lincoln, the guy conducting the interview seemed passionate with his questions and responses. He also enjoyed my answers which shows me that he must agree with me or believes it will make a good story. Anyhow; not sure what the story will say, it will be published sometime this upcoming week prior to the race so I am hoping it will be a good read. Tomorrow will be another recovery day as we gear up towards race week already. Tomorrow folks, we are one week away from getting this indoor season started.

1.6.2018

Mileage 9

35 minute AM run with 2x200s at 30 then a 25 minute PM run with Tom. Nothing too crazy happened today, just kept it light and recovery based. One week till we race. Seems like we just got done with cross country and here we are gearing up for a 1000m race. At cross country nationals our first 1k was 2:42 so hopefully I could run at least 17 seconds faster than that in a single kilometer. Watched some more Peaky Blinders today with AJ and Dustin. Last week where we don't have school, I am taking advantage of being a vegetable.

1.7.2018
Mileage 8

50 minute single run at 6:35s. I planned on doubling today but totally spaced out. Once it got to 8PM it was too late to go out for a run. Six days out from racing, one day out from starting winter term (yuck). After getting a 3.95 last term for my GPA I am tired of school, now that I didn't get a 4.0, I will be happy to pass these last two terms and graduate. If I got a 4.0 last term maybe I would be more motivated. GPA is a funny deal though, because at the moment I do not plan on attending grad school, so why does my GPA really matter?

But here I am convincing myself otherwise. GPAs do matter I suppose, I think GPAs go hand in hand with athletic competition and competing for the best GPA you possibly can. Spring term last year I got a 4.0 and I won the 1500m national title for Div. 2. I don't think either of those would have been possible without the other. Being a student-athlete really is finding the balance and when one is going great, chances are the other one is too. On that academic note, if I want to succeed in track, I should probably go to bed so I can try to succeed in the classroom. In bed 9:55.

1.8.2018

Mileage 9

First day of school, last first day of winter term, I am taking 18 credits, I am ready for this term to be over. Is that bad to say day one? Today's practice:

2 laps 2 laps
1x20 leg swings
2x40 side to side
4x80m jumping rope
1x20 burpees
2x120 stride
3x30m harness
3x300 sprint float sprint 100m/100m/100m
Not focused on the time but on the feel 39.5, 40.5, 40.2
40 minute run 6:43 pace
2x40 strides
1x20 rhll
1x10 leg swings
3x5 drop squats
10 mins of flexibility

After practice I went to the trainers rolled out, stretched the ankles, got in the boots then went to class. In indoor track something I really focus on stretching and strengthening is my ankles. Usually those are the first things to blow out during indoor from the high speeds and tight turns. Doing one leg balance and squats has helped me so much already. After class I had dinner then ran a mile to the pool before jogging around stretching in the water. We race in five days, Drew looks to be in the 1k as well so that will be good. 9:50 = bedtime.

1.9.2018
Mileage 8

Workout day, a better day than I thought it would be. I felt great and felt fresh:

2 laps 2 laps
1x20 leg swings
1x20 jumping rope
2x20 turning side
20 minute run (3.25 miles)
2x20 running high knees
3x5 drop squats
1x40 big skips
1x200 fast and relaxed 28
1x2 laps of 50/50s
2:14 for the two laps, weirdly Dustin and I talked the whole time and it was 4:28 mile pace broken. Weirdly felt easy.

After that we switched to more aggressive spikes 4x600 broken 30/40/30
If you have noticed we do a whole lot of broken work, that is because in a race the lead can take off at any time and you need to be able to respond to a speed change, also rhythmically this makes you very aware of what speed you are going and what target speed you need. Our reps looked more like this

29/40/30
29/39/29
30/39/28
29/37/28
Fast 200 26.47

1x120 focusing solely on lifting the heel and driving
1x20 rhll
Cooldown.

Today was a good fast day. This workout won't necessarily benefit me for this Saturday but in two weeks' time this workout will be all tuned in with my body for the DMR/Mile double. Today I felt calm and relaxed, really really smooth. The last rep I wanted to keep accelerating into the last 200 but today wasn't designed for all-out effort. Saving the speed for Saturday (hopefully). In the 120 I never realized how much speed is generated by just driving the heel and toe up as you sprint. I feel like an uncontrolled spring, I will need to work on that.

If I gained anything from today it was confidence that this December training cycle was exactly what I needed. Coming into workouts like this I am a bit nervous after training blocks like December. If you recall when I was in France I couldn't spike up or get on a track for about 10 days, I also couldn't run for 3 days at the end of our trip. I get a bit freaked out when I can't run for multiple days so taking that time off seems to have zero negative effect on my legs now. I probably needed it to be honest. Tomorrow is a circuit then we are home free for the weekends race! Entries should be released tomorrow for the race! Let's go! This morning's workout I also used cues I will be using for the race. **Contact, Execute, Finish**. Contact through the first 600m. Execute 600-800. Finish last 200m faster than previous 800m. I am ready! In bed 10:10

1.10.2018
Mileage 7

I keep doing this to myself, Wednesday are always my hard days. I have class from 9-9:50, I do homework or go to trainers from 10-12, 12-2 I have practice, 2-3 I go to trainers, then from 3-4:20 I have class, track meeting at 4:30 then class from 5-7:50. A rough 11 hours but it is what being a student athlete is all about I suppose.

Warm up 2 laps 2 laps
1x20 leg swings
3x40 side to side turning
30 minute run
Finish run straight into 300 @ 47
3x 100 relaxed stride
1x20 right hand left leg
1x10 lateral lunge
4x100m jumping rope
2x30 walking figure four stretch
2x20 spiderman
3x20 overhead med ball lunge
2x10 pogo
2x10 speed skaters
2x8 jumping jacks
1x15 burpees
1x20 mountain climber
Jog 100m
1x20 leg swings
1x10 way back

Overall, I felt pretty good today, my ankles are sore, maybe I did too much ankle strengthening work too soon the other day, or maybe it was just spike days back to back. All in all, nothing too serious but definitely a bit beat up. My muscles feel great though! The Flotrack article was released today and it was really good, the click bait was, "David Ribich wants you to respect Division II" so I thought it was going to be an aggressive article, but it definitely took a different direction than I thought it would. It talked a lot about my high school development and a lot about my high school coach. I wish it would have highlighted a bit more on Western Oregon but it is what it is, still a great article. Looking forward to this weekend's race. In bed 10:05.

Contact, Execute, Finish.

1.11.2018

Mileage 8.5

Good 40 minute run with brady this am, forecast showed 100% chance of rain during our run but luckily it barely sprinkled. We finished the run on the turf and did 3x80m stride, they felt fast and smooth. A good sign leading into the weekend. I am a bit sore, but I feel very sharp which is a good spot to be in. After the run I went in and booted up/iced, my body is ready to rock and roll. We leave tomorrow, and I am so excited to pack my bag. Drew and I texted back and forth should be a heat we can go 1-2 in, no doubt he will be in speed shape.

Contact, Execute, Finish.

1.12.2018
Mileage 5

First pre meet of 2018, mileage was low but the work was exactly what I needed, tomorrow is the first track race since USAs in June, finally that race will be pushed back on the list, a great experience but I am ready for more track races.

20 minute run
1x10 legs wings
1x15 high knees
2x40 side to side
2x80 stride
1x10 way back
Rhll
Inside on the track
1x250 @ 34
1x200 25.3
1x500 broken 27/20/28 (200/100/200)
1x200 26.6
Cooldown 15 mins

I got a bit anxious in the premeet because I am very excited to race this 1k, not sure what the time will be I assume 2:23-2:24 the race should be pretty fast. School record is 2:28 held by Dustin Nading, he is in the 3k tomorrow and I have a feeling I will grab his 1k record and he will snag my 3k record. Record for record is my prediction. We walked 3 miles around downtown Seattle trying to find food to eat, we are staying in a new hotel area and the food options are so expensive, we settled to eat at KIKI Raman, and wow! It was delicious we all agreed in two weeks we are coming back for another round.

Tomorrow is race day, lights out at 10, asleep by 11, had a good hour long conversation with Freshman Neil. Johnson matched us as roommates, I might as well talk to him, right? He is a good guy and going to be very fast.

Contact, Execute Finish. Let the Big Dogs eat.

1.13.2018
Mileage unsure

Race day mileage I am always unsure how much I do, not really about the mileage you know? I just do enough to where I feel ready and cooldown enough to where I feel good.

Woke up at 6:30 ate a bagel for breakfast and headed on the bus at 7:15, arrived at Dempsey at 7:40 not racing until 11:35. Usually that is far too early for me to get to the meet but the next bus was at 10:15 and I really didn't want to just arrive and start my warm up so I took the early bus. Upon arrival I walked to QFC and got some coffee and bagel sandwich after time flew by it was time for my warm up:

10:40 am started warming up
10 min run
15 minutes of drills
10 min of light stretching
15 mins of strides and spiked up
Raced.

Wow, that race was crazy, the 1000m flew by and before I knew it, we were in our last lap. 2:21.35, something like that. Are you kidding me? Last night I said 2:23-2:24, that's honestly the fitness shape I thought I was in. Moral of that is don't put a time stamp on a race, go into the race fighting for the win and you will impressive yourself. From the gun Drew raced to the front which I have never seen before. That's when I cued **Contact**. Then, the race played out like so: pacer, Drew, me, all the way till the end. The pacer who we didn't know was in the race stepped off around 600 right when I cued **Execute.** We closed our last 200 in 26.xx **Finish**. Honestly, I am a bit shocked. We chose the 1k as my opening event because I told Johnson I feel like I have better speed than endurance right now, so I would rather hold off until later in the year for a 3k. Turns out I have more speed than I thought.

I think it was a good race switch, Drews time of 2:20.xx was the leading time in the world this year, given its January, still really crazy. My only hiccup is once Drew hit a new gear with 60m to go I sort of settled for second, I almost got caught but luckily pulled another gear out to barely squeak for second over my good friend Mick from Oregon. After the race Johnson was talking with coaches from Nike Oregon Project, Bowerman and Brooks. All good things I hope, it was nice to see Coach Mackey again, after the race I was going to do 200s with Brannon Kidder from Brooks, but our timeframe didn't line up as well as expected.

Went to the track for
6 min jog
2x3x200s and 2x200s
28,30,28 walk 100m jog 100m between reps/3 min walk between set
28,29,29
3 minute walk 28,27
10 minute cooldown

After the workout my calves felt a bit sore but the 200s felt fast and relaxed, far smoother than I thought. on normal days 8 200s at 28-30 seems like a workout in itself but doing them after a 2:21 race gives me confidence I am in pretty good mile shape. Went back to the stadium to watch Shalane Flanagan crush a 3k, as well as Craig Engels. He is a goofy guy but someone I hope to become better friends with as the years go on. Dustin Nading broke my 3k record as expected so we swapped. I heard a lot of people today say, "I respect Division II" and a lot of people came up to me introducing themselves and talking to me. They were high schoolers, collegians, coaches it was pretty interesting, a lot of them referenced my Flotrack article, crazy how many people read that. Felt really great about today, there were a lot of school records today. Everyone had a great meet, so I bought 36 ice cream sandwiches from Safeway for the bus ride home. Killer deal, three boxes for nine dollars. The school records were Olivia in the 600m, Suzie in the 1000m, Dustin in the 3000m, Nicole in the 3000m, and me in the 1000m. We got home at 12:30 in bed at 1 am, sleeping in tomorrow so we will see what the runs are like.

1.14.2018
Mileage 10

Great recovery day, woke up at 9 after sleeping soundly, played FortNite and ate breakfast before a 40 min run at 6:35 pace with Dustin and Parker. After we talked a lot about pro groups and FortNite we all went home and played some more FortNite. Before I knew it 6 o'clock rolled around, time for another run 20 minutes with Dustin. We talked about fearing our own fitness. An interesting concept, my side of the conversation was, "I feel like I am so mysteriously fit that I don't know what I am capable of, the minute I find out how fit I am maybe I will get hurt." We talked about how injuries are not inevitable, how you can take care of your body daily to prevent those kinds of things from happening. The 2:21 race yesterday was a weird race for me because it was the first race where I looked at the board shocked how fast I ran.

With that, I am a bit scared of my fitness, am I an 800 guy? Am I a miler? That 1k auto qualified for me USA indoors in the 800m. Never thought my first USA auto would be for an 800m race. All in all, we concluded that if we take care of the daily stuff the big picture will be accomplished. It's like a painting, instead of thinking what the final product is going to be, think about the fine detail of a tree on the hillside or the eyebrow of the person. Taking care of the fine details makes a great masterpiece. I'm no Vincent Van Gogh but I am a certified thinker on runs which pretty much equals the same thing. In bed at 10:03, tomorrow will be a single run of 60-70 mins.

1.15.2018
Mileage 11.5

Good group run with the guys in the AM. 9.5 miles, usually we do speed work on Mondays but today was swapped for a long run because 1) the race and 2) MLK day. I finished some homework I procrastinated yesterday than sat down for an hour to play FortNite before another run. Ran 2 miles at 7 minute pace. In bed at 9:45, a bit tired and I need sleep for another school week. Ugh, only week 2.

1.16.2018
Mileage 10

School was boring, but the workout was awesome. It was quite difficult and a lot harder than I thought.

2 laps 2 laps
1x20 leg swings
2x20 walking alternate toe touch
2x40 turning side to side
20 minute run
3x5 drop squats
2x10 lateral lunges
3x120
Spike up 2x80 strides
3x3 laps broken 29/40 so for the reps we went
40/29/40/29/40/29 (always finish fast) 800m jog recovery
40/29/39/27/38/29
35/29/40/29/38/28

First rep felt good, second rep my shoe came untied so I had to play catch up and it cost me, my middle 600 of the second rep was 1:38, the third rep I recovered enough and felt good. Dustin and I close hard the last lap and we jockeyed back and forth saying, “let's go 1-2” “how bad do we want it?” “Indoor national championships Dustin Nading and David Ribich coming into the homestretch!” I know we are still two months away, but we do this stuff often, just race each other visualizing ourselves closing 1-2 for nationals. Dustin is a great competitor and friend. I hope next year he can get the chance to visit pro teams because he is in a constant state of improvement.

After the cooldown Dustin and I got in the boots and then did ankle work, my ankles are a bit sore from the weekend, but I attribute that to the track and tight turns. Need to keep strengthening them all year if I want to think about a post collegiate season. I also finally gave Olivia her Christmas present, a homemade Christmas ornament. Inside the ornament contains shells, sand, and rocks from the Atlantic Ocean when we were in France, also on top of the rocks and shells was a cork from the winery we toured. She loved it so that makes me happy, every year I give her a Christmas ornament from my favorite trip we do together, two years ago was an Oregon Coast getaway trip we did, this last year was hands down France. I am excited to see what this year will be. Tomorrow is circuit day, bless Wednesdays...

1.17.2018
Mileage 8

Today was a doozy of a circuit after yesterday. I expected something a bit easier, but I am not going to disagree with whatever coach wants us to do.

2 laps
Leg swings
1x20 alternate toe touch
1x20 spiderman
1x15 burpees
1x25 mountain climber
3x80 stride
4x100 jumping rope
2x10 hurdle skip overs
4x5 rocket jumps
2x 50m 40m, 30m harness
Jog a lap, repeat from spiderman-rocket jumps
3 min recovery
5x30 bounding
1x20 forward lunge with med ball
1x20 backwards lunge
2x30 side shuffle
Jog 400
1x20 Rhll
1x10 leg swings

That was the circuit today, as you can see it was quite lengthy, hoping for a good recovery run tomorrow to get ready for the weekend workout. This weekend we have off and a week from Friday we race the DMR, the next day THE MILE.

1.18.2018

Mileage 10

Woke up this morning feeling really wrecked. I felt sore, tired, all around not good. I thought this AM run was going to be just a 25 minute run for how bad I felt but we talked about DnD and ran some funny scenarios while we talked because no one felt very good. We distracted our minds and boom before we knew it, we had a good run. This is a proving factor that the mind is a powerful thing, I thought at the start of this run that there was no possible way I was going to make it to 30 minutes, let alone 50.

Finished off the run at 7.5 before taking on an easy Thursday of classes, the workout tomorrow is all talked up to be a good one, I am excited, potentially 400s (which we never do). Easy 20 minute run alone tonight, thought about next weekend's mile race and clicked off a 5:20, wasn't really paying attention. Going to start developing cues for this upcoming race. First focus is being ready for the workout tomorrow, in bed 9:55.

1.19.2018
Mileage 10

Woke up today ready for the workout, it was extremely hard to focus in class from 9-9:50. All I did in class was write down lap splits for miles, 3ks, 4ks, and 5ks. It was a productive class none the least. After class went to the library tried to read, ended up looking at rankings for track. Went to the trainers amped. Once we got to the track, I knew it was going to be a good day, a little windy, but nothing too bad.

2 laps
Leg swings
3x3 drop squats
2x40 side to side
Campus loop
3x120 acceleration
1x200 fast relaxed 28.7
1 mile of 50/50s (accelerate 50 meters tempo 50 meters)
73,72,72,71 (4:48)
Change shoes from trainers to spikes
3x400 with 600m jog recovery

Before I get into this next part, I want to emphasize that this may have been the best track workout I have ever had at Western. I never find myself able to really click of 400s until today. The group today was eight men strong, and strung out in single file every rep. I took up the rear on every rep and tigered them, tigering is where you find someone ahead of you and you catch them, like a tiger catching their prey. I would get all of them accept Dustin, who would be leading the reps. Shame on me for never doing any of the work keeping the pace, I just got to enjoy the ride and kick:

54.6, 53.84, 54.3
400m jog
1x200 26.8
1x20 rhll
10 mins stretching
Cooldown

After the workout today I felt really good, I ran another 4 miles tonight to just shake out the workout. Today is the first day where I haven't had the thought of running 4 flat in the mile. There is a lot of hype going into next weekend about who will be the "500th miler to go sub 4". I had doubts about my capabilities leading up to this point. Can I even go sub 4? Will I run 4:00.00? Last week's 1000m and this workout today gives me extreme confidence that I can do it. But can I do it after a DMR 1600m leg the night before? We will see. Going to bed super happy and healthy from today, tomorrow will be an easy Saturday going down to Eugene.

1.20.2018
Mileage 11

Good 7 mile AM run with the guys, 30 mins of it was back on the turf with some DnD talk. Some of the guys weren't feeling the conversation but it's not for everyone. If they didn't want to play, they would just stab themselves with a sword (of course in game/DnD conversation). Afterwards Olivia and I went to Starduster before driving down to Eugene, once there I ran with a great friend of mine Mick Stanovsek. We talked about our history and our transition into collegiate running and he had a great story. I respect him a lot for his dedication and rising as a University of Oregon runner. After the run, we went out to dinner with Max Lydum and then went back to Micks house and hung out listening to Russian themed music. In bed 1:15am, had to drive home from Eugene.

1.21.2018
Mileage 7

Today was an easy day, getting back late last night from Eugene gave me a good excuse to sleep in, started my day with an easy 35 minute run. From there I kicked off a 3 hour trip to the library. I don't have much homework for this week, but I want to get as much done as I can leading up to this weekend's races. I am anchoring the Distance Medley Friday night and running the mile Saturday. The plan is Division II auto in the Medley and sub-4 in the mile so this is a big week ahead. 2 mile PM run to settle in the legs for tomorrow's speed workout. I am pretty confident going into these next two races cause this past weekend's workout was pretty dang good. In bed 9:45, sleep is quite important this week.

1.22.2018
Mileage 8

This week will be a low mileage week probably around 55-65, I fluctuate a lot during track season depending on how I feel. I also don't wear a watch, I haven't worn a watch since November. The only time I know my pace is when someone I am with has a watch on or when I come home and calculate the distance and time I was gone. Sometime people get caught up in what the watch reads and not how the body feels. Track is supposed to be a fresh feel good sport and by not wearing a watch I get an essence of that luxury. For the speed development today, we had:

2 laps 2 laps
1x20 leg swings
2x40 strides
2x20 alternating toe touch
2x40 side to side
3x120 accelerations
2x5,7,9s
1x3 laps of 50/50s 77,74,70
3x200s 24.9, 25.3 24.83 (walk 50, jog 150 recovery)
30 minutes on the treadmill
8 minutes of abs
Cooldown strides.

After the workout It started downpouring, I had class after practice and I really didn't want to go to class cold or wet. I wimped out and ran underneath the stadium on the treadmill while the rest of the guys manhandled the rain. I don't know, today was not the day to handle the storm. I just wanted to be warm and dry. After the 200s I felt like curling up in a warm chair by a fireplace as a fluffy white cat walks past me in my living room. Not sure what the cats name would be. I ran 2 miles tonight with Olivia nice and easy then we made tacos. 4 days out till race day!

1.23.2018

Mileage 9

Today was pouring down rain once again and I had no option for a treadmill, so I had to tough it out. My body today also wasn't really feeling a workout today. I don't know why but on part of our 2 minute tempo I just wasn't having it and relatively got dropped.

2 laps 2 laps

Leg swings

2x40 side to side

30 minute run straight into 5 minute tempo, 3 min tempo, 3 min tempo, 1 min tempo

All the recoveries were 1:1 so by the time the 60 sec rolled around I was pretty tired

We then got back to the track and had 500,400,300

66, 61, 47 they were supposed to be rhythmic, well I can tell you my 61 felt like an all-out race effort.

3x5 drop squats

A piss slow cooldown

How the heck am I going to try and run sub 4 this weekend if I was gasping for air after a 61?!?! I have to run a second and a half faster than that three more times if I want to run sub 4. After that rep I thought I was as good as done for the weekend. My legs were not feeling good today, I am not sure why but hopefully a circuit tomorrow and premeet Thursday will wake them up.

1.24.2018
Mileage 8

Today's circuit was a bit different than the past weeks, after a 35 minute run and some strides we went upstairs in the gym and did a lot more core work. For people who haven't done core in a while I am sure their abs were wrecked.

2x10 Single leg bridge
4x30 second plank continuous, push up at 30 seconds
2x40 speed skater
2x20 inch worm
2x5 drop squat
2x15 medicine ball push ups
Repeat two more times.

This was not a lengthy circuit and really one of a kind in comparison to what we usually do. I surprisingly feel really fresh after it and my legs feel really recovered, thankfully we didn't do a lot of explosive work this week and my legs can work back under my body again. 2.5 mile double tonight gearing up for a pre meet tomorrow. Mileage should be easy for the next few days.

1.25.2018
Mileage 8

Premeet 2 laps
2x 40 side to side
3x5 drop squat
Leg swings
20 minute run
2x200 27,28
1x600 broken 29/30/29
1x200 26.4
Cooldown for 2 miles

PM shake out for 2 miles, I am ready for tomorrow. We start off the weekend with a DMR, first time we have ran it since winning the Division II title last year by .001. This opener is important to show and prove we are back for another year, I think we will run a great race tomorrow. Everyone is focused and excited to get the baton off to the next guy. I would say the DMR is the focus of the weekend, sure I am in the mile the next day, but I have the rest of my life for individual events, indoor is a team season where my focus is the DMR. I will race the DMR like I don't have a mile the next day because the three other guys deserve me to race the best I can.

After packing for the weekend Tyler and I sang karaoke in the living room for a good hour and a half till 10:40.... latest I've stayed up before a meet in a long time. If I had a predictor for the weekend, I would say we run 9:45.6 in the DMR and I will run 3:57.72 in the mile the next day, ambitious saying I'll run sub 4 by a largish margin but I feel pretty fit and I am sure the DMR will carry momentum into Saturday. Cues: **Position, Patience, Kick.**

1.26.2018

Mileage: Unsure

Woke up with a good 20 minute loop shake out before loading on the bus, we head up to Seattle on the day of the meet for this weekend because Johnson thinks we race best heading up same day, taking care of business and moving on. I agree because there isn't as much waiting around if we head up same day. For other meets I like to be up there early but for this, I am totally okay with heading up day of. In terms of the race we ended up winning and ran 9:47, barely snagging the Division II auto for nationals. It was a weird race no doubt. However, what is important is everyone handed off the baton in the top 3.

By the time I got the baton we were barely in third by maybe a few seconds, I closed it immediately and just sat in the lead, **Position**. I led from 300m in to the finish and kept getting clipped, but I waited till 400m to go, **Patience.** Ended up splitting 4:00 flat on my leg but that time didn't come till the last lap, I think my last 200 was 26ish **Kick**. A Stanford guy clipped me multiple times during it, my spikes had little slice marks on the bottom from his spikes clipping mine. I really don't care to be honest, it didn't annoy me, didn't frustrate me, but I just don't understand what was to gain riding that close.

Anyhow, I think Johnson was a bit upset at our time because it was slower than all of us wanted but we raced. The slow time came out of the 800m leg, not our leg but everyone else's leg, this was AJs first DMR 800m leg, but he handed the baton off right on the lead. The other team's sort of controlled that leg to 1:55ish or so for all their carries. We won tonight so we are ready to race, 9:47 is the same as 9: 44... both autos so we are good to go. tomorrow I run the mile, pretty loaded heat, hoping for a sub 4, gunning for a sub 4, but importantly I want to race it. My roommate Josh is pacing it through 1:59-2:00 through 800 so no matter what it will be on, embrace the race and go. tonight, I will be dreaming. **Position. Patience. Kick.**

1.27.2018

Mileage: unsure

Woke up today thinking today is the day. Got up and went straight to the treadmill in the hotel gym for a nice 15 minute run, shook out, stretched, and got all the little aches out from last night's race. After that, had some breakfast and went back to the room. Waiting to go to the meet on race day feels like an eternity. The easiest way to compare the wait is like waiting at the DMV for your number to be called; or the wait at the financial aid office, FOREVER. Once the time came we packed up and headed to the meet, Josh and I warmed up together like we do every day, *bang* gun goes off and we are out the first quarter in 59, okay, we are on, we come around 600 and I felt the pace slipping in my gut, not because of Josh but because he had a good 8 meter gap on the field, no one really wanted to close it so I roll into lane two and fill the gap, **Position**. riding the pace wave.

We come through 800 in 2:00 as he steps off, I am in the lead for about 300m until Lopez and Yomif make their way around me, I was sitting in third and somehow this is exactly how I envisioned this race to look with one lap to go, **Patience**. Sitting in fourth we go through at 3:02 and I just thought "time to race." the whole field accelerates as Andy Trouard flies around and the race goes, I end up running 3:58.88, closing the last 200m hard repeating **Kick.** Finished third in the heat behind Andy and Yomif. I felt a good sigh of relief that my 1500m time is legit and I am no longer a converted sub 4 miler. I got word quickly I was 501st US sub 4 miler. JUST MY LUCK! I CALLED THAT IN DECEEMBER!! JEEEEZZZZ....

I am happy and humble to join an elite club of sub 4 milers. I got an interview tonight with Flotrack too, at the end I pulled my dad into it and he was pretty surprised, but he seemed to enjoy it. You have to spice up stuff like that. Be a character, be different and enjoy just being you. That interview is by far my favorite all time because I got to throw in celebrity guest Michael Ribich into the scene. Tonight would not have been possible if it wasn’t for the support and hard work from my team. As I was getting interviewed, the guys all had their phones out and recorded me getting recorded in an interview, pretty funny really. Going to enjoy the next week of training, this race was a long time coming and now it's time to turn focus to a 3k in two weeks. That will be the real test.

1.28.2018

Mileage 11

Felt pretty good at mile 8 during the run today so I decided to just do 11 miles. Today was going to be a double day but I would rather just run another 20 mins in the moment than gear up tonight for a double. Ran with Josh aka the roommate aka the pacer from yesterday's race. He is in 4:05 shape or better no doubt. I am looking forward to getting to race him outdoor season. He brings a good energy to the races. Today's run was averaged out at 6:43s pretty chill. After the sunset, AJ Josh and I sat on a picnic bench and talked for 40+ minutes. We just talked about life, what matters, what doesn't, what love is, what life is. Deep conversations like that really gets the brain active. Going to bed tonight in pretty deep thought. I hope tomorrow is a good day, see if I am wrecked at all from the weekend.

1.29.2018
Mileage 11

Training room prior to practice 30 mins of ankle rotations and lunges to get the lower legs warmed up. My muscles above the knees feel great, but my calves are sore, and my ankles are pretty wrecked. Next week will be consistent ankle exercises. For practice we really didn't slow from the weekend:

2 laps 2 laps
1x20 leg swings
2x40 side to side
2x4 drop squats
1x10 lateral lunge
2x20 twirling
1x15 burpees
1x20 mountain climbers
1x30 quad stretch
3x 120 stride buildups
50 minute run felt decent but nothing too special
1x200 at 33, felt terrible
1x400 float sprint float 66 felt worse
1x200 30, felt decent but not good enough to where I could do that for another 200m
Cool down with strides

Tonight's double was a good 15 minute run with 3 strides, I felt much better than earlier today, earlier today I did a 30 second 200 and I was gasping, how did I do that 7 more times after that? That pace was rough today. In bed 9:40 looking for 10 hours of sleep.

1.30.2018
Mileage 10

Today we did a different workout than what we had planned because Johnson sensed general fatigue for the group. (rightfully sensed):

Mile warm up
side to side
leg swings
20 minute run
11 minute tempo, mile 1 (5:13), mile 2 (4:57), last two minutes at 4:47 pace.
After the tempo we switched shoes and got onto the track, I meant to switch into Avantis, but I switched into MDs. The aggression between the two spikes is huge, usually the MDs work the calves a little much for me to practice in them. However, since I accidently put them on, I just rolled with it.
Broken 1000m, 30/41/31/38/29
1x400 @ 63
Cooldown

Felt better after we got done with the 1k. that 63 was really relaxing as well, I wonder if I can do that 6 more times because that's the goal right? If I go into a 3k I want to just rock it! PR big time! Eh, who knows. I took a good nap and ran a 20 minute double nice and easy. Overall, I would say I feel pretty good after the weekend, looking forward to train through this week no doubt.

1.31.2018
Mileage 9

Another Wednesday means I didn't get home till 8:20. If I make it through this term I will be surprised because academically wise these 18 credits are going to kill me. However, I am a STUDENT-athlete, right? Right! Today's circuit looked exactly like last weeks. Honestly as I write this log in bed, I just want to go to sleep so just turn to last week's circuit it was exactly the same. I'll make you guys do the work now. After the circuit I got a great leg message, tomorrow should be a good recovery day gearing up to the workout on Friday. I can't believe tomorrow is February.

2.1.2018
Mileage 9.5

February baby!! It's the month of love, conference month, and the 2nd month of the year (duh)! I cruised a 65 minute shady loop today, just did a solo run to start off the month. Remember, running with people is great, but some days take a day for yourself and do what you gotta do. My run had a good 6:20 minute mile and had a solo rolling 7:30 mile. Good speed change and overall relaxing to just be out in my own thoughts. I don't think todays run would have felt as good if I was with a group. Tomorrow's workout is going to be great I have a good feeling.

2.2.2018
Mileage 8

I woke up and felt a lot worse than I thought I would feel. Overall my legs just felt taxed and the thought of running a 60 second quarter seemed impossible. As the day went on my legs warmed up a bit. I wore tights to class just to give me the edge of feeling good. We got to practice and I read the workout sheet. I thought it was going to be incredibly difficult but in reality, this just turned into one of my favorite workouts I have ever done.

Originally the workout plan was supposed to be 1x1200 broken 30/40 the full way through. We substituted that for:

2x1200 first 600 in 1:40 then break it into 30/40/30 making the total 1200 time 3:20
After the 2x1200 we transitioned into the good ol 3x600 broken 30/40/30
3x120
2 mile cooldown.

Overall I felt really good, we went through the first 400m tempo around 63-65 and I felt comfortable at that pace so I am quite confident when I run a 3k I will be able to hang on at 65s. I think my favorite part of the workout was transitioning from 600 tempo to a 30 second 200 into 40 second 200 into 30 again. It felt like a classic race scenario when someone just drops it or the pace quickens all of sudden. Two times this week we altered the original plan to better suit our needs. By doing so, all of us benefit with the confidence of getting the right kind of work in. Tomorrow will be a recovery day once again before we start up another week of training leading into a race.

2.3.2018
Mileage 7

Ending this week with just 7 miles. Low, but it is what my body needs. After the run watched the Millrose Games at the Armory. It would be so cool to be able to compete there, my entire indoor seasons have been Washington and the National Meet. I have never gone to these big premier locations, hopefully next year I get the chance too. Tomorrow will be a good day to sleep in. I am going to use tomorrow as another chance to get ready for a race week and school week. I am already over this term. Is it spring break yet?

2.4.2018
Mileage 9

Good 8.5 mile run at 6:20s this morning. First run since the DMR/Mile double that I felt like my legs were under me. We had some speed changes down to 6:00 felt pretty good to get going, other than that today was just another day. I don't have much to share to be honest, might have been the most boring day of the year. For a good thirty minutes today, I bounced a tennis ball off the wall as I sang Christmas carols. 6 days out till race day. Ready to go.

2.5.2018

Mileage 10

Warm up 2 laps 2 laps

Leg swings and side to side.

I forgot my shorts today, so I had to run home during our run and put shorts on. I wore tights over my underwear, not too comfortable.

40 minute run

3x120s fast relaxed

12x10 small hurdles (the ones sprinters go over, the super short ones)

3x300 @ 40,39,38 with 300m jog in between.

Cooldown 10 minutes

Talked with Johnson and we decided I won't do USA Indoors in New Mexico. I am happy we had an actual discussion about it because it was a possibility. However, my reasoning was I would rather go to conference and help the team point total as much as possible. We decided on mile 800m double at conference so that's exciting. Looking forward to tomorrow's workout, should be a good tempo day gearing up for this weekend's 3k. I think I could legit run sub 8 right now.

3 mile PM run 7:20 pace

2.6.2018

Mileage 11

Tuesday tempo! This was a fun day, Johnson is incorporating turf tempos into the weeks and I am really enjoying them. Last year a lot of our work was on the track so being able to come on the turf and accomplish a hard few reps is refreshing.

Campus loop
2 laps stride walk
Leg swings
3x40 side to side
3x120 fast and relaxed
15 minute run
Onto the turf for 6 minutes, 3:30, 2 minute tempo
On the 6 minute tempo we went through 1 mile at 4:38, 4:35 pace for 3:30, then 4:25 pace for 2 mins.
Run back to the track for 3x500s @ 65, 62, 58 through 400.

Felt good today, body is really sparking up for the weekend. We started talking about the 3k during the tempos and I couldn't help but want to drop it. I am excited to see the accepted entries and the heat sheets. In bed 10:14

2.7.2018

Mileage 8

Today was circuit day once again, I am sure you are pretty annoyed reading all these drills, but they are an important part to our training and well I try to document each drill as much as I can. My body was feeling really good, sometimes during circuits I opt out on a drill if something is too sore or bothering me. Today, was not one of those days. I blasted through each drill singing and dancing. I love being a part of a team where I can express myself. I am sure they are also annoyed of me and just thinking, jeez can David just leave already.

Full campus loop
1x20 leg swings
2x15 spiderman
3x5 drop squats
5 mile run
2x15 rhll
2x30 walking overhead med ball
2x10 med ball push ups
1x4 position plank
1x10 hip twists
1x20 mountain climbers
1x10 burpees
Stride 100
2x10 hurdle walkovers
Stride 100
2x 30m harnesses
Rest 5 Minutes
Repeat planks to hurdle walkovers

Cooldown.

Today's circuit was long, I also didn't get home till 8PM so today was a very long but good day. I'm excited to relax tomorrow, enjoy a light day before we travel on Friday. Tomorrow will be an EASY RUN.

2.8.2018
Mileage 5

Easy 5 miles today and three strides. Dustin and I just chilled and it was so nice to just relax. I think both of us are ready for a good weekend. We feel fresh and are both ready to go, we don't race till Saturday so tomorrow will be a good pre meet. In bed 9:47, My cues for this race are simple, **Tempo, Race**. Its funny, this is the longest race of the indoor season, but I only have two cues instead of three. Not sure why but these are the only two that make sense to me. I will go into more detail tomorrow.

2.9.2018

Mileage 7 or 8

16 minute AM run before traveling up to Dempsey. Once we got to the stadium after a good ol drive Dustin and I ran 3 miles:

Spiked up
200 @ 27
500 @ 63 pace
600 of 30/40/30
2x120s 17-18
10 minute cool down

Overall, I feel pretty fit for tomorrow, I wanted to do more work today or just be on the track longer so that is a good sign, if I run a good 3k tomorrow I will do the DMR/3k double. In all honesty I am not too confident. A lot of my thoughts are mixed, I have thoughts of running 7:55 then I have thoughts of running 8:15. 3k is a bit out of my normal routine so I need to think of this like a mile. Coping with my nervousness I am confident in my cues. These cues were selected for very specific reasons. **Tempo** for 2k and **Race** for 1k. I know for a fact I am the fastest 1k runner in the field so why not try and turn it into a 1k race. I am racing some big names, like Craig Nowak but mostly collegiate athletes like Ben Saarel, Colby Gilbert, Sydney Gidabuday. As well big names I have never raced before. I plan to sit in fourth or so and enjoy a pace for 2k. Just gotta stay tucked in and gear up for the final 1k. I have used a lot of self-talk today. Hoping for the best tomorrow.

2.10.2018

Mileage: unsure

Woke up to a good 12 minute shake out on the treadmill visualizing the race, I did this for the mile and it seemed to work so I gave it another go. I then walked to whole foods for a breakfast burrito. The waiting game continued because I didn't race till 4:55 pm. Once it got to 2PM I boarded a van and headed to the meet. The races were on Flotrack so most of my day was watching races. I was hip 16 and there were 24 guys so I was pushed to the back. What was annoying was they didn't really organize us by our numbers, so I was sort of just pushed to the back, but I didn't care too much it's a long race, I could sneak in. The gun goes off and we go through 400 in 60 seconds. I just remember laughing in my mind thinking here we go...thanks to Sam Prakel's pacing, we rolled through 400 and the field was immediately strung out in a line. I am thankful for Sam's hot pace because it put me in about 5th and from there I could just ride the train through the mile.

We clicked off 63s going through the first mile in 4:11-4:12. The whole time I just told myself "**Tempo** 2k. Tempo 2k. Tempo 2k." 2 laps to go, I sort of doubted myself and I went into about 6th place, my **Race** cue didn't materialize till the last 300m where I closed pretty hard getting back to 4th. With 60m to go I hit another gear and finished fast which felt really good. I definitely could have; maybe should have gone earlier, but that's where mentally I disengaged. I ended up running 7:50.81. I was pretty shocked with the time, turned out to be a Division II All-Time record and a 23 second PR. Unreal. I cooled down with Sydney and George, looking forward to recovering tomorrow and learning more about the 3k as the weeks go on.

2.11.2018
Mileage 10.5

I forgot to mention this last night but after the 3k I got on the track and did a brief workout. Honestly, I felt better immediately after the 3k than I did after the DMR/Mile

2x300 @ 47, 47
2x200 @ 28, 28
I meant to do 2x120 but then some SUU boys and Jeff Thies from Portland were working out, so I hoped in on 2x400 @ 62

Now back to today, today was a good day for miles, we went to Green Lake in Seattle 55 min run with 90 second tempo towards the end. The whole time I was imagining myself maybe being a local here in Seattle, maybe Green Lake will be my usual loop or my workout spot. We got 8.5 miles out of this morning and then I went to the track for a massage from Kurtis. We left the meet at around 2 getting home at 7. Dustin and I went for another 15 minutes. It's Sunday and we leave for our conference meet on Thursday, not a whole lot of time to recover so the next few days will be very important.

2.12.2018

Mileage 8.5

Nice and easy day, 7 mile run at 7 minute pace, 3x120s. Aiming for 60-65 miles this week but it may be difficult with traveling to conference (about a 9 hour bus ride). Today Johnson and I decided I will be running DMR/3k at nationals as well. It was a decision we talked about in December and it was decision I never thought was truly a possibility. My reasoning is I want to give my main effort in the DMR and double back and race the 3k. I think at this point I can learn a lot more in the 3k than I can the mile. The focus is a season in July and August. Johnson knowing the plan as well agrees that keeping this indoor season as a preseason to outdoor helps. I know it is the right thing to do. Tomorrow will be a circuit/workout combo.

2.13.2018
Mileage 10

The day before Valentine's day always a fun day. Except I have had my valentine's day gift for Olivia since January. She is getting a sloth trinket, supposed to be a good luck charm. She is also getting a pineapple necklace and a necklace that has a D on it. The charms on the necklace are very small like smaller than your thumbnail so I just got both. In case she doesn't like one there is a backup plan. She isn't picky, I am sure she will like both.

When I got to practice Johnson walks up to me and says, "Dyestat will be here to interview after practice." I thought oookay? I was told out of the blue which is fine, but I was definitely caught off guard.

Campus loop
2x40 side to side
2x5 drop squats
1x10 burpees
2x10 mountain climbers
1x200 @ 28
Campus loop
3x20 second strides
6 min, 3:30, 2:30 tempos on turf
3x400 58,57,58 200 walk 200 jog recovery
3x120 cooldown
4 laps on the grass

So, before I talk about the interview something that needs to be said is my team are jokesters. Rarely ever do you get something serious out of them. Today, I was the butt end of the joke. Every 400 rep I would be in the lead, until 50 meters to go someone would just drop the rep and act like it was a race. I was so confused, the first rep Dustin did that, second rep Justin did that, third rep, Josh did that. I was so confused and annoyed! Why are you racing these reps! Finally, after the third rep everyone cheers when we finished. Confused I asked what was going on and Dustin said, "we decided back on the turf that if you lost every 400 rep you have to buy a FortNite skin. If you win at least one, we will all pitch in for a FortNite skin." Annoyed and humiliated I laughed it off and chased down Justin and Josh. Days like today make me appreciate my team because we work hard but are friends.

After practice I went up and had an interview with Dyestat it ended up lasting an hour and a half. I then dropped all my stuff off at the trainers and ran 2 miles home. I learned that doubling back 2 hours after a hard practice is stupid. Don't do it. It was a very hard 2 miles. Once I got home, I showered, ate, turned on the Xbox and bought myself a FortNite skin.

2.14.2018
Mileage 8.5

Good recovery based run with Dustin and AJ before we leave for conference tomorrow. This is my last time making the trip from Monmouth to Boise and I am quite excited. We board at 6:10 and it is 11:15 so its best I get to sleep. Tomorrow will be hopefully a decent day for miles.

2.15.2018

Mileage 9

Today was travel day! We boarded the bus at 6 am on the way to Boise for our conference meet, three weeks till nationals. I am excited for tomorrow finishing up my indoor collegiate conference experience. I am running the 800/mile double with 800 prelims tomorrow, then hopefully 800 and mile the next day. This weekend for me is about bringing up the team. I want to see four guys in the 800m final and I want to see us sweep the mile. We have such a good middle distance program that works hard and enjoys each other's company that there is no way we can't do those things. I have Neal, a freshman on our team, who is in my 800m prelim. My hope is to get him through to the final.

For runs and workouts today I ran 30 minutes in The Dalles before boarding the bus for another 6 hours. Once on the bus we played DnD the whole way to Boise from Pendleton. It was like four hours of role play and stories. It was really funny and fun but mentally I was a vegetable when we arrived at the track. At the track I did another 30 minute run into 120 strides

On the track:

4x200 @ 30, 27, 32, 30

The first 200 was solo, second 200 was with the guys, third 200 was with Kennedy and the last 200 was with Olivia and Suzie. Today was a fun day on the 200m track.

2.16.2018

Mileage 8

15 minute AM run before breakfast, then hung out at the hotel until I went to the meet at 1. Today was the 800m prelim and I was super nervous. I don't know why but I am far more nervous for conference meets then I am national meets. I think it is the general expectations people have for me at this level. During the prelim I led from the gun and glanced back with 50m to go hearing someone yell, "Go Neal!" I turn around to see Neal about 20m back, I yell at him and waved my arm to tell him to catch up as we went 1,2. He makes the final finishing right behind me. That was a really cool moment for me, seeing Neal make the final at our conference meet was pretty inspiring. He was fourth fastest in our heat and ran so smart to put himself ahead of the other guys. 2nd heat we got two more. We have 4 of 8 competitors in the 800m final tomorrow. Olivia also ran a 2:09.10 for an indoor PR! It exactly ties that of Suzie for a school record.

2.17.2018
Mileage 8

Mile final at 11:25. 20-minute run, drills then got to the line and led it in 66,63,61,60. Dustin and I talked through it keeping the pace relatively honest from 1200 to go. with 100m to go I look back and see Justin and Parker coming in hot, 1-2-3-4 that was pretty wild. In the mile we went 1-2-3-4-7. We had 5 of the top 8 spots in the mile. Our middle-distance program has evolved from just 800m to milers as well. After the race I cooled down 20 minutes, ate a bar and sat for 15 minutes before I needed to warm up for the 800. It was only about an hour separation. This weekend's focus was treating the mile like the first mile of the 3k then treating the 800 like the last 1400m of the 3k. after 200m in the 800, I took the lead and ran 1:50.81. it ended up being a new meet record and put me 11th on the national list. In all honesty I was aiming for sub 1:50 but my first 400 was too slow I went 56, 54.

After the meet I was honored with Male Indoor Track athlete of Meet, as well as Performance of the Meet. I really was not expecting that. I even told my parents to take off after the last event because I told them I wouldn't be getting any awards. Johnson apparently stopped them and had them stay because he already knew. The bus ride home was a good 10hr reflection on this weekend and I am so thankful we decided our conference meet instead of USAs, looking at USAs not a whole of collegians went anyways so it makes sense really that I didn't. Johnson and I are still relatively new to the USA scene.

2.18.2018

Mileage 6

Today was a nice six mile run after yesterday's races. 41 minute run then watched Drew Windle make his second world team and Craig Engels make his first team. Tonight, I also went to the pool. Boring day, but no tennis ball and Christmas carols.

2.19.2018

Mileage 11.5

Mile warm up into a 10 mile run in 64:21 pretty fast run but the last two miles were 5:50 to 5:40. Kurtis gave me a good message until my foot cramped up. I then went to the library till my eyes bled from reading (figuratively). After that, went for a mile and a half shake out to the stop light and back. Another boring nothing to report day.

2.20.2018
Mileage 8

Pretty solid day, didn't expect a workout but I am glad we did one

Mile warm up
2 laps 2 laps
Drills
Campus loop
Twelve minutes of X's on the turf
3 min jog
Eight mins of Xs on the turf
5 mins to the track,
Because it was cold, we switched the workout around to 2x3
200s @ 29 with 100 jog
Then 1x200 @ 28 for 7 total.
Cooldown and drills upstairs

I would have doubled today but I feel a bit stuffy. I am in bed at 9:45 calling it a day early. To be honest, last few days I have been really tired right before bed and its been hard to journal, ill pick it up more after I clear my darn stuffiness.

2.21.2018
Mileage 10

Today was a good day although I woke up feeling relatively stuffy. I will be taking the next few days smart. I need to be 100% leading up to nationals.

½ campus loop
1x10 lateral lunge
1x20 alternate quad stretch
2x30 light skipping
35 minute run
3x120 acceleration
2x2 40m harness
4x20 backward lunge
2x5 rocket jumps
1x30 mountain climbers
2x20 side shuffle
1x15 burpees
2x30 speed skaters
2x20 med ball lunge
Repeat from lateral lunge to med ball lunge
1x20 HLL
Achilles stretch
10 min cooldown

Today's circuit was once again a doozy. Circuit days usually are like this, I have no idea why I'm still surprised at the amount of drills we have to do. After the circuit I went to class until 8PM and decided to go for a 20 min run. Tomorrow I am going to sleep in and just try to rest as much as I can. Going to bed with a cold.

2.22.2018
Mileage 10

Sick. Stuffy and scratchy throat. We ran 42 mins today, 20 minutes out the bike path then 20 mins back. We had a massive head wind on the way out, so the way back felt good.
My double was 30 minutes solo. I feel really fit but this cold is a little bit of a drag at the moment. Tomorrow will be a full recovery day because I need to get this cold out of me especially being two weeks out from nationals.

2.23.2018
Mileage 5

Today dropped my weekly mileage but that's fine. Mileage is like a pizza. Some people like anchovies some people like cheese. Ultimately mileage and pizzas are largely individually enjoyed. One tastes good to one person and may be disgusting to another. What works for one person may not work for another. That was my poor attempt at a metaphor. Maybe mileage is like making nachos...never mind. I don't want to explain myself right now. I HATE THIS COLD!

2 laps 2 laps
Jog to turf
Leg swings
Side to side
3x X's at 75% effort
Back to the track
1x200 @ 27
Jog 400 3x400 supposed to be 56
Went 54.3, 56.8, 56.3 400m jog in-between.

I ended up doing this workout alone and I am surprised it went as smooth as it did. The 54 was the easiest rep because I was trying to run a 56. I thought, I gotta get out fast if I want to run a 56 because 56 sounds really difficult. To my surprise the 56 was quite easy.

Campus loop cooldown into the trainers to roll out. I had a breakfast burrito to top off the day so that was nice, I feel better than yesterday.

2.24.2018
Mileage 11

Today could and should have been a productive day but instead I ran 8 miles with Dustin at 10 am then he come over at 2PM and we played Xbox till 7pm. We then ran 3 miles then played Xbox from 8:30-10 so that's what kind of day it was. I should have been working on homework, but I honestly needed a day to veg out and not worry about anything. Sitting on the couch all day was nice. Today the team went up to Seattle and raced in the Last Chance Qualifying meet. This was the first time I haven't gone to the race. It was weird getting results and not being there. Justin Crosswhite a Sophomore ran 4:08. Big time PR. He is going to have a good year I know it.

2.25.2018
Mileage 10

Just about ten miles for a single run this morning, not a long run but a good moderate distance run. Ran at 9 am so I had the rest of the day to chill and do homework. Olivia and I went and watched Black Panther and it is BY FAR my favorite superhero movie. Holy cats (no pun intended) that movie was awesome!

2.26.2018

Mileage 9

Good day of practice, sickness is relatively gone:

2 laps 1 lap

Drills

3x120 strides

2x5,7,9

5xwickets

3x200 @ 28.4, 28.2, 25.3/walk 200m between

30 minute run with Justin and we talked about declarations for indoor nationals.

We are two weeks out from the national meet and here I am fully committed to scratching the mile. I am confident. I HAVE TO BE CONFIDENT. Dustin in the mile, myself in the 3k, we could pull off two victories.

2.27.2018
Mileage 11

Today was a classic Mike Johnson workout, 30/40s and broken 600s. Looking at this workout I thought it was going to be a big time struggle but we took it a rep at a time and it went better than expected. It was the first time I really spiked up since conference.

7k worth of track work.
2 laps
Drills
20 min run 6:23 pace (we were all talking about races, so we were feeling good)
2x30 side to side
1x10 lateral lunge
2x20 running high knees
2x200 28, 26
1x1200 40/30
Jog 700m
1x1000 30/40
3x600 29/38/28
3x150 sprint float sprint
Cooldown two miles

Pretty crazy workout, we hit all the times prescribed and even a bit faster on some. The PM shakeout was short and sweet just shaking out the legs from the workout. Tomorrow will be a circuit day, chances are it'll be a doozy. Today's workout made me super pumped for nationals. I am excited to open with the DMR the first day of the meet.

2.28.2018

Mileage 6.5

Warm up ½ campus loop + 2 laps of stride walks
1x20 leg swings
2x40 turning side to side
1x10 lateral lunge
1x20 alternate toe touch
2x30 skipping
30 minute run @ 6:38 pace
3x120 acceleration
2x2 40m harness
4x20 backwards lunges medal overhead
2x5 rocket jumps
1x20 mountain climbers
2x20 side shuffle
1x15 burpees
2x30 speed skaters
2x20 overhead forward lunge
Repeat backward lunges to forward lunges
1x20 rhll
4x60 acceleration
2x20 high knees with twist
2x20 alternate toe touch
Achilles soleus stretch
10 full complete breaths.

Seems as though every Wednesday I say something along the lines of, "as you can see this is a long circuit." But in reality, this is normal, and these days are so important for development. These days challenge all the muscles we often underutilize in running so strengthening every aspect of ourselves increases our race capacity. Today's circuit took a while to get through but taking each exercise one at time and enjoying it through each exercise makes it far easier to complete. Tomorrow will be a good recovery day on my own. Tomorrow is the first of March. Jeez, Indoor Nationals is close. In bed at 10:04

3.1.2018

Mileage 8

Nice solo day to start off March. I wore a watch today for the first time in two months. Ran 6:35s. I didn't look at it often until I had to poop then I looked a lot, but for the most part today was a great day relaxing. From mile 5 to mile 7 I zoned out completely just thinking about racing. It was one of those runs where you come back into reality and think, how the heck did I get here? Last thing you knew you were turning the corner at the cemetery and now your two miles away. I really didn't remember running for two of those miles I was completely zoned out. Once I got home, I turned on NBC Gold and watched the World Indoor championships. Katie Mackey finished 8th in the 3k. Shelby Houlihan finished 5th. Tomorrow are the prelims for the men's events. I am excited to see Drew, Craig and Ben race. See what they can do. In bed 10:15.

3.2.2018
Mileage 11

Woke up to incredibly sore quads and calves I guess this circuit needed some time to set in. I thought today was going to be a run but turns out it was a workout.

Campus loop
Side to side
Head to turf
2x100 stride
3 mins of 20 sec on 20 sec off
3 min recovery
6 min tempo 5:00 pace
3 min jog
6 min tempo 4:40 pace
3 min jog
6 min tempo 4:35 pace
Jog to track
3x300
Sprint Float sprint
15/17/15
14/18/15
15/16/13
Mile and a half cooldown.
PM 3 mile with Dustin

Last big workout before nationals. going into this I had the mentality it was going to be really tough, after the first rep I said screw it because going in with a mental attitude of it being tough will make the rep tough. So instead, I switched mindset and just focused as if it was a 3k or the mile leg of the DMR. I felt more rhythmic, smoother and overall better. Looking forward to the next few days gearing up to nationals. I am mind blown how fast this season has gone by.

3.3.2018
Mileage 9

Drew Windle got silver! DREW WINDLE GOT 2ND IN THE WORLD!! It was a crazy few hours because immediately after he showed up as DQ and it was like what!? However, after an hour or so of contesting he was reinstated and got the medal he deserved. Awesome to see Coach Mackey fight for Drew. My run today was fast because I was so excited from Drews race. 9 miles in 61 minutes. We have speed development tomorrow, hoping for 300s or something. This is the final tune up before indoor nationals. In bed 10:34.

3.4.2018

Mileage 8

Today is Sunday, 5 days till the DMR and 6 days till the 3000m final. We are under a week now folks. For today's practice we had a pretty crazy speed development day:

20 mins after 2 laps 2 laps

Drills

1x200 @ 27 (with Olivia) she was fast relaxed and cookin!!

Full recovery until heart rate and breathing is back to normal

1x300 @ 42.3

1x400 @ 53.7

1x300 @ 42.1

2x200 @ 25.2 30.28

My last rep was at 30 because I wanted to feel what 4:00 mile pace was again. After doing speed work it's always nice to do a rhythmic race pace rep just to get a feel of what it feels like. Typically, after a good speed session like today when I do a 30, I feel as though it was a 34, smooth and slow enough to where I feel comfortable. For today's reps I really didn't think we would run that fast, but everyone was comfortable and smooth. The 53 was the easiest 53 I have ever done. 15 minute cooldown and then a PM 20 minute run again to just shake out the legs. We travel in a few days and I have not done laundry yet.

3.5.2018

Mileage 9

2 laps 2 laps

Side to side

Leg swings

Hurdle walkovers

3x120 warm up sprints

30 minute run

5 minutes of 40s/40s (40 seconds tempo. 40 seconds regular pace)

1x200 @ 30

3x800 40/30/40/30 (all on pace 2:18, 2:20, 2:20) 800m jog recovery in between

1x200 @ 28

15 minute cooldown

Mile run to Dustin's for my PM run, today was a pretty big day, I'm surprised we did a workout this close to the weekend however we are a speed-oriented team. I am not sure the last time I went into a meet completely fresh. Johnson tends to train us through indoor nationals because come outdoor we continue to get faster. I'm thankful for his style because it makes each month feel like progression towards May or June. Today I also got nominated for West Regional Track Athlete of the Year. Last year I thought I deserved it. In reality I really didn't do anything last year to deserve it. I am thankful this is my first year receiving it. I ran fast but I never had a real breakout to be honored with the award. I am thankful I didn't get it last year because this year I had zero focus on the award. I just wanted to run fast and race.

At the start of this year if you would have told me I would hold the Division II national record in the 1000m and the 3000m I would have laughed because never could I of imagined. After each race I was told I got the record and I was in shock. That race mentality is something I need to remember going into outdoors because the 1500m record is on my mind. However, if I focus solely on the time, I doubt I will be able to get it. If I focus on the race I am in and not worry about the time. I am sure I can break it. Going to bed anxious to travel. Now I am packed for nationals. Even though we don't leave for another two days

3.6.2018

Mileage 8

Last day in Monmouth before we travel to nationals:

2 laps 2 laps

35 minute run

3x hills (30 seconds) in reality I didn't push myself up these because this is the first time we have done hills all year and being 3 days out from racing, I wasn't really feeling it

2x mountain climbers

2x10 burpees

2x10 pushups

1x15 lunges

3x100 jump rope

1x200

Cooldown

18 min PM run with Dustin, tomorrow we travel.

Tomorrow we travel to my final collegiate indoor national meet. Time to defend that DMR.

3.7.2018
Mileage 5

Travel day made it safe and sound to good ol Joplin Missouri. The meet is in Pittsburg Kansas, but we decided to stay in Joplin because there are more food options and it's only a 30 minute drive. We are staying in a different hotel this year and I am extremely happy about that. Two years ago, the one we stayed in had mold in the jelly packets. This year I am rooming with Justin Crosswhite, aka Phil because we brought him as an alternate for the relay. It is so good for him to see the indoor meet because I guarantee if he was racing in the mile prelim, he would make the final. In bed at 12:10 (10:10).

3.8.2018

Mileage unsure

Today we shook out two miles in the morning looking for some Goodwill finds. Nothing good, nothing in my size at least. We then headed to the track at 3PM and we commenced our premeet.

20 minute run
1x200 @ 30
1x400 @ 63
1x400 34/27
1x200 29

After the reps we did a few 120s with exchange handoffs for the DMR. Crazy that my only race tomorrow is the DMR. Watching those mile prelims is going to be a new experience but I know it is the right decision because the DMR is the focus. I want to have a good leg in that. After the premeet we attended the national banquet and I received the West Regional Athlete of the Year award. When the announcer started listing my season accolades, I sort of spaced out and didn't hear a single thing. I felt extremely nervous and just tried to focus on looking out into the crowd which was made difficult with how bright the stage lights were. Now that that is over, we can focus on tomorrow. I have no idea what is going to happen. I just need to make sure I do my job for the guys. Last year we predicted it would come down to us and Adam State and we were right, .001 right.

This year, I have no idea what jersey will be in the lead, I have no idea where I will get the baton. I can see me getting the baton in first and I could see me getting the baton in 8th.

Wherever I get it I want to race with my heart because this could be my last relay ever. I am going to bed prepared to run 3:58 or 3:55 whatever I need to do I know I can do it. Tomorrow the weekend begins. Whether we have a 10 second lead or a 10 second deficient I don't care, my race plan is the same. My cues are simple: **Heart, Kick.** Racing with heart for 1300m and then whatever the last lap brings; that is when I will kick. Title or Bust for us. Time to defend. Let the Big Dawgs EAT.

3.9.2018
Mileage unsure

Today is done. Our team was 3/3 on individual qualifiers for the finals, Suzanne in the mile, Olivia in the 800m, and Dustin in the mile. Dustin was a small q to advance so I gave him a hard time about that. Now for the DMR, we won. Back to back national titles. The feeling crossing the finish line this year was by far a better feeling than last year because when I crossed this year, I knew we had won.

What I explain next is how the DMR went down, I don't want it to sound like I am the reason we won so I will say this first. Each of the guys gave their all to defend the national title. I got the baton in 9th and the reason is because every other team was ready to win a title for themselves. This year was an open year in terms of who could win it so the fact that I received it in 9th shows how much more competitive the relay has gotten. Right when I received the baton, I heard the announcer say, "Keep an eye on Ribich his team is 9th. He is the national leader in the mile and the Division II record holder for 1000m and 3000m." hearing that right off the bat gave me confidence that I could do it. **Heart.**

Each lap I focused on staying relaxed, I was about 90m behind the leaders after the exchange and it was difficult not to just sprint after them however, I stayed relaxed and patient each lap. Every lap around I would look over and see Phil yelling at me saying, "you're closing!" "stay relaxed" after about the third lap around I wanted to tell the guys on the infield "We can do this!" however I just looked ahead, my last 600m was 1:26 and I split 3:54.76 to give us another national title.

The craziest thing about it was I felt great doing it. Never once did I feel pressed or out of control. Being able to be in my own stride and my own rhythm helped me. With 300m to go I was roughly 30m back on the lead 2 guys. They never kicked it in and with 200m to go I just told myself to **Kick**. "go go go" was all I could tell myself. Having the guys cheering, the girls and my family made it possible. I remember finishing and hearing a roar of the crowd. Did that actually happen? I am so happy I scratched the mile and I am so happy we got the baton in 9th because I surprised myself and just raced with heart. That was the confirmation I needed in terms of my mile speed. Going into tomorrow, I want to be in a position to win. It will be tough, but everyone is energized so I know tomorrow is going to be a good day. Whatever happens I am taking only positives away from this weekend. Onto day two. My cues are **Tempo** and **Kick**

3.10.2018

Mileage unsure

Well today was better than yesterday! Not necessarily for me but for the team! We finished 6th as a men's team, DUSTIN WON THE INDOOR MILE! Olivia and Suzanne earned All-American Honors and I finished 3rd in the 3k. Immediately after the race I knew what I did wrong and that was swinging a bit too wide around final turn and as well waiting too long to kick. I can kick from 600m out, but I really waited till 300m. The entire race I had no idea how fast I was going, I was leading the chase group to chase down Ngandu who went out fast. I knew he would come back so I just remained patient. Now finishing 3rd I should've just gone out with him, he went out in the pace I ran 7:50 but I was unsure with how my legs were feeling from the night before. The final turn I swung wide and got passed on the outside and the inside. 3rd by .44ish.

I panicked a bit getting passed on both sides and from there it was over. Our last 300m was 41.xx so it was still a quick finish. I learned a lot and I am happy in my decision for DMR/3k double because I learned a lot more in those two races than had I done DMR/mile. Driving to Kansas City now it's about 1am, I can't help but think only of the upcoming outdoor season. Indoors was great but that book is closed. Most incredible season up to date. Now it is time for my final collegiate season and whatever is to come after.

3.11.2018
Mileage 0

Took the day off today, we flew home and traveled today so I decided to just relax today and get a beer at the restaurant downtown. We posted in our group page, it was an "indoor celebration dinner." It was a great night two beers and lots of laughter and support from the team. Looking at Dustin tonight I could tell he gained a new-found confidence which is well deserved and important. He is a great training partner and there is no one I'd rather be working with day in and day out. I wonder if any Division II school has ever had a mile champion and 1500m in the same year be different athletes.

3.12.2018
Mileage 4

WOU West Regional Championship game tonight. We got honored at half court and it was awesome. Standing ovation from the crowd and it was a full house. My Achilles is a bit sore and I think it is time for a down week to heal up. These next two weeks are going to be extremely stressful for school because it is dead week this week and finals week next week.

3.13.2018
Mileage 5

A good 35 minute run today nice and relaxed. Some tempo work when Dustin and I felt like it but for the most part we are doing our own thing this week working out the last weekend of races. This week my right leg has and will be getting some work on it. The Achilles and calf are pretty wrecked. This Friday, Mark Rowland from Oregon Track Club Elite will be visiting for our workout. Hoping for a good day that day.

3.14.2018
Mileage 8

First day since the meet that I felt like I had my legs back under me. It was also the first day where I came close to normal miles. Good 40 minute run @ 6:10s. that pace really got my legs moving. After the run we did circuit work here and there whenever we felt like it. Tomorrow may be a workout, or it may still be on Friday, not sure but I'll be ready. Mile shakeout tonight after a couple hours in the library. 18 credits this term wasn't too terrible until now. Prior they were difficult but nothing like what dead week is like. So many assignments due. In bed 10:04

3.15.2018

Mileage 10.5

First day back at full miles. I thought today was the workout, but it turns out tomorrow is the workout. It will be a doozy no doubt. Mark Rowland from OTC will be in town to watch practice. OTC is Oregon Track Club Elite. It is a Nike sponsored group based out of Eugene. Their current athletes include athletes like Ben Blankenship, Hassan Mead, Nigel Amos. Tomorrow will most likely be a hyped-up workout because Johnson will be excited to have Mark on campus. Afterwards I hope I can sit down and meet with him.

My first run today was just 7.5 miles easy with Kennedy and Parker, I then ran 3 miles at 8PM with Phil and Tyler. My Achilles is pretty shot right now but I think it's just flared up from racing back to back days. Going into outdoor I want to take the time to let this heal up by going in training room regularly before and after practice. What we have been doing for it is ultrasound and heat packs on my calves and shins. I'll be good to go come Stanford (fingers crossed). Last fun fact of the day, my march madness bracket is absolutely busted. I'm in the bottom 7%. That's how busted it is.

3.16.2018

mileage 12

Today was the first workout since nationals. This last week as you know has been runs and recovery. Today was also the day Mark Rowland from OTC came up to campus to watch me/talk with me.

For the workout:

Mile warm up

drills

20 minute run (we then had to go back to Dustin's because he forgot a shoe...)

1x200 @ 27

3x80m

1x200 @ 28

1x1000 @ 30/40/30

800m jog

5x600 30/40/30 w/ 600 jog recovery.

(last 600 was 29/38/27)

Cooldown

After the cooldown I went and sat down with coach Rowland. We talked about his philosophies, his athletes, his training staff so on and so forth. We talked for a good two hours and I really enjoyed our conversation. Talking with him made me excited to go down to Eugene to visit his team and staff. We will be planning that trip for the upcoming week or so. Overall, I was really impressed with him and his team. Going into this meeting I was a bit nervous for a couple of reasons. 1) Because he was coming to our campus to talk with me. At first I thought it was strange that he would rather come here then me go down there.

However, after chatting here in Monmouth, I am happy we established a relationship before going down there. 2) I was nervous about the Nike bit. Nike is such a large company and corporation that to be honest I am a bit scared about, I just don't know a whole lot of information on them. With Nike being such a large company, if I were to sign with them would they appreciate me and value me as a person? Nike products and people that run for Nike are freakin awesome, but this is a genuine concern. I look up to those guys, but I voice my concern as an athlete looking in. When I look at their groups do, I see it as a place in which I can develop athletically and socially? I just don't know. Which is why I am so thankful for Mark coming up here and chatting with me. Extremely excited to learn more about Nike as the process continues.

What I liked most about Mark was his honesty and his nationality philosophy. He never has more than two event runners from the same nationality on his team. After that discussion, we went through some of his scientific backing, and his methods used for lactate testing and stress level testing. We then talked about Eugene itself. I am familiar with Eugene, so their training areas and sites are known. Overall, I am really looking forward to going down to Eugene and seeing the team, facilities and staff. Mark seems like a brilliant coach, I am just really excited. 1.5 miles nice and easy to clear the thoughts and finish out the day.

3.17.2018

Mileage 12

Today was another good day, woke up and ran Shady Loop with Dustin. We slow rolled and talked about yesterday. Dustin is a good guy to bounce my thoughts and ideas off because he will answer honestly and give me his genuine thoughts. After the run I got a breakfast burrito before going to Dustin's to play DnD. We are starting up a campaign so that will be fun.

3.18.2018

Mileage 10

AM run with Brady, nice easy 8 miles before submitting my final work for my practicum. We are going into finals week! I worked in the library for a good 3 hours then right when I got home, I ate a bowl of cereal as Dustin and some of the guys came in to go for a spontaneous run, so I joined but it was surely a miserable two miles.

3.19.2018

Mileage 4

First day of finals week and I woke up feeling pretty hurt. My right leg (my perineal) is extremely sore as well my achilles tendon and calf. The last few days felt fine but waking up told a different story. After getting work done from Kurtis, I decided to just take a day for recovery the team did a speed workout today, but I need this day to come back stronger this weekend for the workout. However, after getting worked on I ran 30 mins and felt relatively pain free.

3.20.2018
Mileage 8

Back on track, went in and got worked on same thing yes yesterday only this time I woke up feeling much better. I got to practice and did the "special 1500 group" workout which was just me.

30 minute run
3x40 side to side
3x5 rocket jumps
2x20 spiderman
2x5 drop squats
6x120 in flats (fast and relaxed nothing pressed)
Jog 2 laps
1x400 @ 67
3x80
Jog two laps
Cooldown stretches

I got in the ice bath then went to dairy queen for free cone day. WAHOO! Ice-cream after an ice bath! I ran again tonight for 20 mins with Dustin and felt pain free the entire time, I think Monday was just a late soreness hit from the weekend. Two days down with finals week three to go!! I can make it!

3.21.2018
Mileage 8

Circuit day getting back to a normal routine, looking forward to the next month of progression. Time to gear up for "peak" number three of the season.

Warm up 40 minute run
2x20 alternate toe touch
1x20 rhll
1x20 monster walk
3x80 acceleration 60-70-80%
3x10 hurdle walkovers
2x10 hurdle skips
Jog 300
1x10 med ball lateral lunge
1x10 way backs
2x20 med ball forward then backward
2x80 stride
3x5 rocket jumps
1x20 mountain climbers
1x20 burpees with pushup
2x20 speed skaters
2x3 harness
Jog 400 cooldown
PM 20 mins

Felt good today, the circuit was nice and the last two days have been easy. The hardest part about today's circuit was the burpees. Sometimes those get to you and you start feeling pretty tired but you just gotta push through and get it done. Tomorrow I will be doing Mondays workout since I skipped out on that.

3.22.2018

Mileage 9.5

Today was pretty much the workout the guys did on Monday that I missed out on. I went into the trainers again and got more work done on my legs. This treatment is definitely helping me recover and bounce back from the last two weeks:

20 minute run
Warm up stride
1x20 leg swings
2x5 drop squats
2x40 side to side
2x5,7,9
Stride 120
3x300s
2x300
1x300
3 min jog in between each rep and 5 min walk in between each set. I was not a big fan of the weather today, but I was zoned in once the workout got going. It was just Johnson and I at the track, it was nice to have him calling splits. First set 42,44,39. Set two, 41, 41, final set of one 39.4. the last rep was definitely the most difficult because by then the wind started really picking up.
15 minute cooldown
30 minute rollout/boots

After the workout Dustin and I had a co-op interview with the Itemizer Observer. They do a great job of covering our successes. 20 min PM run with Dustin.

3.23.2018

Mileage 9

Another day another workout, also I have finished winter term!!!! It is officially SPRING BREAK! Except its downpour rain, so that sucks. Today's workout was a combo from Tuesday.

2x6 minute tempo 3 min recovery
2x30/40/30
1x200
1x120
15 minute cooldown

Overall this workout felt easier than the 300s but still taxing considering I did that just yesterday. This week is a pretty hectic schedule from finals and workouts. My PM run consisted of a nice and easy 3 mile run with Dustin. I don't know if you guys have caught on yet, but I run a lot with Dustin, and a lot of those runs are 3 miles.

3.24.2018

Mileage 10

8 mile AM run in 53 minutes and then a PM run with Dustin for just two miles. We are one weekend out from San Francisco and I believe I will be opening in the 800m. Going for a pretty fast time, hopefully around 1:47. Fingers crossed I draw the fast heat and rip it with the big boys.

3.25.2018

Mileage 9

Speed day on a Sunday. Switching around the schedule because tomorrow I am traveling down to Eugene to visit with OTC. Mark came up here before and it's time for me to swing down there and see what they got. I am excited to go down there because they will be my second team visited. I visited Brooks if you remember so now, I'll have two under my belt. For today:

30 minute run after mile warm up on track
2x80 warm up strides
3x300 3 min walk/jog
39.8, 39.2,38.7
3x150 fast last 50 focus
3x120 cooldown
10 min jog

15 minute PM run after playing some DnD with Dustin. We are gearing up for the new campaign, we are getting everything situated before we start playing.

3.26.2018

Mileage 8

Went down to Eugene today to visit Oregon Track Club Elite. Solid 50 minute run on Amazon trail with Neal Cranston. I bet he runs 1:52 this year. As him and I ran I couldn't help but remember the first time I was on Amazon trail. It was spring of my sophomore year of college, Zach Holloway and me. We talked about running professionally and all the teams in the country. That run was the first time I truly believed I could and was the day I set focus to pursue it. Once I met with the team, I watched them workout and do their weights/circuit work with Jimmy Ratcliffe. Coach Row took me through their routines and it was really awesome watching.

The team seemed to be cohesive and energetic with each other. Coach Row and I then went out to lunch and we talked about my future. Something I loved about him is his ability to listen. We talked, I talked, he talked, and we ate for almost 2 hours. I see myself really improving under his coaching. He seemed purposeful and passionate about track and field. Comparing the two places Seattle and Eugene is hard. I really like the team atmosphere and location of Seattle, but I liked Oregon Track Clubs team size and resources available. I need a lot more info from both groups before I make an ultimate and sound decision.

It's hard, being a collegiate athlete, especially being a track and field athlete. I can't see numbers, or specifics about a contract until I am out of eligibility to stay in compliance with NCAA. This means I won't be able to know how much I can make and what my contract entails until I am done. So as of right now I don't know where I will live, how much I will make, what my options are. I still have about two months until I can see the contracts so as of right now it is just time to stay sharp and focus on finishing out my collegiate career. These decisions are tough but being able to have options is important. I am thankful already Brooks and Oregon Track Club has reached out to me. Tomorrow is a speed workout and I am excited to get that going. Opening in the 800m this week.

3.27.2018
Mileage 8

Solid workout this morning, wasn't expecting this work load:

Mile warm up
Drills
20 minute run
2x200 @ 28,26
1x600 30/40/30
1x800 @ 2:03
1x600 @ 30/40/30

Today felt really smooth. The speed element of my fitness still seems like it needs some tune up, but my aerobic fitness feels great. The 800 felt smooth and I wanted to pick it up but today was about feel and 62/61 felt great. Tomorrow we have our circuit, after today I imagine it will be pretty tough, circuits always are.

3.28.2018
Mileage 8

Solid circuit but I lost the circuit sheet. Top 5 hardest circuits ever so I am bummed I didn't save it. I will be pretty sore tomorrow but that's okay It should be worked out of the system by 800 on Saturday. Hoping for the fast heat.

3.29.2018
Mileage 7

Travel day to San Francisco. Did all the basics, coffee and a mod pizza at the airport, journal on the plane, and listen to podcasts. Dustin, Josh and I went to Stanford for our premeet. I don't run till Saturday so today is an early pre-meet for me, I'd rather do it today than tomorrow when I don't have as much time.

20 minute run after 2 laps 2 laps
3x200
27, 27, 24.4
120 @ 17
15 minute run

Today I felt pretty good, took two of the reps to get warmed up then finally felt smooth on the 24.4. I think it was the fastest 200 I have ever done. I do a lot of 200s at 25 and 26 but rarely do I dip under 25. Stanford was overcrowded as usual, and it was funny how many people were on the track and how many people felt entitlement to lane one. Now we get out of the way for people, but some people were straight A holes. Oh well, we let the track do the talking.

I finally ate dinner at 6PM first thing I ate since 9:30 am. After dinner Dustin and I went 20 mins on the path in San Francisco.

3.30.2018

Mileage 7

Good early 35 min run with 4 strides then a 12 min PM run with strides.

Pretty nervous to be honest not sure why. Tomorrows race is a bit lower in distance but that's okay, I want to be able to race it. I have Nigel Amos in my heat, OTC member, Olympic Medalist, so I know it will be a good race. This is my first race since Indoor nationals, I assume it is just outdoor opener nerves. If I can run 146-147 that would be great, if not it will all be good. Going to bed excited to race fast. Race cues: **Get up, Ride, Finish**

3.31.2018

Mileage 9

Race day. Cinnamon French toast, race at two.

Waiting around all weekend I was really ready to race; the race went out in about 52,53 fastest first lap I have ever had. I was almost shocked at the first lap speed, my **Get up** and **Ride** cue blurred and all I could really do was **finish.** I moved into 3rd with 250 to go and tried to close. Nigel Amos, Olympic Silver Medalist closed his last 200 in 25-26 so the gap grew. I ended up running 1:48.09. Just shy of going 1:47. The last 100 felt great but I had no idea how fast I was going because of how gapped I was from Nigel. Nigel ended up running 1:44 so a lot of that gap was made up in the final 250. Cooled down with Drew Hunter.

Later I did a 20 minute run with the guys before we played "King of the Ring". We named the game ourselves but what you do is you stand in the pitching ring on a baseball diamond, pick up the baseball and throw it straight up into the air. You look at each other and can't look up. If you look up or step out of the circle you are eliminated. If you are hit with the baseball, you are also eliminated. It was pretty fun because it was dark, and because it would hurt if you got hit. I never got hit so I had a blast.

Overall, I am relatively happy with today's opener. It was a full second PR and it was a good race. Of course, I wish I would have gone just a bit faster to dip into the 1:47 range but there will be a time for that. last year at this time I ran 3:45 on Friday then a 1:49 the next day. I know I have better speed than a 1:48 on fresh legs. Taking only positives from this race because I am healthy, I feel fast, and am surrounded by an incredible group. Next outdoor race will be a 1500m in three weeks at Azusa Pacific.

Part IV: Spring

April: California Races

May: Last Conference & Nationals

June: Contract & Post Collegiate

4.1.2018

Mileage 4

Ended up getting an X-Ray and unfortunately, I have a stress fracture. This entire year has been so great. I have been health and focused, this injury came out of nowhere. I am not sure what the plan will be other than rest. Stress fractures are not something to mess around with. APRIL FOOLS! I am healthy, I just didn't run much today because today is Easter and I ate too much food at Olivia's. Stress fractures however are not something to joke about. If you have one, relax and repair because you must heal up to improve. Rushing stress fractures happens too often. Take time, recover and enjoy a break because when you come back, you'll be ready to rock it. My run was only 28 minutes today and I am sure it was at 7 min+ pace because I felt the ham, potatoes, wine and everything sloshing in my body. Oh well, recovery day today, tomorrow will be a good run at Saddle.

4.2.2018
Mileage 7

Saddle loop first and foremost. I haven't done this loop since cross country so getting a fresh run in was nice. After we got Market of Choice. A classic go to after the saddle loop. I get the same thing every time as well. A MOC burrito, maple bar, and a white mocha. Wow is it the perfect combo... First day of spring term so it's time to saddle up and ride this last term. In bed at 10:10

4.3.2018
Mileage 8

Second day of spring term went well. Practice today was speed development

2 laps 2 laps ½ campus loop
Drills
6 wickets
2x3x200
First set: 25.4, 25.8, 25.5
Second set: 24.7, 25.12, 25.5
Cooldown 20 minutes with stretching and rolling out

In reflection of today's workout this was the fastest and most consistent I've ever been with 200s. To add, our entire distance team was hitting these times within .5 of a second. We had 10 guys going through these reps together and it is so awesome to be a part of such a deep squad. I think our outdoor season as a team will be tremendous in terms of PRs. I left the track today pretty pumped.

4.4.2018
Mileage 8

Circuit day once again, crazy we are already in the month of April, next month is nationals and I am out of eligibility. Next month after that is graduation. That same month I run at USAs and will be representing a different kit. WOW, trying to remind myself to keep focusing one day at a time. Today we had a fun day:

40 minute run
Into 3x200 @ 28-30 in trainers
4 laps of 50/50s
3x full circuit
3x30 sec jump rope
2x5 rocket jumps
1x10 burpees
1x30 mountain climbers
1x10 inch worm
2x40 bounding
Cooldown mile.

Today was a good circuit. I haven't felt that good on a circuit in a while so coming off this weekend and feeling this good is a positive. I made nachos for Olivia and me for dinner. We have been dating for a grand total of 21 months! I know some people find it annoying to do monthly stuff in a relationship, but Olivia and I do it because we will take all the chances, we can get to celebrate us. Celebrating us is the best kind of celebration! Tomorrow is a solo day before getting ready for John Knight Twilight, I may be pacing the 1500m.

4.5.2018
Mileage 11

Today was a good day but my throat felt a little sore. Not sure why but I am taking it easy today and ran alone. My first run was 9.25 miles at 6:34s so it was relatively faster than normal, it felt good to work up rhythm to kick this sore throat out. Tomorrow will be a workout because I won't be pacing after all.

4.6.2018
Mileage unknown

Today was a day of mix ups. The other day I was planning on pacing but then Johnson called it off this morning. Then at noon today I went to the track for a premeet type workout. 30 minute run 3x300 at pacing duty. I told him I want to do it for the guys. I then show up to the meet at 4PM thinking senior recognition was at 4:45 because earlier in the day I was told it was at 4:45. Turns out it was at 3:45 and I was told the wrong time, so I missed my own senior recognition day. That kind of sucked but oh well. After that mix up I paced the guys 1500m we went 2:34 through the first k. Justin went on to run 3:54 which is a PR, Tyler ran 3:55. Hunter also hit a PR just shy of going under 4:00. After the pacing job Dustin and I hopped on the turf for a 15 minute tempo. We did 13 turf laps in 15:24. The day was a good one, but I am still bummed I missed senior recognition.

4.7.2018

Mileage 9.5

Good single recovery run from yesterday. Not too sore which is surprising. My sore throat also went away but now I am super stuffy in the nose and have to blow it every 30 or so minutes. Ended up doing Shady our 9.5 mile loop and left the watch at home so I'm not sure what the pace was, I just wanted to go by feel. In bed at 11:20 pretty late night but I'm going to sleep in tomorrow.

4.8.2018

Mileage 6

So today was just 6 miles but it was about a 10-12 mile effort day. We went to Peavey and ran Bonzai. Bonzai is a muddy, steep hill that climbs for about 15 or so minutes straight. You go from the base of McDonald National forest to the top. We came down Powderhouse trail and my quads were burning. Hopefully this doesn't impact us tomorrow for the workout but if it does oh well. Today I also scheduled a phone call with Flynn Sports Management. That will take place Tuesday, I am looking forward to getting this agency process going. Only a month and two weeks left of eligibility. Not that I'm counting down, just that it flies by. Wow.

4.9.2018

Mileage 10.5

Yesterday I felt a bit stuffy and today was a tad better. Today's workout was a nice gear up for tomorrow's workout.

Campus loop
Side to side
Drop squats
2 laps stride walks
2x hurdle walkovers
2x20 monster walks
2x5,7,9
3x200 25.7, 25.6,25.1
120 @ 80%
5 mile run @ 34:21
1x15 pushups
3x4 position plank
1x15 spiderman

After today's work I rolled out and got some recovery in. When you're a bit under the weather and sore that is when you need to take care of your body the most. I was pretty tired today, so I took a quick nap in between classes. At 7PM once it cooled down, I went for another 3 miles. I felt strong in the 200s and thought about Azusa Pacific the whole time. We are getting closer and closer to the meet and I'm getting more and more excited. I hope I draw the fast heat, I would love to draw the same heat as Kerr and race a deep field. I am in bed at 9:40. I feel fit and now all I need is normal health and good recovery.

4.10.2018

Mileage 10

Today's workout was something different than we have ever done before. This workout gave me a lot of confidence for the 1500. Sometimes you need to trust your coach and roll with their plan. We have been doing a lot of the same things for the past few weeks, so I was a bit nervous how a newish workout would feel but boy did it feel good.

Campus loop

Drills

3x120s

Campus loop

Spike up 3x120s

3x500,300,200 (300m jog between 500-300) (200m jog between 300-200) 800m jog between sets

Mission of the day was to cut down each set, each set completely faster than the previous. First number is through 400m of the 500m rep.

Our goal: 63/46/29 |61,44,28| 58/43/27

I led the first set feeling great hitting each time perfectly. The next set was a bit slower on the 300 we went 45. Last set I asked Johnson if I could tiger the 500. I started in the back and went 53.8 through 400 on the 500 rep and finished off the set with a 43 and 26. The team finished together on the 26. All in all, it felt good and our cooldown we got soaked as it downpoured. After drying off I went to class and had a phone call with Flynn Sports. I talked with Matt and we chatted for a good 45 minutes. He seemed genuine and interested in my successes. He said he was interested from Portland Track Festival before USAs entirely.

We talked broadly about companies and what a contract consists of and how it is best to keep my coach and compliance director in the loop on all conversations and questions. We then talked about my post collegiate season and what that may consist of. We kept it all within NCAA terms and I appreciated the loyalty to that. This is the first agent I have had contact with and it is a good starting block. A little over a month before I have to make a decision. Looking forward to this next month of the process. What I want to know now is what is included in contracts. Is health care? Life insurance? So on and so forth.

4.11.2018

Mileage 8.5

Circuit day felt good, a single run kind of day.

½ campus loop

1x20 leg swings

2x40 turning side to side

2x10 lateral lunge

2x30 light skipping

40 minute run

3x80 stride

3x40 harness

Four position circuit

Position 1

2x15 med ball lunges forward

2x15 med ball lunges backward

1x15 med ball push ups

Stride 100

Position 2

2x10 hurdle walkovers

2x10 hurdle over under

2x20m monster walk

Stride 100

Position 3

2x10 burpees

1x20 mountain climbers

1x20 spiderman

Stride 100m

Position 4

2s100 jump rope

2x30 spiderman

2x20 box jumps
Repeat.

Got a Blizzard tonight because today was such a big day. This was a long and difficult circuit. To top it off it started downpouring through the second set, but Dustin and I kept each other accountable and I said, “what would the mile champ do?” he said, “What would the defending 1500m champ do?” We finished the whole sheet and called it a day. After practice I got in the boots and rolled out a bit. Less than 10 days till Azusa Pacific meet and rumor has it will be a fast race. Looking forward to it but right now I just want some sleep. In bed 9:49.

4.12.2018
Mileage 12.5

Higher mileage day, 8.5 mile run in the morning solo. Just a nice easy rhythm piece to get the body in a groove. Then Dustin and I doubled for four miles. We talked about US and Russia's involvement in Syria. Political talks make runs go by just as fast as DnD talks. Forgot to eat dinner, just realizing it as I journal. Going to get up and have a plate of nachos, who cares if it's 9 o clock. I was going to go to bed at 9 for how tired I am but food is food, so I need to get that in my system. 9 o clock nacho party it is. Tomorrow is some form of a workout.

4.13.2018
Mileage 10

Workout did not disappoint

Campus loop
Drills
To lift our spirits, Johnson turned on the loudspeaker and we listened to music through the stadium audio as rain continued to pour.
1x200 @ 28
400 jog
4x600 @ 28/39/28 600m jog between
1x300 @ 43
Jog to turf
6 mins of Xs as cooldown

Then a 3 mile PM run with Dustin. Today was pretty difficult and I was really tired. Maybe eating nachos that late was a bad idea, but I needed to eat something. Went home after practice and took a good 40 minute nap. Tomorrow will be a full recovery day (hoping for easy runs). Playing FortNite a lot tomorrow if I don't have any homework.

4.14.2018
Mileage 8

Good solo run recovery day, relatively low this week in terms of mileage but that is okay because the work was exactly what I needed. Olivia and I went to Portland today to just get out of town for a bit. Gearing up for a good week leading to Azusa. Tomorrow I'd usually take for a longer run but we are going to have a light day tomorrow working into race week.

4.15.2018
Mileage 9

Today was a perfect Sunday! Seven miles in the am at 7:35 pace then two miles in the PM after DnD. My legs and health feel back to normal so I'm ready. It's hard not thinking about the future. Talking with agents and teams I have had a hard time focusing on the present. Focus on the now and the future will take care of itself. That is something I try and tell myself every day. I get caught up thinking about next year when if I don't take care of the now, next year won't be as promising. This week I am focusing on the now, focusing on the race. Just like at DII nationals for indoor. I am prepared to run a 3:54 mile equivalent if needed. I want to do whatever I can on that day and I know I'm fit right now. I am ive days out from race day and I already know my cues. **Contact, Execute, Finish.** Familiar words for a familiar race. PR or bust.

4.16.2018
Mileage 9

Good Monday done. Woke up at 6AM to watch the Boston marathon. Wow talk about inspiration! Des Linden wins are you kidding me!? Her acts were so selfless in that race I couldn't believe it. When Flanagan had to go to the bathroom Des slowed down to help Flanagan catch back up to the group. A couple month ago I said Shalane's race was my favorite when she won the New York City Marathon, but this is my favorite now. This was absolutely incredible; Women's Marathon is the best thing to ever happen in the sport of running. The weather was crazy bad in Boston and so many people couldn't handle it. People dropped out constantly, for that I would say this is a prime example of whether or weather. Weather shouldn't be a deciding factor whether or not you are going to be great. Be great in bad weather and you will be able to rise through any adversity.

On the men's side the unlikely winner was a man from Japan named Yuki Kawauchi. At the start of the race he gaped the field by 50 meters and the announcers roasted him for it. They said things like, "Does he realize this is a marathon?" "He has world class competitors looming behind maybe he should get that hint." "Come around 5k he will start fading." Here is the thing, first the announcers should never put down an athlete for taking risk and doing something "out of the norm." What else is out of the norm is winning the Boston Marathon which is something Yuki also did. BLOCK OUT THE HATERS YUKI! Never be diminished for what others say about your racing. Everyone is critics when they see something out of the norm. Be confident in whatever you do and know that greatness comes with risk.

After watching the marathon, I go outside to find it was downpouring here on the west coast. I put on my rain coat and smiled because I figured it wasn't a good day to complain about the weather since Boston was far worse.

Half campus drills
Fast 30 minute run (maybe a bit excited from the race)
6 min tempo @ 5:05 pace
Jog to the track
500,300,200
57.6 (through 400) 42.34, 27.5
10 min cooldown
Stretch and roll out
35 min nap to follow practice.

Tonight, we had our honor society dinner as well, I will have honor cords for graduation which is pretty neat. That was something I was working for since my sophomore year, so I am excited to finally have those. In high school I was .01 point shy for my cumulative GPA. With falling that short in HS, getting cords for my degree was a priority. Four days out **Contact, Execute, Finish.** Record or Bust.

4.17.2018
Mileage 9

Different Tuesday than normal. Yesterday was the bulk of the workout so today was:

30 minute run into circuit drills
3x120, 1x200 @ 28, 1x300 @ 38.7
15 min cooldown

I left the workout sheet at the track and I can't remember the drills off the top of my head. However, during the track work 100% of my focus was imagining me in this weekend's race. Picturing Dustin as Josh Kerr and riding the wave and racing the last bit. Looking forward to traveling on Thursday, I feel fresh and ready. Three days, here we go, **Contact, Execute, Finish.** Record or Bust.

4.18.2018
Mileage 8

Entries are out and the whole run I was amped. Some names listed are Josh Kerr, Justyn Knight, Sam Prakel, Robert Dominic so on and so forth. This is easily the deepest collegiate field I will be a part of. These names are the 2018 middle distance names. When you think of collegiate track these are the names I think of. Last few days I have been visualizing a win. I know that sounds crazy but visualizing an achievement is the first step in making it a reality. I never want to go into a race counting myself out. Not trying to sound arrogant, I just always want to put myself in a mental and physical position to win. I just know my team and coaches have complete faith in me so why shouldn't I? The run was 52 mins so relatively fast but nothing crazy. Felt good the whole time before I went to the trainers, rolled out and booted up. In my mind I am trying to hear someone yell "57" through the first lap of this upcoming race. Two days, **Contact, Execute, Finish.** Record or Bust.

4.19.2018

Mileage 6

Mileage dropped a bit due to travel, but we still got a really good pre-meet in. We worked out at Cal-Poly Pomona so a decent facility, enough to get the job done.

30 minute run

1x200 @ 29

1x500 120 on, 80 off, 120 on, 80 off.

1x300 @ 42

2x80 relaxed.

2 lap cooldown

Too be honest today's pre-meet didn't wasn't great, the 300 was what finally felt good and the 80s felt great. Overall it felt like a typical pre-meet, but I know if I feel bad today I will feel great tomorrow. Went to the track meet today to watch the 5ks. Didn't get back till 10:30 in bed around 11:15PM typically I wouldn't stay out that late, but I wanted to watch Tyler my roommate PR in the 5k (which he did) and watch Sydney Gidabuday run the 5k. Syd Ran 13:29 for a #2 all time in Division II. Tyler PRed by more than 8 seconds and I couldn't be more amped for tomorrow, tracks hot so I am ready to get this show on the road. Going to bed tonight excited because tomorrow is race day. Tomorrow is go time, no more room for anything but confidence. **Contact, Execute, Finish.** RECORD OR BUST!

4.20.2018

Mileage unsure

I slept decent but felt exhausted right when I woke up. Shook out, ate breakfast and went back to the room debating a nap. I took a shower and shaved my legs, felt better after that so I decided to just relax. We played Exploding Kittens from 1-4PM which was fun, but my mind was exhausted. As we drove to the meet, I plugged in my usual artist Russ and visualized the race. Repeating **Contact, Execute, Finish.** Once I was warming up, I knew tonight was going to be a good night. The atmosphere, weather and how I felt all seemed right. The gun goes off and we go through 400 in 55-56 **Contact**, 1:55-1:56 through 800. The race then really took off and the fight for position became more difficult **Execute**. I wish I would have engaged with 500 to go and attempt a long grind to the finish but this was toughest field I had ever raced. I close the final 120m as fast as I could to run 3:37.35, a new DII record. **Finish.**

Best part was right when I crossed the line and saw the time, I was immediately swarmed by hugs and cheers from my teammates. They were waiting in a large group just meters behind the finish line. Those embraces are something I will remember forever. As excited as I was, I finished 6th in the race, I wanted to race to a higher finish. During the race I was focused on the race, I had a great talk with Knight after the race and he congratulated me on the record. This goal was something I focused on since last June and to see it all come together in front of my team was incredible. Next 1500 I want to be in position with 500 to go

Guys like Knight are the future of track and field, being able to toe the line next to him and race is always a great time. However, next time I gotta beat him. He is 2-0 against me!

Knight and I also got in a twitter convo which is summarized by, "Never categorize yourself as an event runner categorize yourself as a racer. Race the race you're in and fight for the win." Knight is a RACER. I hope I can be as well. That is one point I hope you take away from this journal, if you're still reading it, I can never tell.

For all I know I am just talking to myself in this journal, but I hope I am talking to someone, someone like you because if you are still reading this than running is more than just a sport. It is a passion and you are learning just like you would any subject. Like I said in the intro, it takes a special kind of crazy to be a distance runner, but it takes a special kind of crazier to read about a distance runner. I am no expert, but I hope my words can help develop your dreams and passion. After the cooldown the team and I went to In and Out. It was delicious! However, In and Out at 11:00PM is a little rough on the stomach but it's worth it. Going to bed blessed to be surrounded by the team that I have and the competitors I have raced that make me better. Better as a runner and better as a person. Looking forward to the rematches with these Division one icons.

4.21.2018
Mileage 8

Could have raced today, woke up feeling really great but Johnson wanted me to relax today and not amp up for another race. So, we scratched the 800m I was signed up for. Instead we went to a track and got a good 25 min run in and 3x200 @ 28.1, 26.3, 25.3 cooldown 10 mins
They felt fast and they were, but they were fun. AJ, Dustin, Tyler, Phil, Josh and I were cruising on them. After the shakeout we got some food and went to the track to watch some track. Around 4 hours later we went back out for 30 min run at the beach, an annual tradition. Talked with coach on the flight home and he told me from here on out we need to focus on enjoying each day and get ready for nationals. In a few weeks I will come back down to California and race at the Payton Jordan Invite.

4.22.2018
Mileage 9

Woke up and ate with Olivia, an unspoken tradition we have is going out to breakfast the day we get back from meets. I always look forward to these meals because it gives me a chance to finally love and talk with Olivia. We rarely see each other on track trips cause typically we are all business. These catch up breakfasts are so nice because I get to just listen to her talk about her weekend. After breakfast I ran with the guys 9 easy miles some tempos here and there to get the legs moving. Finished the run at the track and got some good strides in before DnD.

4.23.2018

Mileage 9

A speed substituted day, still feel the weekend. Looking back at the last four months I couldn't have asked for a better training and racing result. Each and every day this journal has proven to be one of the most valuable training items I put focus to. I truly believe had it not been for this journal, none of what i have done would have been accomplished. So in a weird way, thank you future reader. Thank you for keeping me accountable and helping me achieve my dreams one day at a time. Put the book down and high five yourself, we did it. For today:

Campus loop

Leg swings

Light skipping

2x40 side to side

Alternate toe touch

30 minute run

6x150s sprint/float/sprint

3x40 harnesses

2 laps jog

3x15 box jumps

1x20 light skipping

1x10 side lunge

3 min inversion

After practice went to the trainers and got a really good massage from Kurtis. Easy 1.5 mile run to shakeout the legs tonight... Over social media I have been getting tons of messages congratulating me. I don't need the public acknowledgement, but the recognition is nice. Tomorrow will be a workout then easyish next few days I believe (I hope).

4.24.2018

Mileage 9

Workout day and I felt surprisingly well. I had my tai chi class this morning that went out onto the tennis courts for all to see. The professor said, "Let's do our exercises for all of campus to see." Besides feeling awkwardly judged, I felt surprisingly good. For the workout it was:

3 laps 1 lap
Leg swings
Side twists
Quad stretch
Toe touch
Side to side
10 min run into 10 min tempo
1x600 @ 29/38/28 600m jog
1x1000m 30/40/29/28/27 800m jog
1x600m 29/36/27
1x400 @ 57
10 min cooldown
3 barefoot strides

After class I went home and facetimed our old athletic trainer Tyler (Tyler is at Iowa State now.) We facetimed for a good 90 minutes and it was good to catch up. I ran to the stop light once again and overall I felt pretty good. Tomorrow I hope I feel better. rest recover repeat. Those will be my cues for the next few weeks. Far less intense than race cues.

4.25.2018
Mileage 7

Today was a circuit day and it was a good core day none the least:

Mile warm up
Side to side
Leg swings
Toe touch
23 min run
3x80 stride
Section 1
1x20 mountain climbers
1x20 burpees
1x10 rocket jumps
2x10 jumping jacks
2x10 crab walks
1x30 speed skaters
Section 2
2x20 high knees
15 each side unbalanced pushups
1x20 med ball catches seated
1x20 inch worm
4 position planks
2x10 hurdle walkovers
Jog 100
1x20 box jumps
2x100m jump rope
Repeat.

After the long circuit we had a meeting and then I ran again at 8:40 for 20 minutes, it was a good run but definitely felt today. The race from this last weekend I believe is out of my legs. Tomorrow should be just a regular run. Turns out I'll run an 800m race this weekend.

4.26.2018

Mileage 8

Good off day, no regular practice. Today I ran 6 miles in the am with Tyler before I premeet tomorrow. I ran 2 miles tonight after I DMed the girls DnD game. Today was a pretty boring day really. I was planning on running more tonight but my stomach hurt pretty bad. I think it was from the bubble tea I drank. Tomorrow is a premeet for the OSU HP meet.

4.27.2018

Mileage unsure

Premeet today, racing the 800m tomorrow last little tune up before the championship season. I will race down in Payton Jordan, but this is my last 800m before conference. This will be my last shot at a fast 800m this year, hoping for a fast time but in reality, I will go for the win and hope to be in a position to run fast. Forecast calls for wind and rain tomorrow, potentially thunder so it will be a waiting game to see what tomorrow brings.

30 minute run
1x200 @ 26
1x150 @ 18
1x80m
6 quick starts off the 800m start line
10 min PM run

4.28.2018
Mileage 9

Woke up and did a good 20 min shakeout, ate breakfast and waited around till noon before heading to the meet.

15 min jog warm up
20 mins of drills and stretching
5 min strides

On the start line I have never felt less like racing, I'm not sure why but in the moment before the gun went off, I was thinking jeez again? I have to race already? Luckily it as just an 800 but first 200m I wasn't feeling it. I go straight to the back and as the race progresses, I move up to the front, I raced to the line winning in 1:50.xx not sure exactly what the time was but at 600m I knew I needed to just focus on the win. After the race we went and did hill repeats on campus, I then had dinner with Olivia's family before a 25 min PM run with Dustin. Overall today was a good day, I race at Payton in five days so that's the real focus. Hoping for a good race down there.

4.29.2018
Mileage 9.5

Single 63 minute run relatively fast with Dustin. We threw in 3 tempos at 40 minutes to spice up the pace a bit, 30 sec, 40 sec and 60 sec tempo. After the run I just relaxed and did homework before the guys DnD session. They ended up fighting a Drider, which is a cursed Drow that takes on the lower half of a spider. It's like a centaur but half elf half spider, look it up on the internet! Pretty crazy stuff.

4.30.2018
Mileage 7

Today was circuit day, even though it's Monday we pushed the circuit to today because I race on Thursday night.

2 laps 2 laps
3x120s
30 minute run
3x Xs
Back to the track
Rhll
3x80m stride
3x40 harness
1x20 lunge med ball
1x15 med ball push up
2x15 rocket jumps
1x4 plank
1x20 mountain climbers
1x10 burpees
2x10 hurdle walkovers
Repeat x2 lunges-walkovers
Cooldown.

KGW swung by the track today and gave Dustin and I interviews, after the interview he said alright, I should have this story up and running tonight on KGW News Channel 8! That is such a fast turnaround! We fly to San Francisco in a few days, we will be meeting with Flynn Sports Agency Thursday too. Hoping for the best down there!

5.1.2018

Mileage 9

Fly out tomorrow so today turned into a premeet to the premeet

30 minute run after 2 laps 2 laps
3x200 @ 28, 28, 24
2x120s
2 mile cool down

After words I went to class and then home before doubling for the evening with a 30 minute run. I am so done with school right now, I am so close to finishing like a little over a month left but it is so hard to stay motivated. These classes I am taking are so easy that I have zero motivation to do anything. The only difficult class I am taking is Rhetoric in Western Tradition. It's a hard class but I still enjoy the topic. Tonight, I went and watched Infinity War, wow, so good. If you haven't seen it yet Spiderman and Black Panther disappear. Like die? I think they are trapped in the soul stone but I'm not sure. You could be mad at me for spoiling, but you've had half a year to watch it so boohoo.

5.2.2018
Mileage 5

Low low mileage day with travel and pre-meet.

Landed in Palo Alto first time ever coming down here two times in the same year. Overall, I feel pretty terrible, you know what they say, bad premeet good race right? My legs don't feel under me and I don't feel rhythmic on the track. Today's premeet was supposed to be smooth and control focus but I felt pretty pressing the whole time. Not sure what's up but hopefully it passes by tomorrow night's race. Names in the race are Chelimo, Centro, Jenkins, Engels, McGorty, Fischer, Ingebrigtsen. This is the deepest professional heat I have been in so hopefully I can represent Western and give a good showing of DII. For today:

20 minute run
1x200 @ 28
1x600 @ 30/42/30
1x200 @ 26
Cooldown

Overall I am excited for tomorrow, mentally preparing for this off feeling to pass. Tomorrow is the day, it's just another business trip. 500 to go I want to be in a position to win it, at Azusa I was off a bit with 500 to go and I couldn't race till the finish. Tomorrow hopefully I can be in a position to do some damage from the front. Going to bed with the focus of success. **Relax, Position, Finish.**

5.3.2018
Mileage unsure

Well today started out great, 15 minute run in the am honestly felt ready to race. After the shakeout, got some breakfast then headed out to a Starbucks to meet with Flynn Sports with my coach. After the meeting I hung out in the hotel room till race time which was not till like 8pm. Got to the track and high fived and met with people like Craig Engels and people I don't often see. We get to the starting line and in the first 100m I sprint out to try and get position but find myself in the front. I look around and just laugh right off because two weeks ago at Azusa I would have been in 5th off this start but today I'm in the front, we go through 400 in 58-59 and through 800 in 1:58-59 I felt great moving up the back stretch and with 500 to go I was in about 3rd put myself in the position I wanted then all of a sudden the last 400 I started going backwards, never in my entire time racing have I been spit out the back that bad.

I race down the homestretch for the final time alone glancing at a shadow to my right, I pick it up to beat whoever is racing me on the final 100m. I cross the line turn around to see no one, turns out I was racing my shadow. I look up to see the entire field walking off together talking and high fiving. I ran 3:45, a few seconds back but I felt like I was in a completely different race. I watched as the group walked off together embracing while I just had my shadow. I was feeling so alone. I have never really gotten last before in a race and this was a huge perspective switch.

I could care less about the result honestly if I got last and someone came back and high fived me or gave me a pat on the back. I would have felt better about myself if that were the case but instead I walked off feeling so alone it hurt. Hurt bad.

The drive back to the hotel was Johnson talking and me really just zoning out. Looking back at the last five days my training wasn't ideal for a race today but I am so thankful this experience happened. Even at the hotel I was roomed alone, slept alone, ate dinner alone just an epitome of the day.

This race put so much perspective in my pocket of experience. Every race I hope I can congratulate and high five as many people as possible. Not being over the top of course but showing enough courtesy to everyone in that race that they deserve to be there and that they are appreciated for their effort good or bad. What a day.

5.4.2018
Mileage 6

Two mile shakeout this morning boarding the plane to Eugene to watch the rest of the team compete at Oregon Twilight. After gate changes and delays, I finally make it on the plane. I was sitting at the wrong gate for a good 20 minutes before realizing they switched on me. I was watching Doha Diamond league and had to run over to my gate mid races. However, they were delayed so that helped. Reflecting on last night's race, the week leading up to it was rough but in the race I never felt rhythmic. Every time I accelerated, I felt as though the race decelerated. My problem with 500 to go was I accelerated to get into a position then once I settled into a position the race took off and I wasn't ready to speed change again, had I stayed consistent pace throughout I think I would have had a better result. That was a shock of a race for me and I am happy with the learning experience.

Once I got to the track Kurtis our trainer gave me a massage and it felt great, I am wrecked. I think what I need is a few relaxed days, put in good miles tomorrow then relax for a bit after. I warmed up and ran with Dustin today he ran 3:47 or so and got second to last in his heat. I wanted him to do good but looking at everyone's performances I assess that everyone is kind of in this slump. It'll shake off by championship season.

5.5.20118
Mileage 11

Normal day today and I felt good. Surprisingly, I figured I would be most sore today, but I feel good. Dustin and I both had track work and a run

2 laps 2 laps
30 minute run @ 6:13s
Spike up
1x600 30/40/28 jog 500
1x300 39 jog 600
1x600 30/40/28 jog 500
1x300 41
10 min cooldown

Today's workout felt great I did it solo and the focus was a rhythmic day. I wanted to do longer reps or Ks but because I just came off of travel and a race, I knew shorter quicker stuff is better. Dustin soloed a 2:58 1200m rep today. He said he wanted to feel good going fast which is something he never felt yesterday in the race. Looking back at the training our two circuit work and track work of last week took a toll. Talking with everyone we all feel pretty tired, but Johnson has got a plan and I am sure it will pay off for Nationals.
23 min PM run to shakeout.

5.6.2018

Mileage 7

Woke up to an easy 50 minute run exactly 7 miles, slow, nice and easy but deliberate. I've gotten more contact from agents, Hawi and Chris Layne from Total Sports both reached out this morning. I am surprised honestly, I figured after this weekend's performance I would be erased from the chalkboard but it's good to see interest. After the run I did some homework rolled out and played some FortNite. Got four wins in a row before going to the library to do more homework. Tomorrow will be a busy day but we are back on the track for a workout so that'll be nice.

5.7.2018
Mileage 8

Waited for Dustin to get done with a meeting. Dustin and I worked out together just us two. We haven't had a workout with just the two of us in a while so this was a super fresh feeling. Looking back at the last three weeks we are deep in this workout cycle but today just added another layer on the cake. At some point this cake will be finished and we will be able to indulge.

Drills
Campus loop
1x200 @ 28
2x200 @ 27 walk 400
1x1200 59/81/59 walk 200 jog 400
1x1000 60/80/28 walk 200 jog 400
3x400 relaxed rhythmic effort 63,63,62

Dustin and I raced the last 50m of the last rep we were probably on pace for a 66 but we dropped the last 80 m to try and win. He won. Overall today felt incredible and I am surprised at how I am feeling after this last week, doing reps over 600m was nice.

Gearing up for this weekend I will be entered in both the 800m and 1500m for conference. I have double duty to try and pace the guys to qualifying marks AJ and Josh are both on the bubble right now so hoping I can help them get to nationals. This is my last conference track race ever... wow 12 for 12 after this weekend. Today I also got a call from Paul a sports rep for Nike. He wants me to come and visit the Nike World Headquarters in Beaverton and I agree, I hope that progresses. 10 min shakeout in the PM feeling good.

5.8.2018

Mileage 7

Tuesday before conference, I'll be running both the 800m and 1500m as mentioned yesterday. I was a little nervous about the double last night but I'm confident it is what I need mid-season. I need that double excursion of the 800m and 1500m to gear me up for a single race at nationals. The hardest part of the season now is keeping the body fresh. Am I tired right now? Yeah, I am, but settling back for just the 1500m for conference won't prepare me any better for nationals and what comes after. I still need to press that button of fitness to continue to peak in June. Today I also called Paul back for Nike and we arranged a meeting up in Beaverton, I look forward to that as well.

For today's workout:

Mile warm up

Drills

40 minute run

3x 250 @ 36 Sprint/Float/Sprint

1x300 @ 48

Jumping jacks

Burpees

Forward and backward lunge

Mountain climbers

Box jumps

Planks

2 lap cooldown on the grass

Tonight, we had a student leadership night I was nominated as a finalist for the Delmer Dewey award and Student Leader award for Students at Western Oregon University however I didn't get either. That's okay, the other nominees were incredible deserving and I understand why I wasn't selected. Also, I am trying to journal, but Olivia is distracting me with Ellen DeGeneres. Tomorrow will be a good run day gearing up for this weekend.

5.9.2018
Mileage 8.5

Just a regular run day 8.5 with Brady. We talked a lot and it was the first time I have talked with Brady about the future in a while. We were running 6:35s and hit a 6:08 mile the last mile. Which isn't unusual with Brady. Tomorrow will be a light premeet and then 800m prelim on Friday.

5.10.2018
Mileage 6

Super light day but tomorrow starts my last GNAC meet. I want to be fresh for this weekend, put on a good show for GNAC. It's been a wild four years and I will be attempting to win the conference title in the 1500m for the fourth year in a row. Not sure if it has ever been done but it's exciting none the least.

30 min run
2x200 @ 29,27
1x400 @ 58
1x120 @ 17
Cooldown 2 laps.

Overall, I feel good, I feel recovered from Payton, my focus this weekend is be appreciative and thankful. I hope to high five and congratulate everyone that crosses the finish line and just be a part of the meet entirely.

5.11.2018
Mileage 8

Good first day of GNACs a nice and easy 20 minute run in the am before pancakes. Today I talked with Phoebe Wright over the phone, we talked for half an hour about agents and coaches. She was a such an incredible resource. I hope I can be that kind of resource for collegiate athletes that have questions about going post collegiate. I am still new to the process but in a month from now I know my team, agent, and future will be decided so I hope I can give honest insight to anyone who needs help. After the phone call I warmed up for the 800m prelim, I won the heat and we ended up getting 7 WOU 800m athletes in the final, seven of nine in the final are from WOU. Middle Distance University!!!! I ran 1:54 and felt really good in it looking forward to tomorrow's races being pacer for the guys.

5.12.2018

Mileage unsure

When I say unsure about the mileage, I say that because my focus on that day is feeling good. I don't record mileage on race days my only focus is performing and competing if I do that off 10 miles I do it off 10 miles if its 3 miles its 3 miles.

For the finals today, we ran 3:49 in the 1500m just off a time for Josh to get in. Then an hour later we were in the 800m and I ran 1:52.xx I won both, but I'm bummed I couldn't get any of the guys to nationals. So much pressure is placed on us to pace the guys that I feel bad when I can't help them. I really tried to press it in the 800m to make up for the 1500m. With 200m to go in the 800m I felt the tallest and sharpest I have felt since Azusa, I look over at coach with 200m to go and he said fast and fluid. I did just that and won (barely) apparently Dustin was cruising in the last 120 and almost got me. Nationals will be fun racing with Dustin, if there was a time we could go 1-2 its now, well, because it's the last time we could ever do it.

We are both fit. Today showed that, 1-2 in the 1500m. 1-2 in the 800m. Let's hope for another 1-2 finish in two weeks. Is it too early to say 1-2 or Bust? I don't think so. Dustin if you're reading this, I am sorry, but I have to win. You can get second, but I will lean on you if I have too (insert tongue out emoji). If you beat me, you beat me! You are an incredible competitor and out of the entire field if I was worried about one person winning it's the guy I train with every single day. I wouldn't want it any other way. Don't let this inflate your head. Olivia split 54.7 in the 4x4 and the women's team qualified potentially for nationals in the 4x4! That would be absolutely awesome!! It will be an exciting next week to see who scratches and who is selected for the meet.

5.13.2018
Mileage 9

Good solid 60 min run with Dustin, but this morning started with a Mother's Day breakfast with my mom and dad in Salem at a restaurant called Annette's. Mothers are so special you know, if you are reading this, before you put the journal down for the night, the day, whatever, text your mom. Text or call you mom and just say I love you I hope you have a great day. If under circumstance you don't have a mother, text the closest person to it. I think Moms can be described as role models, caregivers, and biggest fans. Text that person and wish them a good day. You know my biggest regret growing up is not calling my parents more on the phone or just talking with them more. I mean shoot, I talk with my parents all the time over the phone, but I wish I did more. Role models and support systems are the best.

For today Dustin and I chose the hottest time of the day to run and I guess it is only fitting getting ready for North Carolina. We did strides and talked about the future, our immediate future was Dairy Queen which was icing on the cake after the weekend. Overall, I feel pretty good, not as good as a cookie dough blizzard but that complimented my fitness for the weekend well. Only two weeks left of eligibility. Time to make the best of it.

5.14.2018

Mileage 8

Kurtis worked on my leg today, it was sore. Dustin and I had a 40 minute run just a regular relaxed day after a mile warm up. 3x40/40 tempo at the end making the last mile fast. Josh also got into nationals so that's awesome! He is 19th and they take 20 so looks like we have 3 guys heading to nationals in the 1500m! Two days till I meet at Nike, also scheduled a phone call with Brooks Sports Marketer for Friday. The championship season is underway and so is the phone calls for next year! Exciting times. Taking deep breaths and focusing on the present.

5.15.2018
Mileage 9

Turns out I spoke to soon for Josh getting into nationals. They only took 18 guys in the 1500m and josh was 19. He missed it by .03 in the 1500m, such a stupid selection process. Went to the trainers to get my right leg worked on. Nothing devastating but a bit annoying. It's my right calf and ankle. Feel a bit stressed where my Achilles and calf connect. Kurtis is working great on it, so I am not too worried about it. Just trying to get it worked on before it gets any more serious. Once the training room was done practice went well.

2 laps leg swings
Side to side
RHLL
20 minute run
Side to side
2x200 28,28
Walk 300 before starting workout
3x500 going through 400 in 57
1st 500 we went through 400 @ 57, finishing 500 @ 71
4mins recovery
2nd 500 broken, 28 first 200, tempo 100m, 27 last 200
4min recovery
3rd 500 30 first 200, 39.7 last 300m. Dustin and I wanted to flow the last 300m, we went 55 through 400m focusing solely on last 300m it felt great and felt race simulation.
Jog 200 walk 200
3x300m broken
47 15/17/15
45, 13/18/14

42 last 300m this rep was broken as heck, but I have no idea our splits.

We were moving first and last 100m, we treated it like the 1500m final for nationals. I legit think we can go 1-2 and if we do, I can see it being Me-Dustin or Dustin-Me. This guy is going to be hard to beat. 1-2 or Bust!

Mile cooldown on the track joking with Dustin, even after 9 grueling workout miles we still laugh, joke and have fun. Dustin is a huge part in my successes this year and I know next year he is going to shine. Tomorrow I go to Nike for a tour around the Headquarters.

5.16.2018
Mileage 4

Today was an off day but a good day I went to my class at 8am then headed to Beaverton to meet with Paul from Nike. We had a two hour tour before an hour and a half conversation at a table. I met some great people today. My favorite building today was the Pre building not because of the building itself but because of the woman I met working within the building. Her and I talked for a good twenty minutes and it was so nice talking to her. She was sweet, kind and a humble Olympian before the 2000s. It was so awesome chatting with her.

After the tour Paul, my coach and I sat down and talked about my expectations and my goals moving forward. I made mention to them that a priority of mine is giving back to my high school. I want to be able to give Enterprise High School some sort of amount due to my athletics. Whether that is a gear stipend or a scholarship, I want to be able to help them. Paul was all for helping out which was great to hear. We then talked about the Nike Groups, OTC, Bowerman and NOP.

For each, I told him OTC is a great group, I really like Mark, I think Mark is a brilliant coach and I think the team is great however the location isn't ideal. It's not because I think Eugene is a bad place, but I can't see myself there in the future. Next year as well I know Olivia will be wanting to go to grad school for Psychology and I don’t want to limit her options by placing her in Eugene.

Ideally Portland or Seattle will fit her needs and mine. I also just can't see myself starting a family in Eugene. That is something I hope to accomplish eventually, and I want to be in a location where that is possible. For Bowerman, I have incredible interest in Bowerman however that is the extent of it.

I haven't talked to Schumacher yet, I know of the group and I know their training is a bit different than mine, but I still fascinate the idea of that being a possibility. I want to be able to have a conversation with them.

For NOP I said I think their 1500m training group is close to the best in the world right now, but I am not too sure if NOP is the team I can see myself on. I like the guys but with that many American 1500m runners on the same team I am not sure how I can facilitate their needs. However, a conversation with NOP would also be great. In order I said my interest goes 1) BTC 2) OTC 3) NOP. Hopefully conversations can be arranged with Bowerman and NOP.

I really enjoyed today's tour. Once I got home, I went for a 4 mile run and mini circuit. Easily the most difficult circuit I have done, ironically it was the shortest. I think the only reason it was difficult was because I was mentally exhausted from the day. Nike has so much to offer and I'm incredibly thankful for their interest. I have no idea where I stand on this whole Nike and Brooks decision. If I had to choose today, I am leaning towards Brooks only for the sure aspect of having a team in place that fits me. This whole process is a bit stressful to be honest, but the decision is becoming more and more of a reality. Whether I select Nike or not, I have tremendous respect for Paul and really look forward to future conversations.

5.17.2018
Mileage 10

Felt good to get a full run in today. Started out my morning by spilling coffee all over my laptop. I didn't go to class today, I missed the morning ones trying to fix my laptop. I was typing up my journal as it spilled. My heart dropped as I tried my best to clean up the coffee, but nothing would turn back on. I took it to BestBuy to get it fixed but it would have costed 400+ dollars. I took it to a mom and pop computer shop and it only costed 80$. I left it with them and got a call later today saying they've restored everything, all the memory is saved, only thing permanently damaged is the keyboard. So that was a wild day, but for running I ran 50 mins today then talked with Drew Windle over text about pro teams. He said, "you will be successful wherever you go. At the end of the day it all comes down to you and what you're willing to put in. Work within transcends group factors."

That text meant a lot and definitely made me think about where and what I wanted to do. The word transcend is an incredible word. I then had a 20 min PM run with Dustin after I DMed the girls DnD game. Tomorrow I will drive down to Eugene and watch Oregon High School state track.

5.18.2018
Mileage 6

Today was a short and sweet speed day. I will definitely feel it tomorrow

Campus loop
Drills
10 wickets
2x200 tiger with Dustin. 26.2, 24.15
6 min recovery
2x300 tiger 43.3, 38.17
Cooldown

I then went down to state track with Brady and watched small school state. It was incredible! In order to grow in this sport for the future you need to look back and appreciate the past. Trees grow from their roots. We are just trees. Didn't get home till midnight but it was well worth it. I talked with so many people that gave me hugs and congratulated me and it was exhilarating. My best memory of today was a guy named Shane was in awe that I was in the stands next to him. He reached into his backpack and pulled out an old pair of my spikes and said, "Look David! I have your spikes!" I say this to emphasize that to the world you are just one person, but you never know if you mean the world to one person. Shane went on to be the first leg on the state 4x4 champion team. As he walked to the podium he pointed at his spikes and said, "David it's the spikes!" I yell back. "No, it's the person in the spikes!"

I also got a call from Paul today and we talked about pro groups. Essentially OTC is my Nike option he said he reached out to the other groups and said OTC has the most interest and likelihood for my training. That phone call I wish would've waited till tomorrow but overall the day was good. Going to bed happy to be from a small school and happy to represent the little guys.

5.19.2018
Mileage 11.5

Today was hard but good, last big workout before we race. Our track was occupied by football, so we did a workout at a different location. Our workout was:

2 laps 2 laps
Warm up drills
20 minute run
Into
5 min tempo 3 min recovery 4 min tempo, 3 min recovery, 3T, 3R, 3T. 3R
Jog to the track
1x500 going through 400 in 57.35
Cooldown then a nap

Had an easy 20 min double after playing Minecraft for an hour.

5.20.2018
Mileage 8.5

Good single 55 minute run before traveling tomorrow for nationals. Looking forward to traveling with the team. We are bringing nine athletes this go around, Dustin and I in the 1500m, Alani in the long jump, Hailie and Darian in the Javelin, Suzie in the 1500, Megan and Olivia in the 800, and Grayson on the 4x4. We hit the road tomorrow around 10:30 so we won't be getting in over there till late. This is my last national trip and I hope it's the best. Memories, achievement and all. Focusing on the present all week. I don't care about next year or what happens in a month, I care about now.

5.21.2018
Mileage 7

35 min AM run and a 10 min PM run to Jimmy Johns at 12:30am in North Carolina. The flights weren't too bad today, the runs felt good so overall, I solid travel day. I would say the worst part of today was trying to fall asleep. I wrote this entry on 5.22 because I could not fall asleep after the day of travel. Awake till 3am which typically never happens. On the plane we watched Disaster Artist and it was just as cringeworthy as The Room. Excited to get on the track and get some work in, feel It out.

5.22.2018

Mileage 9

20 min AM run before breakfast. As Dustin and I were running a homeless man yelled at us and said, “Dogs are cold blooded not warm blooded.” So that was interesting enough. The rest of the day we played FortNite in the hotel room because Dustin brought his Xbox. Then around 3 we went to the track:

2 laps
1 lap stride walk and drills
35 min run
3x120
1x200 @ 30 in trainers
1x120
Cooldown

Dinner pizza was good t*hen I had the best combo: Boots and Bed. Compression boots felt great then straight to bed.*
*FOCU*SING ON THE NOW!

5.23.2018
Mileage 5

Light day but a solid premeet. Felt a little heavy warming up but felt great as the stride walks continued. Dustin and I did two lap two laps on the track into a 25 min run to familiarize ourselves with the local area. After the quick run, we hopped on the track. Visualize and mimicking the prelims each rep representing a part of the race.

200 @ 30
300 @ 43
Broken 300 @ 12/18/12
200 @ 25

Felt good the last 300m and 200m reps. The final 200m insinuating the final 200m of the prelim. Surely if I close in 25, I will make the final. This is my first national prelim race since USAs last June. Crazy I have gone 11 months without an intense prelim, but the nerves will carry me through the race no doubt. My hope for the team is we all make it through to finals. Dustin, Suzie and Is prelims are tomorrow. Then the 800m women Olivia and Megan and 4x4, Grayson, are on Friday. Tomorrow is the second to last day repping the W. Hoping this prelim is smooth and Dustin and I can both glide into the final.

5.24.2018
Mileage unsure

Prelim day, AM 15 min shakeout visualizing this afternoons race. Head to the track at 3pm, played a friendly game of cornhole with the Adam State coaches. Next was warm up with Dustin. He drew heat 1, and I was in heat 2. As Dustin lined up for his start, they announced him as "The Division II record holder for 1500m." I couldn't help but laugh because I knew on the start line he was feeling himself after that. The guys around me all laughed and I went with it. Dustin controlled his heat incredibly, winning it with ease as it looked.

Once we got on the track the announcer didn't say a single thing about our heat. I sort of liked that though, took the pressure off and made it just another race. As my prelim went out, it went out like Dustin's. Almost identical in first 1000m. We hit bell lap and around the first turn I get clipped from behind just slightly. It woke me up and I gear changed and tried to get in an open lane. As we come off the final turn Eli from Adam State flew onto my outside and three of us raced to the line. I took second in my heat, 55.2 for the final lap. First fast finishing speed since Azusa that felt natural. Right across the line I chuckled at the race because everyone felt like they had to win the heat. I surely was trying to win the heat but with 10 meters to go the top three were separated so there was no real point. I could hear the deep aggressive breathing and just thought relax relax relax alllll gooood.

Heading into the final I need to be confident in myself and never doubt my ability. I say this because when the pressure is turned up how do you respond? When all eyes are watching you how do you react? I try my best to give the mean mug game face but sometimes that is hard. This weekend is a tossup of emotions, so confidence is something I need to build before Saturday. In the shower I repeated to myself, 3x national champion, 4x record holder, USATF finalist. NOTHING TO BE AFRAID OF! Dustin and I talked about the final. He wants to beat me, I want to beat him and I think if we work together one of the two results will happen. 1-2 is in reach if we work together. Tomorrow night we will talk about race plan. Excited to watch the girls compete tomorrow. Kennedy got 4th in the 10k tonight, closing her last lap in 72. Suzie also advanced to the final for the 1500m! Onto tomorrow!

5.25.2018

Mileage: Unsure

Woke up today feeling pretty good. Yesterday were the prelims so todays focus was feeling fresh for tomorrow's final. Dustin and I went to a park and nature conservancy for a new location to run. I wish we would of came here on other days too. The trails were super nice, clay/dirt and soft surface everywhere. Dustin and I ran for 5 mins before we stopped and stretched. As we stopped and stretched, we saw guys circled in the softball field fighting, full on swinging fists. We were far away so I couldn't tell if they were just playing around boxing or if they were seriously out for blood. Anyhow one of the guys turned and looked at Dustin and I so we quickly began running again. We ran 35 mins and felt good at the end of it.

Dustin and I talked about race plan and he said he will lead the first 800 and I will lead the last 700. I have no problem doing that because we both agree that out of the final, we may be the only guys in PR fitness. Dustin wants to lead it through in 2:02 and I want to lead the last lap in 55 or faster. I think it is a real possibility of going 1-2. I want to win, but if Dustin ends up winning it will be because he out raced me. We workout every day together, almost every run together no way we can't race together. I look forward to tomorrow especially after today.

Today was Olivia's prelim in the 800m, let's just say she balled out and ran a 2:05!!! Holy cats I was screaming and cheering and WOW! That was one of the most exciting races I have ever seen her run. What I love most about our relationship is it is not track driven. Without track we would still be perfect. Track is something we have in common but never put pressure on each other to perform. We are the springboards to each other's thoughts and motivation. THEN an hour later the girls

4x4 team balled out and ran 3:41. Olivia split 53.9 and they qualified for the final! WHAT!! They were the last team into the meet but now they are heading to the final!!! So awesome. This is what I will miss about collegiate track and field. The breakthroughs and togetherness of a team. I hope next year I can be a part of a team that has this atmosphere of success and comradery. Going into tomorrow this week has already been a success. This has been the greatest week of my career and I look forward to putting on the W one last time tomorrow and representing DII and Western Oregon. Here we are, one last Hoorah! 1-2 or Bust! No race cues for tomorrow, I am feeling the race out and that's it. After Dustin leads 800m I am going to go to the front and tell myself, **Home free.**

5.26.2018

Mileage: Unsure

Put the jersey in the frame, it will never be worn again. Today I concluded my NCAA eligibility in the best way possible. Finishing 1-2 in a national championship with my everyday training partner. I crossed the line first and Dustin followed less than half a second behind. During the race it was exactly how we envisioned. Dustin goes straight to the front, I sit in second as we go through 800m in 2:04. After his job was done, I knew it was up to me. I go into the lead with 700m remaining and begin to press the pace. **Home free.** With 170m to go Dustin clipped me and said, "David if you're gonna go, go!" That woke me up a bit and forced me to accelerate the final 150m. We both closed our final lap in just under 54.5 Dustin and I embraced after the finish, what a fairy tale ending to my collegiate year. Tomorrow will be a recovery day.

5.28.2018
Mileage 4

Holy cow, I'm done. My eligibility is out. What the heck. If you are a watchful reader you notice I skipped from 5.26-5.28, what happened to 5.27? We traveled from North Carolina back to Oregon and it was my first day without any miles so rightfully I didn't log about the normal muggle activities. That was my first off day in a while, not sure when my last off day was. I had one glimpse of retirement yesterday to see if no running is what I wanted to do, it is safe to say I had anxiety and felt bored all day long. I will surely be running post collegiately.

Crazy to think this journal started almost a year ago and here I am sipping a beer, feet in the sun getting ready for another game of cornhole on Memorial Day. Before you know it, you slip on your university jersey for the final time, look in the mirror and say this is it. Am I retired? Is it all over? Hell nah, just getting started. Enough running talk today is my RnR day. I have arranged a ton of phone calls this week with Flynn, Hawi, Layne, Lilot, Mackey, Moser, Rowland. I told them today I'm going to take for myself and be with Olivia and the team. I'm incredibly thankful for Memorial Day. For the men and women who serve/served/and will serve.

Today we had a team memorial party. A nice closure to the last week. Burger, beer and cornhole. Dustin and I did meet up today and run 35 mins with 6x120m to finish. It felt good to just shakeout and get some strides in. Tomorrow will be a relatively chill day. Next few days will be all business. Going to do my best to be as real as I can with you through this next week.

5.29.2018
Mileage 7

50 min run with 6x120s to start the day then it was all business. After class (because it is dead week) I went to the library in a room I reserved to take phone calls from 2-5pm. Today's phone calls were with Matt from Flynn Sports, Chris from Total Sports, and Hawi from HAWI Management. Talking with Matt was great, it was like catching up with an old friend. They were the first agency group I talked to so having that in person connection has helped a lot through these conversations. We talked about my future teams of choice, how I thought the weekend went etc. I told him that my top team is Brooks, next OTC and I would still like to have conversation with BTC. I asked Matt about contract negation and the ability to negotiate a contract to facilitate my needs. Some of those needs include giving back to my high school, the ability to be involved in speaking engagements and the opportunity to be involved in promotional opportunities. Something I really appreciate with Matt is his interest in the journal. He loves my journal idea and Matt is someone I hope I keep close, whether I choose Flynn Sports or not Matt is a good guy I want in my corner if not as a representative, surely a friend.

After the phone call with Matt I immediately hopped on a new call with Chris Layne. I talked with Chris about the same thing as I talked with Matt about. Keeping it consistent of course and letting him know my priorities. Through this process I've tried to keep these next few things in mind 1) not being afraid to explain what you want. If you ask and they say no, that is the same result as if you never asked. My mom always told me, "it's always worth the ask, least they can do is say no which is where you will always be if you never try." 2) knowing agents work for you, don't feel twisted by agent representation that YOU need them. Your agent should represent you, they work for you and should be willing to do work for you. Going through this process I'm choosing an agent that I feel the most connection with and potential to grow. As an athlete and person, I want to be with an agency that can further represent me as a human being and as an athlete.

Athletics aside I want to have and be a part of a damn good team, willing to do anything so I can succeed. 3) take a deep breath and enjoy the process. I would say this has been the most difficult part of the process. I have gotten a bit stressed, even just today about the whole thing. I need to remember this is WHAT I ALWAYS DREAMED OF! I shouldn't be stressed I should be excited and smiling that all of this has come together. Sure, it is a life decision but it's a decision that should be made as natural as possible. College is over, have fun you're done. Something I've tried to repeat to myself. Anyway, back to today. I told Chris one of my first priorities in contract negotiation is getting something installed for my high school. I told him a gear stipend or scholarship would be ideal. He replied back with, "David, you are something special. Most athletes I talk to at your age bring up money and companies but the first thing you've told me is you have a team in mind and you want to give back. That's incredible." Talking with Chris I feel a sense of realness. He has a subtle convincing tone to him that anything I wish to come true he can accommodate. I plan and talking with him again later this week.

I then talked with Hawi Management. Our initial conversation was relatively brief, but we will talk again later this week. Again, I pitched all the same priorities to him and he was on board for all of them. He sent me a template and mission statement of his organization and that helped a lot. As he talked about his agency I could follow along on a template and spark questions about his representation. His honesty and ethics immediately stood out to me and I felt as though he is a genuine guy. After we hung up, I went on a quick 2 mile run. I tried my best to keep it chill but would find myself unintentionally picking it up. My plan was to run 7 minute pace or slower but when I got to mile two at 12:18 I shook my head and walked the last quarter mile in. I think walking was really the only way for me to take a deep breath and relax.

If you are an athlete going through this process, I encourage you to look up who your potential agency represents. Look at those athletes, their social media pages, their websites, their accomplishments (on and off the track). I want to be represented by an agency that has a good representation of likeminded athletes. Athletes that I look up too, compete with, and respect for more reasons than their athletic abilities. Who an agency represents says a lot. Through today I've talked with good agencies but next few days I plan to talk to more and talk with more coaches. My goal in the next week or so is to close off every possible conversation so every stone is overturned. I can make a confident decision with the knowledge that every conversation has been made. Next weekend is the NCAA Division I National Championship. I hope to be finalized with a decision by then before Division I gets out, so I'm not lost in the jumble of those athletes turning post collegiate. Lots on my mind tonight but hoping for a good day tomorrow to work through everything. I'll probably annoy Dustin with some questions and ask for some guidance.

5.30.2018
Mileage 8

Today was a good work day, actually wasn't expecting it but it went really well. Was the first time we've had a workout like this so coming off nationals and having a new workout was refreshing.

2 laps 2 laps
Drills
30 minute run
1x200 @ 28
2x600 @ 29/40/28 5 min jog
1x200 @ 27
5x 10 wickets
2x600 30/40/27
5x10 wickets
1x600 28/38/27
Cool down

This was the first day we have ever incorporated wickets in the middle of the workout. The purpose was to focus on good posture and foot strike in the middle and latter parts of the race. After the first set of wickets I felt like my posture was better. However, the 600m reps following that first set of wickets was quite difficult. First 200m of the first 600m was difficult to get in rhythm but after that my posture and foot strike felt inline. After the cool down I went into the training room to recover. I hopped on the vibration platform and hopped in the boots before having phone calls with coach Rowland and Paul Moser of Nike.

With Rowland we talked about the future of OTC and my concerns with Eugene. I told him the location isn't necessarily ideal for me because Olivia plans to attend grad school wherever I end up. Both of us agree that Eugene isn't the most ideal location for grad school and I wouldn't want Olivia to have to attend Oregon. Olivia is sacrificing a lot for my career and last thing I want to do is put her in a position of uncertainty. To add, I personally don't see myself living in Eugene. I love Eugene, but I don't see it as a home for myself or for starting a family, which is also a focus of mine (in the future, not anytime soon). I hope wherever I go it can be a place where little Davids can be running around. However, Eugene isn't out of question, it's just not ideal. I told him I'd still like to talk with more members of the team, talk with Paul and talk about contracts, agencies and all. After coach Rowland and I hung up, Paul called.

Almost immediately, over the phone with Paul I told him about my Eugene questions/concerns and he was understanding and told me he would love to help make it work out. Nike, Eugene and all. He asked me how my agency process is going and I confidently told him Chris Layne seems to be at the top of my list and if he is an agent he is capable of working with. He loved Chris and only spoke highly of Chris which is a huge plus.

Tomorrow I have more phone calls lined up with Coach Mackey and Steve Dekoker. Steve is involved with Brooks Sports Marketing. Once again going to bed with a full mind but tonight Olivia laughingly shook me by shoulders, gave me a kiss, looked me in the eyes and told me to HAVE FUN STOP OVER ANALYZING.

5.31.2018
Mileage 8

Easy recovery day which I am thankful for because I did enough work in school and over the phone today to feel like I had a workout. 55 minute run before lining up the day with more phone calls. Steve and I talked and I told him straight up that Brooks is at the top of my list for interest but out of respect I still want to be able to have conversations with other companies before making an ultimate decision. We talked about my high school, a recurring conversation as you can see, it is a big priority for me. He loved the idea and said no doubt there is something Brooks can do to help my high school.

After the phone call I called Coach Mackey and we talked about my future and my interest on the team. I told him as well Brooks is my first priority, but I'd like to finish off the discussions with other groups. I asked him what he would have me do for the summer and he told me that is entirely up to me. He said if I wanted to call my season now I could, if I wanted to run USAs, I could do that, if I wanted to skip USAs and run in Europe that is also an option. He told me my 2018 job is done and he would respect any decision I had to continue racing or not. That was reassuring because I was never really sure what the next step would be. With Brooks Breasts it seems very accommodating to my long season.

As I ran, I felt 99% sure my decision was to go with Brooks. I ran and sat in class all day before finally going to Olivias and telling her I have made my decision. After I got to her house, I received a text from Kimbia Athletics an agency that has representation with both Brooks and Bowerman. Two groups I have incredible interest with. I have a 50 min phone call with Alistair Craigg before he says Jerry would like to give me a call within the next few days to chat. With Alistair I told him all the same things, I told him about my high school, my goals, etc. he was all for all of it. He asked me how my decision process was going and I told him as of right now Brooks is my top option. He seemed to agree and said he has athletes with Danny at Brooks and what Danny has going in Seattle is world class.

For me it was reassuring that agencies and other coaches are respectful to each other, at least to the athletes. Shows a sense of community in the sport. Once we hung up, I got a text from Jerry Schumacher. I thought jeez the weez here we go. We talk on the phone for over 70 mins. I jokingly told him we talked for the duration of my track season long run. Throughout the phone call it was constant conversation. I asked him about his training and how I would fit into the mix. He opened up and told me his training is different. It is endurance based and it focuses on aerobic capacity. I told him my last four years have been speed oriented with three to four workouts a week. I asked how I would transition into his group and he told me it would be a process overtime. I wouldn't immediately jump to high mileage maybe each year focus is adding 5 miles a week to my weekly average for the year.

Overtime chances are that I would transition to 5k or 3k steeple. 1500m is an event I can do but it's not the focus of the group. He told me I remind him stature wise as a young Evan Jager. When he told me that I immediately felt overwhelmed like, holy cow. This coach is the coach of Olympian's and he told me I resemble Evan? Jeez.... I asked him next about his interest in me and when it started. He told me back at Portland track festival last year and even at USAs when I talked to him in person. He told me his son is a big fan of mine. He said he remembers in March of this year his son was hollering about something, so he goes downstairs to see his son watching my

DMR anchor leg at indoor nationals. That story also overwhelmed me because it shows you never know who's watching. Athletes are under a microscope and I know people follow me and I want to be able to best represent myself for them.

We said our goodbyes and he said he will keep in touch the next few days to try and get a day we can meet in person. After the long talk I sat on my floor for bit. More so laid on my floor looking at my ceiling, reading the letters of encouragement pinned on my wall from the past year. I looked in the mirror shirtless imagining being a part of both teams. No shame I even announced myself as both athletes in a British commentator voice raising my hands, waving to the crowd, seeing myself in a Bowerman kit and a Brooks kit. I exhaled a large sigh and laid back on the floor where I started to tear up a bit.

Not out of frustration but out of realization that a year ago I told myself I hope I'm down to a decision between Brooks and Bowerman. Here I am a year later in an incredibly tough decision and I can't believe it. This journal has helped so much on my mental aspect. This journal has given me a place to speak, vent, think and write. Whether this is even read by anyone or not, journaling is something I will do for the rest of my time as an athlete. Thinking of today though I am looking forward to closure with an agency, team, contract, company all of it. I want to be done with it and I know the decision will be naturally made but here I am chillin in short shorts acting like a British commentator.

I'm getting DQ. Double Fudge Cookie Dough Blizzard on deck. Time for a walk.

6.1.2018

Mileage 11.5

Sup June, nice to see you so soon. Today was a really good workout to start the month off right. This was one of the longer workouts in the last few weeks and I felt pretty good doing it.

Mile warm up
Drills
20 minute run
4 min tempo (4 min jog off)
2x3 min tempo (3 min jog off in between)
2x90 sec tempo
Back to the track
4x250 @ 35 with 150m jog recovery
800m jog
4x250 with 150m jog recovery
34,35,36,37

This set was designed to slow down each rep because the first set was so successful. This was the first day in a while where I surprisingly had a clear mind. Yesterday's phone call with Jerry was insightful and I look forward to our conversation in person. I'm postponing all phone calls till tomorrow going to take today for myself after a busy last few days. From Tuesday-Thursday I had a total of 27 phone calls. A lot of those are repeated with the same people but all of those phone calls were future oriented for post collegiate career. Tonight, we had the Goodwill Awards. The first annual event held by the men's team. I hope this is something the team keeps around. It was super fun, started the night out with karaoke then we had some honorable MCs before the awards. It was awesome to see everyone laughing and having a good time. The team is close and looking around the room I'm going to miss this crew. These guys dream and grind harder than anyone I've met. Of course, all teams are bias, but these guys are the best. They make me proud to be Wolf.

After the awards we told corny jokes over the mic. Something that is super fun to do is have a group fill their mouths with water while a duo or trio reads corny jokes to them. The purpose is to keep all the water in the mouth. If you laugh, you're out till only one stands. After a while you just get overwhelmed with giggles and laughs. I lost it when the joke started with, "two hunters were walking in the woods......" just by that saying I soaked myself with water and it took three attempts before I could even hold the water in. The joke itself wasn't even funny. Tonight was a good night, tomorrow is a light day with a mini circuit and our athletic auction for donors. I'll be MC-ing some of that event as well.

6.2.2018
Mileage 7

Super light day, light circuit, athletic auction. To start the run was a nice and easy 50 minute run into light circuit work from two weeks ago. I left the sheet at home and it is pretty late tonight so I don't want to type out a circuit sheet. Sorry. However, once at the auction I got up on stage and helped with the student athlete panel. I asked athletes questions and they responded accordingly for the auction to hear. The auction consists of a bunch of faculty, athletes and donors. Being a small university, a lot of our athletic funding is made through this night. We made roughly 35k last year and it all goes straight to athletic funding.

As the Q and A went on it felt a bit dull towards the end so I decided to go off script. I sort of just spoke. I sort of vented. I told the donors that as a Division II athlete we are in a constant comparison with other universities. We get on the line and other universities look at a Division II as a beatable team. Or you get in a game and because your team isn't wearing the same shoe, the other team thinks they have the upper hand. Psychologically it's frustrating as an athlete but something we as Division II athletes do is block that out. I said on stage in front of all the donors. "We face teams with full rides for everyone, state of the art facilities, unlimited sponsorship, top national talent, but we face them, and we beat them. We don't give a shit about that. What we care about is waking up, competing and doing our job and for us to do your job, we want you, the donors to help facilitate that." I got a lot of cheers, whoops and hollers after I said "shit". Totally unintentional, I was just kind of rolling off my thoughts and before I knew it, I said it.

As the night ended, I stayed to thank donors and they said that was their highlight of the night and I'm a gifted speaker. I didn't get any shuns only appraisal, so I guess I didn't offend too many people. Olivia and I also sat at a table with doctors, the man I sat next to asked about my career aspirations and I explained to him my process of becoming a professional track and field athlete. He asked me questions about each team and we talked for a good 20 minutes about it all. He finished off with, "with those two teams Brooks and Bowerman, which team do you see YOU in.

"Ultimately a team is a team but who you are as a person is far more important." He said, "You've been journaling, and it's been fun right? What happens if something happens and it is no longer fun, what will you be journaling then?" He continued, "Both options sound incredible from an outsider's perspective but when you make a decision make the decision where you can represent WHO YOU ARE." I looked at him blankly, shook his hand and thought how I am so lucky to talk with people like this. Tomorrow is a solo run day with Dustin. Time to pick his brain.

6.3.2018

Mileage 10

Solid 10 mile single run with Dustin. We ran shady for old time sakes the whole time we talked about NCAA records and whether or not records should be combined for in and out of season. I argued that they should be separate (like they currently are) because level of competition and availability to run fast. Our "arguments" always end on good terms too which is a sign of a good friend. That you can have conflicting views but still agree to disagree.

After some strides and stretches I went and got a breakfast burrito before heading to help setup for the Wolfies. The Wolfies are an annual award night for WOU student athletes. This is only the second year of existence, so we are still in the trial and error stage but already it is more successful than last years. Tonight I spent the night reading over my journal and reading my thoughts from a year ago. Perspective helps, and I recommend everyone to journal. Hopefully my next step will be making a journal template for readers and other people to journal. I think journaling is a huge reason for my successes this last year. I also texted Schumacher about a meeting time so now I will wait for a response. This week is decision week. I know it's close, Division I ends in 6 days, I race a week from today. Will I be racing in a Western uniform or a pro kit?

6.4.2018
Mileage 7

Today was a good speed-oriented day. Tiger 200s and that was it.

2 laps 2 laps
Drills
20 min run
3x200s 23.7, 26.1, 24.3 my fastest 200s with walking 200m in between

Felt great to get up to speed and tiger some of the guys, the 26 was when the guys tigered me and they did a good job as well. In terms of Decision, I am still in a decision between Brooks and Bowerman. Next few days I am going to ask Danny his vision for me. That is a conversation we have actually never had, and I want to hear his plans for me. Tomorrow I will commit to Total Sports. I have been on the fence for a few days now and I know it's the best possibility for me. After going through all the agency conversations. Chris made me feel the most at home. That is of course nothing against the other agencies. The other agencies are incredible and have their pros but for me personally I like Total Sports. Today Brooks also sent me a contract to look over and get an understanding of the figure and make up of a contract.

6.5.2018
Mileage 8

Today I committed to Total Sports. As the words came out of my mouth, I felt this huge weight off my shoulders. The excitement I have to work with Total Sports and Chris Layne is surreal. I look forward to the next steps in contract negotiation and everything.

The workout felt like a glide. Like I was 20lbs lighter.
2 laps 2 laps
30 minute run
1x200 @ 29
3x500 fast/slow/fast 200/100/200
27/18/28
28/20/27
30/17/26
Cool down two miles

Still haven't heard back from Jerry so it's now a waiting game for that conversation. To add pressure, Brooks gave me a contract offer deadline for end of day Friday. I told myself I wanted to decide before Division I gets out but now with this deadline it's scary. However, business is business and I need to respect their end of the bargain. I sent the base contract over to Chris for him to look at, now that he's my agent and all.

6.6.2018
Mileage unsure

Drove down to the NCAA DI meet and watched some of the races and boy was it crazy, Ben Flannigan wins 10k. Was a crazy day none the least. While I was there, I met Chris Layne! That was pretty cool to shake his hand in person and thank him. Later I sat with Schumacher in person for a good hour after the meet concluded. He asked me what I want to accomplish in the sport. He asked me who I want to be, who I am, what do I desire. Some of the deepest questions anyone has ever asked me. He didn't want immediate answers, but I couldn't help but feel compelled to talk to him for hours.

I overlooked Hayward field for a final time before the demolition begins and I couldn't help but feel so lost. On one end I have Bowerman, on the other I have Brooks Beasts. Two dream teams! Through this whole process I let Danny know I was waiting to talk to Schumacher and I told Schumacher my other team choice is Brooks Beasts. Both coaches said they have tremendous respect for one another. Schumacher told me whichever choice I make it wouldn't be a wrong one. I drove home utterly lost and contemplated going for a run along the highway but of course I didn't because that would be illegal.

6.7.2018
Mileage 6

Circuit day
2 laps 2 laps
Leg swings
Rhll
30 minute run
Back to the track
Rhll
3x80m stride
1x20 lunge med ball
1x15 med ball push ups
2x15 rocket jumps
1x4 plank
1x20 mountain climbers
1x10 burpees
2x10 hurdle walkovers
Repeat x2 lunges-walkovers

Today I talked with Danny on the phone and we talked about his vision for the Beasts and my vision as a professional athlete. With that being said I am choosing Brooks as the company I will represent. Their philosophy, staff, coaching and athletes is everything that I see myself in. Danny's ambitions are to make one of the best track and field groups in the world. Hearing his plan for just 10 minutes convinced me. We talked for another 50 mins about my goals and my ambitions which only made me more confident. I am excited to take this next step and move to Seattle. I didn't tell him I knew at that point I just told Danny tomorrow I will make my decision and give him a call. I didn't want to flat out commit right away. I wanted a good 24 hours of thought to flow through me before "pressing the button." As Chris would say.

I then called Chris Layne and notified him that Brooks is my choice. He told me about contracts of opposing companies and said Brooks is the best option all around. I then called my mom, dad and Olivia. Told them my decision and of course extremely excited and supportive. From there I went into Johnsons office and we talked about the decision. He knew from the start that Brooks was the decision, of course he did. We quickly transitioned to talking about races. The race schedule looks like PTF, USAs, then a quick European Circuit through July. We will take it one meet at a time and race each one with the excitement like it's the last race of the year. I went home to the roommates and told them of my decision. Soon I will sign a contract and this journal will be over (sad face).

Crazy that this journal started as an idea and here it is as an almost finished product. This may be the most committed thing I've ever done. Besides being in a relationship, running and stuff. I mean like diligent work. Like holy Toledo I pretty much journaled for a full year... Wow a Brooks Beast, I feel like a new man.

6.8.2018

Mileage 8.5

This morning I committed to Brooks, the next step now will be finalizing my contract and getting everything set in place. Just an easy 40 min AM run and 2 mile shakeout this afternoon I race on Sunday in two days so trying to keep today chill and relaxed. I will debut in a Brooks singlet for the 800m at Portland Track Festival. There was some talk of waiting till USAs to debut, but I thought it was best to represent Brooks and race for the first time professionally in my home state.

I know family, friends, and everyone will be there so this is a good time to show. Because I haven't fully signed a contract, I am going to keep this journal going cause I have something pretty exciting being negotiated in my contract as we speak. Or I guess as I write. So, once I see that finalized and my signature is solidified on a piece of paper, I'm going to let this journal roll.

In regard to choosing an agent and company to represent I want to let everyone know that I have tremendous respect for the agencies and companies that reached out to me. They communicated professionally and personally to me every chance they got. The coaches, agents, sports marketers are class acts and I look forward to having relationships with them throughout my time involved in this beautiful sport. I made sure to thank everyone that spoke with me because I know for a fact, I will see them around the oval. Going to bed mind blown I am signing a contract.

6.9.2018
Mileage 6

Easy day leading into tomorrow's race. I drove up to Portland to pre meet with the Beasts. On the way to Portland I got stuck in a pretty bad rain storm. I turned the Subaru's windshield wipers on full blast and that would barely do the trick. Suddenly, I heard a loud thump and my windshield wiper flew off the windshield, wedging itself between the driver side mirror and the door. I look around on the road and can barely see anything. All I can see is two giant semi-trucks right in front of me spraying me with water. A car then tucked in behind me trapping me between the two giant metal death traps. I slowed down a bit and turned on my hazards. One hand on the wheel the other hand manually wiping the windshield with the busted windshield wiper. It was an intense moment. Finally, I pulled over at a gas station, popped the hood and tightened the screws for the windshield wiper. Luckily that did the trick and I made it to Portland safe and sound. One of the scariest moments of my life happened to be on the day I signed a contract.

Once I was there, I had a nice and easy run with Garrett, Drew, Henry and Izaic.

35 mins

2x80

1x250 @ 33

1x200 @ 26

2x120

Also did a mini photo shoot with Brooks and got some gear. Their gear is SO NICE!!! (This is not a paid advertisement.) looking at tomorrow's race I am not too worried about the result. Of course, I am going to try and go for the win but more importantly I'm going to have fun and be as stress free as possible. It's been a wild two weeks and I contemplated sitting this meet out, but I know this is the right thing to do.

6.10.2018

Mileage: Unknown

Race day. First race day in a new kit. My journal is near its end. This last year has been a whirlwind of events. So many ups I can't list them all. Tonight, I ran 1:49, my second fastest 800m time. I'm thankful to represent Brooks for the first time in my home state. I have never been hungrier in the sport of track and field. A new journey begins with the same ambition. Mentally I am ready to take on the world, physically I need some help and I know Danny and the guys can arrange that.

A big reason I am so thankful for Brooks is their commitment to development (like my background). In my contract I wrote in giving back to my high school. I originally asked for gear or scholarship and Brooks agreed to do both. *Brooks will be giving a $12,500 MSRP gear stipend to the track team, as well a $2000 annual scholarship to graduating track seniors for the duration of my contract.* You can't grow if you don't take time to develop your roots. By years Enterprise High School is in the past but I will do everything I can to help them succeed. Looking forward to USAs and a European circuit. After the circuit, a much-needed break to rebuild for my first year as a pro. I am going to have a lot to learn in the next year but by taking it one step at a time I am ready for the adjustment. My hopes from here are to develop a website and build more publications to help athletes pursue their dreams. Over Twitter and Instagram my name (handle) is dmribich! Give me a follow and continue to be a part of my career. Every year I hope to be the best version of myself. With the support I've received since the start I know anything is possible. My last words of advice are be patient, have fun, and be confident. Just because you are from a small school, doesn't mean you have to have a small dream.

2017-2018 Race Library:

USATF Championships Jun 22-25, 2017
1500 3:40.95 11th (P)
1500 3:45.44 9th (F)

San Francisco State Invitational Sep 22, 2017
8K 24:47.0 1st

2017 GNAC Cross Country Championships Oct 21, 2017
8K 24:54.9 1st

NCAA Division II West Region Cross Country Championships Nov 4, 2017
10K 29:49.2 1st

NCAA Division II Cross Country Championships Nov 18, 2017
10K 31:47.1 30th

2018 UW Preview Jan 13, 2018
1000 2:21.38 2nd (F)

2018 UW Invitational Jan 26-27, 2018
DMR 9:47.56 1st 4:00 split (F)
Mile 3:58.88 3rd (F)

2018 Husky Classic Feb 9-10, 2018
3000 7:50.81 4th (F)

GNAC Indoor Track and Field Championship Feb 16-17, 2018
800 1:54.35 1st (P)
Mile 4:11.08 1st (F)
800 1:50.83 1st (F)

NCAA Division II Indoor Track & Field Championships Mar 9-10, 2018
DMR 9:41.40 1st 3:54.76 split (F)
3000 8:01.55 3rd (F)

Stanford Invitational Mar 30-31, 2018
800 1:48.09 2nd (F)

Bryan Clay Invitational Apr 19-20, 2018
1500 3:37.35 6th (F)

OSU High Performance Meet Apr 27-28, 2018
800 1:50.52 1st (F)

Payton Jordan Invitational May 3, 2018
1500 3:45.74 10th (F)

2018 GNAC Outdoor Track and Field Championship May 11-12, 2018
800 1:53.47 2nd (P)
1500 3:49.22 1st (F)
800 1:52.07 1st (F)

NCAA Division II Outdoor Track & Field Championships May 24-26, 2018
1500 3:51.01 3rd (P)
1500 3:45.34 1st (F)

Made in the USA
Monee, IL
31 October 2019

16123702R00270